French America

French **America** was produced with the generous support of:

Mrs. Arrieta de Blaquier
Central Color
The Cultural Services of the French Embassy to the United States
The Michel David-Weill Foundation
The Firestone Foundation
The Florence Gould Foundation
The Huguenot Society of America
The Anna-Maria and Stephen M. Kellen Foundation
The Kress Foundation
Lyric Opera of Chicago
Société Générale

© Editions Didier Millet
121 Telok Ayer Street #03-01
Singapore 068590
email: edm@edmbooks.com.sg

First published 2004 for French Heritage Society
14 East 60th Street, Suite 605
New York, NY 10022
www.frenchheritagesociety.org

Text © Ron Katz

© Ron Katz for the following photographs: pp. 34; 39 top and bottom right;
49 bottom; 55 bottom; 68 bottom; 76-77; 80 bottom; 81 bottom; 90 bottom

© Arielle de La Tour d'Auvergne for all other photographs, unless otherwise specified

Designer: Louise Brody
Production Manager: Sin Kam Cheong
Colour separation: Colourscan Singapore
Printed in Singapore by Star Standard

ISBN : 981-4155-15-2

FrenchAmerica

French architecture from colonization to the birth of a nation

Text by Ron Katz

Photographs by Arielle de La Tour d'Auvergne

French Heritage Society

EDM

CONTENTS

FOREWORD

To write the Foreword for this magnificent work dedicated to French America is an honor and a pleasure for me. Those close to me know how fond I am of Louisiana, that incomparable country that I rediscover with growing admiration on each of my numerous trips. For a painter, to be impregnated by the aquatic light characteristic of this region, to admire the sunsets flooding the horizon with a purple hue contrasting with the dark clumps of trees, to intensely experience that palpable tranquility, to savor the poetry of the vast marshes, disturbed only by passing alligators, or serving as hunting grounds for the numerous cranes and other pelicans – all of this is an authentic enchantment.

But this deeply physical sensation, this osmosis of my artistic being with an entire region comes from elsewhere, from the core of my family's past. The d'Hauterives family was present in French America from the beginning of the region's history. An ancestor of mine arrived in Louisiana only a few years after the founding of New Orleans: he was an officer from a very old French family – Amédée II d'Hauterives was the first Abbot of Hautecombe, then Bishop of Lucerne and a companion of Saint-Bernard. This first "American" d'Hauterives had, in turn, three sons, all military officers. One of them commanded Arkansas Post, in Indian territory, described in the chapter of this book on the Mississippi Valley. This occurred after the Treaty of Paris in 1763, during the period when western Louisiana had been ceded by France to Spain. The French influence was still very strong in this region, and the French aristocracy continued to play a prominent role in the administration of the territory.

My ancestor, the Chevalier d'Hauterives, a captain, was put in charge by the Spanish governor of resettling the Cajuns arriving in Louisiana on lands belonging to the Attakapas Indians. It was there that he built his home in 1765. This house still stands in St. Martinville, and I have depicted it in one of my paintings. One can well imagine the emotion that grips me when I think of that place, where part of my roots lie.

The great accomplishment of this volume is to synthesize the diverse information, until now dispersed, that we have concerning French architecture, or the French influence on architecture from the vernacular constructions of the Mississippi Valley – that appear to be straight from the Norman woodlands – to the urban architecture of large cities like Philadelphia, New York or Washington, while obviously including the emblematic constructions of Creole plantations, those celebrated "houses with a gallery". The various military constructions must also be mentioned, from which several forts have been reconstituted over the past thirty years based on original plans.

The various styles employed have led little by little to a unique American style. But the French influence is predominant. The history of this country is indelibly linked to France and is reflected in the names of architects or urban planners, such as Gilbert Guillemard and Hyacinthe Laclotte, both of whom distinguished themselves in the early nineteenth century in New Orleans, and Arsène Lacarrière-Latour (the urban planner of Baton Rouge), who were trained at the *École des Beaux-Arts* in Paris.

The journey that unfolds here allows us to better appreciate the origin of the links that today unite France and the United States of America, which doubled its surface with the Louisiana Purchase in 1803, incorporating into this young nation territories spanning from the Gulf of Mexico to the Canadian border – what had previously been French America.

Arnaud d'Hauterives, Secrétaire perpétuel de l'Académie des Beaux-Arts, Paris

(translated from the French by Karen Archer)

The title of this elegant volume is deceptively simple, but the task that the contributors have undertaken is complex and intricate. This task is nothing less than to document with photographs and describe in words a broad range – political, military, architectural, artisanal and cultural – of French influences within the United States, or most especially within what would become the United States, thanks in large measure to French support in the American Revolution.

The range of French-influenced architecture and building techniques portrayed in this volume is breathtaking, and heretofore unexplored in its entirety. In the Missouri chapter, Ron Katz chose to get down to the basics of mud and straw (*bousillage* from the French *boue*) by persuading James Baker of Ste. Genevieve to discuss vernacular construction methods in the Mississippi Valley. This was an audacious and inspired decision for several reasons: Ste. Genevieve contains more French-Creole Style structures than any other locale (not excluding New Orleans) in the United States. And James Baker, having devoted his life to Ste. Genevieve's history, knows more about these buildings than anyone in the world.

Proceeding seamlessly from *bousillage* to the *beau*, this volume spans the range from the vernacular vertical log houses of Ste. Genevieve to the Cathedral of St. Louis in New Orleans. This latter structure was designed by Jacques Nicolas Bussière de Pouilly, who had been trained at the *École des Beaux-Arts* in Paris, and it is in the academic rather than the vernacular style. Fundamentally designed in the Medieval-Revival Style popular during the nineteenth century, the handsome cathedral dominates Jackson Square, which embodies the formal French landscaping style made famous by André Le Nôtre during the reign of Louis XIV.

As Roger Kennedy eloquently puts it, buildings do speak, if only we are willing attentively to listen. The tidy vertical log houses of Ste. Genevieve speak of a French agricultural village populated with habitants who labored (from the French verb, *labourer*, to plow) behind their own plows; the plantation houses of the lower Mississippi Valley speak of a local aristocracy eschewing village life in order to live, as did their French counterparts, on vast rural estates; the Cathedral of St. Louis speaks of a religious hierarchy, extending from the remote parishes of the Illinois Country, downriver to New Orleans, and across the Atlantic back to Europe. The Roman Catholic faith propelled missionaries into the remote Mississippi River valley, and it provided cultural cohesion for the dispersed settlements that dotted the banks of the river.

Two forts speak of a French empire in North America so vast that it was ultimately impossible to defend. These are Fort de Chartres in southern Illinois and Fort Necessity, seven hundred miles away in southern Pennsylvania. There is both symmetry and asymmetry in the relationship of these two structures: they were both erected in the mid-1750s; they were both associated with the French and Indian War; they have both been carefully reconstructed (Chartres only partially); and they are both admirably photogenic, as this volume nicely demonstrates. On the other hand, Chartres was a massive stone structure, erected by the government of Louis XV to defend the Mississippi River valley, while Necessity was a paltry wooden palisaded structure hurriedly erected by George Washington to defend himself against a French force led by Captain Louis Coulon de Villiers. Chartres was never attacked, while Villiers' attack on Necessity forced a surrender after a brief siege. This encounter with the French in the Allegheny Mountains proved to be the most humiliating experience of Washington's life.

Independence Hall, the Georgian gem of Philadelphia, speaks of politics. It was there that the Continental Congress agreed to the Declaration of Independence, and it was there that the Congress decided to dispatch a diplomatic emissary to Paris to beseech Louis XVI's government for assistance in combating the British monarchy. No little irony inheres in the fact that the American revolutionaries were asking the French king to go to war in the name of principles that would eventually destroy the French monarchy itself. This diplomatic coup was engineered by Benjamin Franklin, who persuaded the royal foreign minister, Charles-Gravier, Comte de Vergennes, that with French help the Americans could indeed achieve victory over the largest empire that the world had ever seen. Franklin's Philadelphia – and a remarkable amount of it remains – is lovingly documented in this volume's photographs.

And this victory was largely due to the French army of some 6,000 troops that disembarked at Newport, Rhode Island on July 10, 1780. The force was commanded by Jean-Baptiste Donatien, Comte de Rochambeau, a professional soldier who brought with him engineers, firearms, cannons and ammunition. Vernon House served as Rochambeau's residence in Newport, and it has been faithfully preserved as an emblem of Franco-American friendship. Rochambeau's statue by Ferdinand Hamar, a gift of France to the United States, was unveiled in Washington, D.C. by President Theodore Roosevelt on May 26, 1902.

Marie-Joseph, Marquis de Lafayette, served in the American army at Yorktown alongside Rochambeau's French troops. Although not so important to the American cause as his countryman, Rochambeau, Lafayette's love affair with America has made him more famous in this country. As they were associated in battle, so the two French aristocrats are now linked in their respective commemorative statues in Lafayette Park facing the White House, one on either corner of Pennsylvania Avenue.

Pennsylvania Avenue was itself the invention of a Frenchman, Pierre-Charles L'Enfant, who, like Lafayette, joined the Continental Army to fight for liberty, an idea that was wildly popular among French aristocrats living under an absolute monarch. A trained engineer and architect, L'Enfant became acquainted with George Washington and remained in America after the revolution. When the first U.S. Congress under the new constitution decided to establish a new capital city on the banks of the Potomac, L'Enfant prepared a plan for the city in 1791. This plan, based upon principles of city planning already implemented in Paris (Place de la Concorde and the Champs-Elysées), governed the land surveyors as they shaped the new capital city during the 1790s. L'Enfant's remains now repose close to those of John F. Kennedy in Arlington National Cemetery, fittingly looking down on the city that he designed.

In addressing the extensive and profound connections that bound French civilization to America – especially during the critical period of the gestation, birth and infancy of the United States – this volume performs a timely and signal service. As Thomas Jefferson declared on departing France in 1789: "I cannot leave this great and good country without expressing my sense of its pre-eminence of character among the nations of the earth."

Growing up in Minnesota, I was bombarded by French words: St. Croix River, Hennepin, Nicolet and Larpenteur avenues, Duluth (transmogrified from the early explorer's name, Daniel Greysolon, Sieur Dulhut), St. Anthony Falls (originally *les chutes de St. Antoine*), Frontenac, St. Cloud, Le Sueur (home of Green Giant peas) and my childhood favorite, Prairie du Chien, Wisconsin. I was raised in a household of books, but none of them adequately explained the French connections that lay behind the exotic words and names.

With the appearance of this volume, households from New England to Louisiana, and Illinois to South Carolina, are given the opportunity to have all of these important Franco-American connections conveyed in an appealing and accessible fashion, a feast for the mind and the eye.

Carl J. Ekberg

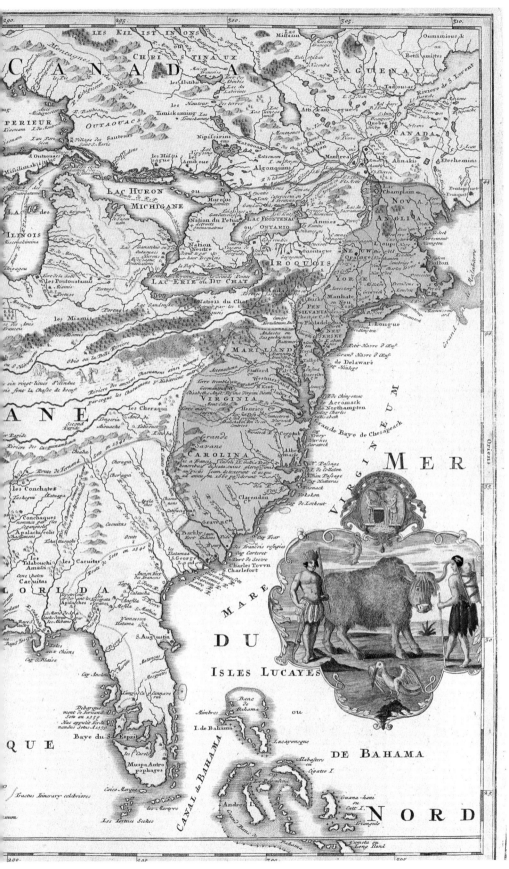

Blérancourt, Musée de la Coopération Franco-Américaine. ©Photo RMN

SPEAKING FRENCH

In the time of Washington, Jefferson, Lafayette and Rousseau, it was conventional to write "architecture parlante" – buildings that talk. Buildings do talk. Fortresses, city halls and palaces bespeak politics. Ashrams and cathedrals and meeting-houses? Religion. Mansions? Social aspiration, and sometimes politics and religion as well. Cottages? Cottages may speak of all these things and more, because often they are built without so much attention to what others may take their meaning to be as do grander structures. The vernacular is candid. It is, by definition, an unconsidered architectural statement.

Buildings impart feelings, ranging from a desperate need for shelter to a desire to show off. Extroverted buildings of all sizes (there are Greek Revival outhouses in upstate New York and Gothic Revival kennels) – say "notice me." Introverted buildings say "please go by and let me do my job of protection." Like us all, many of the structures pictured in this book are a mixture of both, saying both at once. According to *our own* natures, and to *our* mood at any moment, we may listen to their public statements or to their private implications. We may settle merely for easily read style-marks and common qualities, or we may choose to seek out what can be discerned only by learning about the individual persons who built each structure.

Since it is always easiest to hear what is proclaimed rather than what is whispered, the buildings in the first pages of this book are those conveying political messages – and since we humans are so prone to violence in politics, we will immediately be drawn to loud, bellicose buildings. Drums and cannon shots. Fortresses. There they are, demanding our attention to the history of the Franco-American relationship as a sequence of wars and peaces, of conflicts, reconciliations and coalitions. Though from time to time official relations may hang in a suspended frozen courtesy, as if we had not been lovers – or haters – so often, a multitude of private friendships keep us connected when Lafayette is *not* here and Generals Pershing and Marshall are not *there*. Most of the time the United States is not at war with France, as it was in 1798, and nearly was in 1834 and again in 1863. But neither are our leaders embracing each other, as Benjamin Franklin and Voltaire embraced in the 1780s to let the world know in the most direct way of an affectionate geopolitical association between the revolutionary founders of the United States and of the first French Republic, expressed again by many humbler French people and Americans in 1917 and 1945.

The story of our relationship, whose stages have been crystallized and symbolized from time to time in architecture, is not merely the extension of the ancient interplay of British and French peoples. We are both composite peoples, though the French sometimes are less celebratory of their polyglottery than are the Americans. It is well to recall that was true even when, after the world war of which the American Revolution was a part, all but two of the British colonies in North America had set themselves up as an independent confederacy in 1783, leaving out Canada and Florida, which would have added to the complexity of the barely United States. According to European law, Canada had been "French" twenty-two years earlier, and Florida had been "Spanish". The United States were still in the plural, a fragile and febrile coalition; the French had themselves only lately coalesced into a nation; many still thought of themselves as Gascons or Bretons, just as Jefferson always spoke of Virginia as his country, and Ethan Allen was always ready to take Vermont back out of the Union it had joined only at the last minute.

Nonetheless, it is convenient to ground our discussion, if only briefly, in the familiar and conventional story of Anglo-French rivalry in the New World. It commenced with Giovanni da Verrazano's staking a claim to Canada for the French (1524), Jacques Cartier's probing the St. Lawrence Valley (1535), the English sending John Hawkins on his first slave-trading expedition (1562) and Francis Drake's claim upon California (1579). France became the most important European presence in the Mississippi and St. Lawrence Valleys, and the Great Lakes Region, and remained so almost until 1763. That did not mean that the King of France ruled everywhere that maps in history books have colored blue – in contrast with the British scarlet and the Spanish green. Only a few thousand Frenchmen actually lived amid the Indians. Though some traveled widely, most remained in such little stockaded villages as New Orleans, St. Louis, Detroit, Gulfport, Mobile, Québec and Montreal.

Then, after a half-century of conflict culminating in the French and Indian War of 1754-1763, the *fleur de lys* flag went down and the Union Jack went up. A few Englishmen, Scots and Irishmen now strode about in uniform, and lawsuits were pressed in English in these places among the Indians and French and many people who were both – as they had for a few decades east of the Appalachians. Within the present limits of the United States, France was done, though a corporal's guard of Napoleonic troops returned to hold New Orleans for two months in 1803, to collect on the Louisiana Purchase. In the 1860s, south of the Rio Grande in Mexico, France made a last attempt for a North American empire. Here are some useful political dates of events thereafter to set beside those given for the buildings in this book:

The American Revolutionary War – 1775-1783

The First Franco-American Alliance – 1779-1783

The first French Revolution – 1789

The Quasi-War between France and the United States – 1797-1799

The Alliance of Napoleon and President Thomas Jefferson against the Toussaint government of Haiti
      – 1800-1803 – leading to the Louisiana Purchase – 1803

The Third Franco-American Alliance ("The War of 1812") –1812-1815

The American Civil War and the French invasion of Mexico ("The Second Empire") – 1860s

The Fourth Franco-American Alliance (World War I) – 1917-1918

The Fifth Franco-American Alliance (World War II) – 1941-1945

Our subject is in large part architecture in America influenced by France, informing us in a variety of ways, some obvious and some very subtle, of the ways in which Americans have expressed an affinity for things French – and for ideas that were sufficiently French as to find expression in large, inhabitable objects: BIG things French. Even when we have been at war with each other, even where governments were British and the official language English, French taste has guided the hands of people of English whose heritage was Irish, or German, Dutch or Scottish – especially Scottish.

Many of the photographs in this book show French architects' and engineers' participation in the creation of an independent American architecture – though we must not imagine that it required the political break from Britain to provide them clients in America. As early as 1562, Jean Ribault, in the service of French Huguenot colonizers, built the first of the military installations on what is now the Marine training center on Parris Island, South Carolina. Ribault's clients were massacred by the Spaniards, on religious rather than political grounds – the French were Protestant.

During the ensuing century, French royal policy became more repressive of religious dissent, driving Huguenot technocrats to British America, ready to serve Protestant lords of any nationality. Requiring a design for a fort at Yorke, on the York

River in Virginia, the settlers compensated Nicholas Martieu (or Martiau) with a new citizenship and a grant of sixteen hundred acres. His land included the terrain around Yorktown where, in 1781, other French military engineers laid up the earthworks to besiege Lord Cornwallis. Among the lineal descendants of Martieu was a surveyor whose military reputation reached its apogee at Yorktown: George Washington.

Martieu's successor among French-educated engineers in the English colonies of America was Gabriel Bernard, the uncle, tutor and long-suffering guardian of Jean-Jacques Rousseau. Bernard had served in campaigns against the Turks with James Oglethorpe, who became the proprietor of Georgia; he laid out eleven towns for Franco-Swiss emigrants to Oglethorpe's domain, and probably composed the plan for Savannah itself. After his death in 1737, he was succeeded by William Gerard De Brahm, who designed more towns and more forts and led German colonists to Georgia. In the 1750s, he was busy as far inland as Fort Loudoun, in Tennessee, and gave Savannah a new set of fortifications. Claude-Joseph Sauthier was a contemporary of De Brahm's and mapped North Carolina and New York, while De Brahm provided the first detailed maps of Georgia and South Carolina. Sauthier came to North Carolina in the 1760s in the service of Governor William Tryon, a willful, vainglorious and splendid gentleman whose expensive tastes in gardens (designed by Sauthier) and in mansions such as Tryon Palace in New Bern detonated the smoldering resentments of upcountry colonists who rose in revolt in 1771.

The first coastal defenses of the American Republic were largely built by French engineers. So, too, was the academy at West Point that trained their American-born replacements of the Corps of Engineers. "The First American System" – geometric fortresses carrying cannons on earthen parapets – was created by French engineers employed by state governments from 1783 through 1793. After 1807, when war with Britain became likely, the "Second System" commenced, producing the "French" forts to be found protecting every major port of the eastern seaboard. After Waterloo, former officers of Napoleon created our "Third System".

Drawing upon Napoleonic experience with massed artillery, and new concepts in casement construction developed by Montalembert, they stacked decks – three, most often – full of artillery. Civil War photographs of the results of bombardments of these fortresses at the entrances to Southern ports from Newport News to Galveston, showing blackened apertures in their immense walls, cleavages holding crippled cannons like cigars in the mouths of drunken soldiers, are images of Napoleonic engineering put to the test in American civil conflict.

Though outside the period addressed in this book, when these pictures were taken, in the 1860s, France had reappeared in the New World as an imperial power – Napoleon III had installed the hapless Maximilian as puppet-emperor of Mexico while the Americans were otherwise distracted.

Third Order Forts were the speaking architecture of the lingering First Empire. To the confusion of many, the Second Empire was established by Napoleon the Third. His Second Empire was briefly but emphatically influential in American taste. To make way for Napoleon III's artillery to put down rebellions in Paris, Baron Georges Eugène Haussmann created broad avenues destroying the raffish variety of medieval Paris – and exercised a lingering influence upon American city planning. Hausmannizing was the urban renewal of the 1870s and 1880s. A little earlier, in the 1850s, those American towns such as Cambridge, Massachusetts, that managed to prosper despite the depression of that decade, took upon themselves a domestic architecture in the Second Empire Style. Mansard roofs, emerging in Paris to escape the technicalities of the third Napoleon's real estate taxation, swelled and gelled upon mansions and cottages from Oregon to Maine – but, oddly enough, exerted very little influence in New Orleans, Biloxi or Québec.

Redemption from the twin traits of Hausmannizing and mansardizing emerged from Paris as the nineteenth century wore on. Students of the *École des Beaux-Arts* such as Richard Morris Hunt, H.H. Richardson and Louis Sullivan brought French discipline to tame the carpenters' frenzy of late nineteenth century American extravagance. It is no more possible to apprehend the nature of "the birth of [recent] American architecture" without taking account of what the *École* did for Hunt, Richardson and Sullivan, than it is to see clearly the neo-classical world of Jefferson, Latrobe and Ramée, three-quarters of a century earlier, without including within that view the contributions of the French neoclassicism of the 1780s and 1790s.

Some, including Sullivan himself, suggested that *Beaux-arts* neo-neoclassicism chilled a truly American exuberance. Perhaps. Perhaps as well the cool, bleached Columbian Exposition style that followed the European example prepared the way for the chill International Style of the 1950s and 1960s. Indisputably, the more animated but scarcely "organic" art of Le Corbusier won the admiration of sophisticated American clients and American architects. True, there is a direct lineage between Le Corbusier's Fogg Museum for Harvard (1961-63) and Richard Meier's Getty complex in Los Angeles of the 1990s. It is noteworthy, however, that despite the derision with which the Prairie School architects such as Sullivan and his pupil Frank Lloyd Wright derided what they called "bozart" architecture, Sullivan showed considerable admiration for the *Art Nouveau*, and Wright would not be Wright without the presence of the spidery designs of Le Corbusier.

And to return to the beginning – let us recall our long Franco-American association by listening to the architecture of the two great campuses developed in deference to French architectural precepts by architects French in heritage or affinity. Both designs are like great châteaux, centered on rotundas and flanked by pavilions. The first was Joseph Jacques Ramée's Union College in Schenectady, New York, commencing in 1815. Five years later came the University of Virginia, the mature expression of Jefferson's experience in Paris and his association with the genius of Benjamin Henry Latrobe de Boneval.

The brothers Charles and Joseph Francis Mangin, Hamilton's favorite architects, made New York a classically French town with its first great theater building, the Park; its City Hall (in collaboration with John McComb); and the first St. Patrick's Cathedral, fragments of which remain on Mott Street. They probably joined McComb as well in the design of Hamilton's "Creole" house, the Grange. And the most famous of French military engineers to work in the United States, Major Charles L'Enfant, laid out our national capital on the footprint of Versailles itself, with the Capitol in the place of Louis XIV's château and the White House in the location of the Petit Trianon. What could speak more eloquently of a Franco-American affinity than that?

What a long way we have come from the springtime of the Republic, and from the fresh, ebullient spirits of "the Party of Hope" in France and in the United States! Yet we may be refreshed by the memory of great architects working in that spirit. The American Progressive Architects were also members of the Party of Hope. And as we begin a new century, let us hope that the philanthropic impulses of French Heritage Society still unite us, and that we may listen again to the speaking architecture of that time, as well as to the Preamble to the Declaration of Independence and the Declaration of Rights of Man.

Roger G. Kennedy

The idea for *French America* took shape several years ago over lunch in a Paris café. My luncheon companion, Arielle de La Tour d'Auvergne, was a gifted photographer who had done work for several French magazines and for French Heritage Society (FHS), then called Friends of Vieilles Maisons Françaises, a Franco-American charitable organization that had raised millions of dollars to restore French heritage properties in both France and the United States. The 200th anniversary of the Louisiana Purchase was going to be celebrated in 2003, and FHS wanted to mark the occasion. Would I, Arielle asked, be interested in collaborating on a visual history of the French heritage in the United States that would more or less coincide with the anniversary?

The idea intrigued me. As an American journalist living in Paris, I had a foot in both cultures. I believed that living abroad allowed me to view my own country more dispassionately than I had during the forty-odd years I lived there. And I had always been fascinated by the complexities of French/American relations, which vacillated between hostility and grudging admiration.

But there were hesitations. I was neither a historian nor an architect, and wondered whether I could do justice to a subject that required a considerable knowledge of both fields. I was also unsure about how much of the French heritage remained intact in the United States. I knew that after the French defeat by the British at Québec in 1759, the British and then the Americans had become the dominant forces in what had been *Nouvelle France*. Were there enough French traces left to fill a book?

To find out required a several month crash reading course about the French in America. I was fortunate in that a number of respected scholars – Carl J. Ekberg, Roger G. Kennedy, W.J. Eccles – had produced works of outstanding quality that were solid introductions to the subject. Both Ekberg and Kennedy graciously consented to contribute essays to this book, lending it the intellectual heft it required.

My research convinced me that while a great deal had been written on the subject, no book, as far as I could discover, had ever taken on the task of providing a visual history of the French experience in America, one that combined a commentary on French-related sites with a full-color photographic presentation illustrating them. Consider this, then, to be a popular history of the French in America, leavened with commentary by recognized experts in the field. The aim here has been to balance the visual – the lovely photographs of Arielle de La Tour d'Auvergne – with a commentary that enriches and explains them.

After a round of reading and pouring over maps and planning an itinerary, the author and photographer – armed with several reference books, a briefcase full of maps, contact numbers, a tape recorder and a Hasselblad – "lit out for the territory", in Huck Finn's phrase, knowing little of what we would find.

Surprisingly, as this book illustrates, there was a great deal, as we discovered in our visits to more than 150 sites. The preservation movement in the United States, which has picked up steam in the last few decades, has awakened America's conscience to the importance of preserving the remaining remnants of its heritage. Small in numbers, but remarkably determined, the preservationists, with growing success, have fought off developers and the indifference of public officials to set aside a range of historic French properties for future generations. In Dupo, Illinois, for example, a fire chief with a passion for old houses saved the Martin-Boismenue Creole cottage, that had been destined to be replaced by a car wash; in Florissant, Missouri, when the Archbishop said the historic Shrine of St. Ferdinand could not be saved, a non-profit group raised $100,000 to restore it; in St. Louis, a collection of private citizens talked the Missouri Highway Commission into rerouting an interstate highway a few feet to the east in order to spare the Greek Revival Chatillon-DeMenil House. The lesson appears to be that preservation can triumph over thoughtless commercialism if its backers are stubborn and insistent enough.

Other Americans inspired us by their determination, against overwhelming odds, to restore and inhabit authentic French-inspired dwellings that had fallen into ruin. In Louisiana we ran across formidable women in Breaux Bridge and Baton Rouge, who had a deep appreciation of old Creole houses and arranged to have decaying structures disassembled piece by piece and transported dozens of miles so they could be lovingly restored in felicitous surroundings. In

Ste. Genevieve, Missouri, a retired professor and his contractor insisted on using eighteenth-century tools and materials to restore the Green Tree Tavern to its 1790s appearance. There were other stories equally as surprising, which convinced us we were on to something.

Purists will note that *French America* does not include all of the remaining French sites in the United States. The author and photographer would liked to have visited the Grand Portage Monument in Minnesota, Vincennes in Indiana, Fort Niagara in New York, Fort Caroline in Florida, and dozens of other places that might well have found a place in these pages. That we didn't is a consequence of limited space and limited time, coupled with the difficulty of developing a book like this one while living abroad. In Carl Ekberg's introductory words, what *is* documented in these pages is "a broad range – political, military, architectural, artisanal, and cultural – of French influences within the United States".

What we hope emerges from the book is an appreciation of the abiding links between the French and American people, links that have somehow survived in spite of occasional rocky periods, jealousies, angry diplomatic exchanges and mutual incomprehension. The stereotyped views of the French as effete cultural snobs and the Americans as money-driven philistines have always been gross distortions. The fact is that our peoples are many-faceted and complex, and are drawn to one another in ways that go deeper than many of us comprehend.

Special thanks at the outset must go to the French Heritage Society and its President, Marie-Sol de La Tour d'Auvergne, who had the vision to commission this project and who worked tirelessly to raise the funds to support it. Our gratitude to Karen Archer, also of French Heritage Society, whose creative eye lent shape to the final text, to Sharon Delezinski, whose search for sponsors moved the project forward, to Jane Bernbach for her support from the FHS New York office, to George Martin for his legal skills, and to Louise Brody, our designer, who overcame our shifting demands to produce this elegant layout.

Research on a book like this has a snowball effect. One source leads to another, and little by little the broader picture emerges. We also extend our appreciation to those who opened doors for us and put us on to the experts who filled the gaps in our knowledge in more than five hundred pages of personal interviews. Still others, cited below, spent long hours escorting us to French sites and correcting the errors in our text. If mistakes remain, the fault is mine, not theirs.

On a more personal note, my deepest thanks to Arielle de La Tour d'Auvergne, not only for her talent as a photographer, but for her diligence and unfailing good humor during three exhausting trips to the United States – and, above all, to my partner, Madeleine Volpelier, who lived as "une veuve de la Louisiane" during two difficult years and whose love and patience enabled me to complete this book.

The others, listed below, are equally deserving of our gratitude: Steve Anderson, Judge Morris Arnold, Barbara Bacot, Charles Balesi, Daniel Baker, James Baker, H. Parrot Bacot, Monique Barbier, Mark de Basile, Connie Becnel, John Braunlein, Hal Brayman, Stanhope and Libby Browne, Ellen Bush, Keven Campbell, Dr. Paula Carlo, Madeleine Cenac, Arlen Chaleff, Dr. Eugene Cizek, Donna and William Charron, Mary Louise Christovich (and all the staff of the New Orleans Historical Society), Tim Conley, Mary Y. Cooper, Todd Cooper, Helene Crozat, Christal Dagit, Rosemary Davidson, Lola Dunahoe, George Ewert, Dr. Firth Fabend, Dominique Flahaut de La Billarderie, Kim Fontenot, Jan Frederick, Jonathan Fricker, William Fritz, Charles Gray, Esley Hamilton, Dorinda M. Hilburn, Dr. Jack Holden, John R. House III, Bill Hyland, Dr. and Mrs. Robert C. Judice, Elbrun Kimmelman, Isabelle de Larouillière, John Lawrence, Dr. Alfred Lemmon, Meg Lousteau, Jack Luer, Emily Lyons, Donna Oliver, Estelle Powers, Norman and Sand Marmillion, Ruth Menard, Mimi Miller, Molly McKenzie, Bob Moore, Paul Nevski, Dr. Charles Nolan, James W. Parker, Brandon Gerard Parlange, Mike Pecen, Andy Rhodes, Rosemary and Dick Rosenthal, Professor Bertrand van Ruymbeke, Sandra Schexnyder, Rick Seale, James Sefcik, Lloyd Sensat, George W. Shorter, Jr., John Sledge, Robert E. Smith, Alexandra Stafford, Sally Stassi, Patti Teper Sherman, Cheryl Stromeyer, Barbara Turner, Carol Wells, Janet Westervelt, Edward Wood, Jr., Marge and Royce Wilhauk, Anne Woodhouse, and Virginia Young.

Ron Katz, Paris, France, June 2004

The early French incursions into North America were sporadic and tentative. Preoccupied with their own conflicts in Europe, the French were slow to develop an interest in colonizing the New World.

The first French to come were fishermen from Normandy and Brittany, who mined the rich fishing grounds on the Grand Banks of Newfoundland from around 1500. But the growing power of Spain and Portugal in the New World, spurred by Magellan's circumnavigation of the globe (1519-1521), led the young French monarch, François I, to react to the political threat. In 1524, the king sent an Italian, Giovanni da Verrazano, on a voyage to explore the North American coast from Charleston, South Carolina to Maine. Verrazano was not under orders to colonize; he was sent to further French commercial interests by seeking a route through North America to the Indies.

The same motives drove Jacques Cartier, who followed in 1534. Cartier, like Verrazano, searched in vain for a strait that would lead to the Pacific Ocean. Cartier's two voyages, and a later failed attempt by Jean-François de la Rocque de Roberval, led François I to abandon once and for all any idea of establishing colonies overseas.

Some decades later, the first French attempt to establish a colony in North America ended in disaster. This time the motivation was essentially a religious one. In 1562, Admiral Gaspard de Coligny, the Huguenot first minister of Henry II, sent a group of Huguenot émigres to present-day Florida to establish a Protestant sanctuary in *Nouvelle France*. But the settlement, known as Fort Caroline, was overrun by the Spanish and all of its settlers put to the sword.

Samuel Champlain, who followed in the early 1600s, did establish a permanent settlement at Québec, but apart from forays into New England and New York, did not explore the interior of the present-day United States. Only several decades later did French Huguenot settlers, driven by religious persecution under Catholic monarchs, start trickling in to settle alongside the Dutch and British in present-day New York and South Carolina.

The early French had to face unimaginable hardships – impenetrable forests, savage Indians, disease and extremes of heat and cold – to gain a foothold in *Nouvelle France*. Many died in the attempt, but the few who endured laid the groundwork for those to follow.

THE EARLY EAST COAST SETTLEMENTS

THE PATHFINDERS
SAMUEL DE CHAMPLAIN: FATHER OF *NOUVELLE FRANCE*

∧

Champlain, who spent three decades in *Nouvelle France*, set the stage for the French explorers who followed him.

©Photo Library of Congress

Cartographer, geographer, bold explorer and chronicler of *Nouvelle France*, Samuel de Champlain was the first of the French explorers to devote the greater part of his life to the dream of a French colonial presence in North America. He made the hazardous transatlantic journey no fewer than twenty-three times in a career that spanned more than three decades in the New World. Founder of Québec and of Montreal, Champlain is linked with the Canada he helped to create more than with the United States later explored in depth by Marquette, La Salle and other Frenchmen who followed in his wake. But he was the first native of France to make his presence known – in present day New York and New England – and as such he set the stage for the voyages to follow.

The son of a mariner, Champlain accompanied his father on several voyages before he set out for North America. Like La Salle, who followed him by some decades, he appears not to have been motivated by personal gain but by the relentless curiosity of the born explorer. Champlain got his chance in 1603, when the Duc de Montmorency, admiral of France, appointed Pierre de Gua, Sieur de Monts, the vice-admiral of Acadia, a region that stretched from the Atlantic eastward on both sides of the St. Lawrence River. The aim of de Monts' mission was twofold: to discover mineral deposits and to stake a claim to the area against those of the Spanish, the English and the Dutch. As geographer and historian, Champlain accompanied de Monts and created valuable charts of the east coast.

Champlain chose Québec as the most defensible place for a settlement, and ventured on the St. Lawrence as far as Sault St. Louis, gathering information from the Indians about Lake Erie, Lake Ontario, the Detroit River and Niagara Falls. In 1605-1606, he traveled south to the coast of New England and in 1608-1609 explored the Green Mountains and the Adirondacks, and discovered the lake on the Vermont-New York border that now bears his name. While at the present site of Fort Ticonderoga, he engaged the Iroquois in a brief but vicious fight in which the Indians were roundly defeated. A marker at the site bears his name.

Back in Canada, Champlain, like other French explorers, had to contend with the frequent indifference of the French Crown –. preoccupied with internal struggles with the Huguenots and foreign wars – as well as quarrels with the French merchant class. An English force besieged Québec in 1629, forcing his return to France. The colony was returned to France three years later in the Treaty of Saint-Germain-en-Laye.

On his return to Canada, Champlain was appointed governor of Québec and struggled to maintain the colony's precarious existence. He died in Québec in 1635 and was buried in the chapel he had built for the hundred colonists who remained. Honored by the Hurons, whose cause he had championed, he wrote a last message to Cardinal Richelieu a few months before his death. In it he called Québec a capital founded "for the glory of God … and the renown of the French."

French military architecture –
Vauban and the American forts

The French who came to *Nouvelle France* brought with them the concepts for fortifications developed by the engineer Sébastien Le Prestre de Vauban. A protégé of Louis XIV, Vauban was assigned the task of building a chain of forts to protect France's border lands in the northeast.

Vauban, a soldier himself, directed a number of sieges for the king's armies in the years after 1658. As a person skilled in the tactics of attack, he was particularly well qualified to develop fortifications that effectively resisted the sieges that characterized seventeenth-century warfare. Vauban saw that modern weapons, particularly cannons, could be devastating to thick stone walls and towers, which crumbled when frontally assaulted. What was required, in his view, were fortifications that could not only resist attacks, but that could provide the defenders with an edge that would help direct their fire against aggressors.

The solution that Vauban developed was the star-shaped fort, with bastions protruding from the corners that would leave the defenders no blind spots and would enable them to direct accurate cannon and musket fire on besieging armies. To augment firepower from the bastions, the thick walls of the ramparts were slit, allowing the defenders to rake the surrounding moats with gunfire.

Vauban designed more than thirty forts and fortified

walled towns and strengthened a number of others throughout France during his long career – from the Citadel at Lille in the north to the fortifications on Ile de Ré in the west.

So pervasive was Vauban's influence that many of the French forts built in the New World followed his design. Most of the American forts were rather flimsy structures, built in haste of wooden palisades that soon rotted in the earth. The very early French forts – such as Maurepas near Biloxi, Mississippi and Crèvecoeur at Peoria, Illinois – have virtually disappeared without a trace. The stone fortresses, such as Fort de Chartres in Illinois and Carillon (Ticonderoga) in New York, fared better, but even they fell into ruin, though they have now been restored.

But while they lasted, the forts did shield their inhabitants during trying times. More than military bases, they were often – as in the case of Fort Toulouse in Alabama and Fort de Chartres – administrative centers that served a civil as well as a military purpose, and they were a refuge against a savage wilderness. The early French settlements grew up around them and depended on them for sustenance and protection. Their importance is reflected in the scores of fortress re-creations that have taken place in America during the last quarter-century, evidence of a determination to preserve this key element of the French heritage.

∧
Vauban, Louis XIV's chief engineer, was charged with constructing fortifications all over France – from Lille in the north to Marseille in the south. One of his more impressive works is the Citadel at Belle-Ile-en-Mer (*la Citadelle Vauban*) in Brittany, built in 1674 after the island had been attacked and pillaged by the Dutch. The Citadel, which sits on the port, Le Palais, contains an impressive museum and has been restored to its seventeenth-century appearance.
©Photo M. Plisson

<
A model of a Vauban star-shaped fort showing the four bastions at the corners
(University of South Alabama).

THE JOURNEY OF THE HUGUENOTS

They were skilled craftsmen, merchants, artisans and professional people, cruelly persecuted in the religious upheavals that periodically flared in France during the sixteenth and seventeenth centuries. In the late seventeenth century, they sought religious freedom and economic opportunity – in England, the Netherlands, Switzerland, Germany and as far afield as South Africa. Around 2,000-3,000 of them fled to the east coast of America – to present-day New York, Massachusetts, Virginia and the Carolinas. In time, they made a memorable contribution to the building of the American republic.

They were called Huguenots, French Protestants who followed the teachings of John Calvin, with a belief in salvation through individual faith without the need for the intercession of a church hierarchy and in the individual's right to interpret scripture for himself.

The origins of the term Huguenot are uncertain: some claim links to the legendary King Hugo, since during the sixteenth century the Protestants at Tours used to assemble at night near the gate that bears his name. The *Encyclopedia Britannica* claims the word derives from the German *Eldgenosen* (confederates bound together by oath) used to describe the patriots of Geneva hostile to the Duke of Savoy and whose leader was named Hugues.

Corruption and reaction

The France of the sixteenth century consisted of a series of fiefdoms, some of which were but loosely linked to the Crown.

In the struggle to assert a centralizing authority, the Catholic Church accumulated vast power and wealth. Before the Council of Trent (1560), it was also corrupt, with appointments to church office often sold as annuities and churchmen numbering among the richest subjects of the kingdom.

Countervailing forces took root. The writings of John Calvin, born in Picardy in 1509, were fundamental to the growth of French Protestantism. Calvin's book, *The Institutes of the Christian Religion* (1536), was instrumental in sending large numbers of French students to Geneva to experience his teachings first-hand, and on their return, many became Protestant ministers. Calvin's writings were censored in the early 1540s, and Parisian booksellers who sold them were persecuted. But Protestantism continued to thrive; in 1559, the first underground Huguenot Church, based on the teachings of Calvin, was founded in a home in Paris.

Persecutions and reprieves

The French rulers who followed François I alternately persecuted and reprieved the Huguenots. Henri II promulgated the Edict of Chateaubriand in 1551, which speeded the trials of heretics. Catherine de Medici, recognizing the growing power of the Huguenots, especially among the nobility, had the Edict of January issued in 1562. The Edict recognized the Huguenot Church and permitted it to hold services outside of towns and in the country. But later that year, several hundred Huguenots were slain at Vassy, and France entered into more than thirty-five years of religious wars.

The seminal event of the period occurred on August 24, 1572, the Feast of St. Bartholomew, when the organized killing of Huguenots began during the festivities in Paris honoring the marriage of Henri de Navarre (later Henri IV) and Marguerite de Valois or "Queen Margot". In the days

<
Commemorative plaques on the Huguenot Monument in New Rochelle. The monument celebrates the arrival of the first Huguenot settlers to the town in the 1680s.

and weeks that followed, several thousand were massacred, though enough survived to fight on through the wars of religion.

The Edict of Nantes and its revocation

A period of tolerance towards the Huguenots was ushered in when Henri de Navarre, a Protestant who had re-converted to Catholicism to become king (saying "Paris vaut bien une messe," or "Paris is worth a mass"), promulgated the Edict of Nantes in 1598. The Edict provided freedom of conscience and of the press to Huguenots, plus civil and judicial equity, and allowed them to exercise their religion in all but seventeen specified Catholic towns.

But when Henri (by this time, King Henri IV) was assassinated in 1610, the Huguenots lost their royal protection, and under Henri's successor, Louis XIII, they were forced to surrender all of their property. Several unsuccessful Huguenot rebellions followed in the 1620s, one of which led to the long siege of La Rochelle. The peace of Alès, Languedoc, forced the Huguenots to surrender their arms and canceled several clauses of the Edict of Nantes. The entire Edict was finally revoked by Louis XIV in 1685, and the period following saw renewed persecution, characterized by the notorious "dragonnades", where regiments of soldiers brutalized Protestants and forced them to convert to Catholicism. The migration of the Huguenots intensified, with around 200,000 fleeing the country.

<
The Huguenot Memorial Cemetery in New Rochelle has tombstones dating back to the late seventeenth century. Some were engraved in early modern French by Huguenot masons.

Migrations

The first attempt to resettle Huguenots in America occurred in 1562. But this ill-fated effort to settle in Florida foundered when the Spanish admiral Pedro Menéndez de Avilés, under orders from Spain's Philip II, massacred four hundred members of the colony in the autumn of 1565 and placed a marker nearby denouncing the dead as heretics, hanged "not as Frenchmen but as Lutherans".

In the years after 1685, the fleeing Huguenots were sheltered in the Netherlands, Germany, England and Switzerland, though their reception was uneven, especially in England, where they were first welcomed but later regarded with suspicion, particularly by native workers who resented their competition and sometimes superior skills.

In North America, the first refugees arrived in what is now New York in the 1660s. Protestant families founded the village of New Rochelle in 1689. Other Huguenot settlements were established in New York City, Staten Island, New Paltz and western Long Island, followed by settlements in South Carolina, Maine, New Jersey, Pennsylvania, Delaware, Virginia and Maryland. In America, many Huguenot names were later anglicized as a result of the settlers' integration into the Anglo-American world. Some converted to Catholicism, others assimilated into Dutch or English societies. Most, however, converted to the Church of England.

A street of Huguenot homes – New Paltz

Huguenot refugees began arriving in New Amsterdam as early as 1660. Some, like those who founded New Paltz, had lived in the Palatinate ("Pfalz") region of Germany in the vicinity of Mannheim. Most, however, had been born in northern France, in the Artois, in cities like Calais and Lille.

In 1677, some Huguenots, having migrated to North America, purchased from the Esopus Indians around four thousand acres of land in the Hudson Valley on a fertile plain on the banks of the Wallkill River. They were called the "patentees", because they had received a patent for the land from Edmund Andros, the English Royal Governor. New Paltz devised a form of government that demonstrated the importance of the family in managing local affairs. In 1738, the citizens of the town elected a council of "Twelve Men" (referred to as the "Duzine" in early histories) who were responsible for surveying the land and subdividing it

in the patent. The Duzine continued to exercise these functions until the early nineteenth century, when this responsibility was turned over to an elected town government.

The houses the Huguenots constructed were sturdy and simple, built of stone, and passed down through the generations. Because the region was Dutch, there are more Dutch than French features in their construction. Under the auspices of the Huguenot Historical Society of New Paltz, preservation accelerated in the 1950s, and by 1974 seven houses and their outbuildings had been acquired.

Completed around the year 1721, the Jean Hasbrouck House is notable for its kitchen and its large attic, once used for storing grain, and for its massive brick chimney, said to be the largest of its kind in North America. The house has a steeply pitched roof and square dimensions. Its grand scale and extensive use of glazed windows reflect that it was built as a statement of wealth and position in the community. Five generations of Hasbroucks lived here, and for a structure some three hundred years old, it is in remarkable condition.

∧

The Jean Hasbrouck
House is noted for its
large attic, once used
for storing grain, and for
its massive brick chimney,
said to be the largest of
its kind in North America.

>

The jambless fireplace
in the Jean Hasbrouck
House is said to be
the only original
of its kind remaining
in the United States.

The Bevier-Elting House has the appearance of a Dutch townhouse. A unique example of the earliest architectural style of the New Paltz Huguenot houses, its gable end faces the street, a feature of Dutch architecture. Louis Bevier, who migrated from Speyer in the German Palatinate, built the west end of the house, which consisted of three rooms, with a living space and a large fireplace where the cooking was done.

The only reconstruction on Huguenot Street, the French Church, dates from 1972. Based on historical drawings and documents, the church is closely modeled on the first Huguenot house of worship in New Paltz, dating from 1717-1718. Replaced in the 1770s and in 1839, it gave way to the larger Greek Revival Protestant church that still stands on Huguenot Street in New Paltz. The reconstructed French Church, of considerable charm, is a square stone structure

with a highly pitched roof. In early times, a young boy may have climbed the steps leading to the cupola to blow on a conch or sound a horn summoning the Protestants to worship. The interior, too, is plain. Family pews face each other, and a pulpit stands high at one end of the church.

Thanks to the efforts of the Huguenot Historical Society, a number of other Huguenot structures have been carefully preserved. Among others, these include: the Abraham Hasbrouck House (1694), the Hugo Freer House (1694-96) and the LeFevre House, a Federal Style home dating from 1799.

The New Rochelle
Huguenots had their
own French church until
the early eighteenth
century. Afterwards,
they affiliated with
the Church of England
and later with the
Presbyterian church.
The First Presbyterian
Church in New Rochelle
(1928) is the latest
in a line of Huguenot-
affiliated churches
in the city.

The refugees from La Rochelle – New Rochelle

The first Huguenots settled in what is now New Rochelle in the late 1680s. Some were already living in New York, but were frightened that the French government of Louis XIV, which had revoked the Edict of Nantes in 1685, would conquer the area and send them back to France. The purchase of six thousand relatively isolated acres, known as the Manor of Pelham, was negotiated by Jacob Leisler, a wealthy merchant who briefly assumed the duties of Royal Governor of New York in 1689. After Leisler purchased the land from John Pell for 1,625 pounds sterling, he divided it into individual lots to sell to the Huguenots.

Most of the settlers of New Rochelle came from the French provinces of Aunis, Poitou and Saintonge. Some fifteen families came from the port of La Rochelle in Aunis; another five or so came from the Ile de Ré, just offshore from La Rochelle. Although tradition has it that a group of Huguenot settlers arrived in 1690 by ship at Bonnefoy's Point (present-day Hudson Park), it is more likely that their first point of entry was New York.

The Huguenots began settling in, building first simple wooden dwellings, then in 1692 a French church. In time, the French dominance in New Rochelle gave way to English influences, with the majority of Huguenot settlers eventually

Lewis Pintard House.
The house remained
in the Pintard family
until 1827, after which
it became the home of
the Episcopal ministers
and a boys' school.
Moved in 1928 to its
present location next
to the church, the house
is now occupied by the
minister of the First
Presbyterian Church.

joining the established Church of England. The Huguenot heritage, however, remains very much alive. On Huguenot Street, located along the "Old Post Road" from New York to Boston, can be found the sites of the first church, school, tavern and dwellings of the ancient village of New Rochelle. In Hudson Park are memorials dedicated to the early Huguenot settlers.

By 1710, most members of the original French Church had decided to affiliate with the Church of England. The French Church was eventually reorganized and became known as "The Presbyterian Church in the Town of La Rochelle, formerly known by the name of the French Church". In 1862, a new church was built, which served the growing congregation until 1926 when it was destroyed by fire. Another Presbyterian church, The Second Presbyterian Church of New Rochelle, was founded in 1891. In 1974 it united with the first church to become what is today the First Presbyterian Church.

Adjacent to the First Presbyterian Church sits the Lewis Pintard House, dating from the 1720s and originally owned by Alexander Allaire, a Huguenot. The house has links to important events in American history. After passing through several hands, it was purchased by Pierre Vallade in 1765, and shortly after his death by Lewis Pintard, a prominent New York City merchant who used it

as his country home. Pintard, an eminent figure during the American Revolution, was an emissary for American prisoners held by the British in New York.

In remembrance of the Huguenot families who contributed to New Rochelle's early history, there are two commemorative monuments in Hudson Park. The first, the Huguenot Monument, celebrates the arrival of the Huguenots in the town. Erected in 1898 by the Huguenot Association of New Rochelle and the Westchester County Historical Society, it was paid for by local descendants of the Huguenot settlers. Declared a historic site by the city council, the Huguenot Memorial Cemetery has tombstones dating back to the late seventeenth century. Some tombstones were engraved in early modern French by Huguenot masons. Lovingly carved by hand, the early stones are a potent reminder of the Huguenot men and women who struggled against heavy odds to make of this wilderness a refuge from the religious persecution that had driven them from their home country.

∧

New Rochelle. Commemorative monument to the Huguenot settlers in Hudson Park.

<

New Rochelle. Ancient hand-carved tombstone in the Huguenot Cemetery.

The Billiou-Stilwell-Perine
House, an asymmetrical
stone cottage in Dongan
Hills, dates from around
1663. Originally the home
of the Huguenot émigré
Pierre Billiou, the house
has a steeply pitched roof
similar to those found
on some of the Huguenot
homes in New Paltz.

Huguenots amidst the English and Dutch – Staten Island

Another group of New Netherland's Huguenot immigrants settled on Staten Island at the entrance to New York harbor ("Staaten Eylant" as the Dutch explorer, Henry Hudson, had christened it) in the early 1600s. New Netherland's Governor General, Peter Minuit, a Huguenot of Walloon background, allegedly purchased Manhattan Island from the Indians in 1626.

Small numbers of Huguenot immigrants arrived in the mid-1600s, but a series of Indian raids forced them to move to elsewhere on the island or to other locations in what was then called New Amsterdam. The English took over the island in 1664, and their rule brought new English settlers to mix with the French, Dutch and Walloons who had earlier made the island home. By the 1680s, French-speaking Protestants were numerous enough to have their own congregation, and a church building was constructed in 1698.

The original church of the Huguenots on Staten Island no longer exists, but its site on Arthur Kill Road is indicated by a state historical marker. As in other Huguenot settlements, adherence to the French Church weakened in the early eighteenth century, and in 1734 the church was closed down. In 1849 the Huguenot Park Reformed Church was organized, and the current church building, which has some architectural similarities to colonial-era Huguenot houses of worship, was erected in 1924. The names of early Huguenot settlers are memorialized in stone on the walls and pillars of the church.

There are many reminders of the Huguenots on Staten Island. Foremost among them is a community in southern Staten Island named "Huguenot" in honor of the French settlers. Numerous street and place names also evoke memories of prominent Huguenots and Walloons, including Guyon, Poillon, Seguine, Mercereau, Du Bois, Latourette and Androvette.

In Richmondtown, the St. Andrew's Church, where some Huguenot families gravitated after leaving the French Church, resembles many twelfth-century Norman churches.

A magnet for early Huguenot settlers – Charleston

Along with Boston and New York City, South Carolina was one of the sites attracting Huguenot settlers who fled Europe in the late seventeenth century. Encouraged by pamphlets stressing religious tolerance and commercial opportunities, Huguenots started arriving in South Carolina as early as 1680. By 1699 close to five hundred of them lived in the area, split among several settlements – at Santee, Orange Quarter, Goose Creek and Charleston. The Huguenots of Charleston (then called "Charles Town") were numerous enough to build their first French Church in the 1680s. In farming, trade and politics, the Huguenots of South Carolina exercised an influence far beyond their limited numbers.

An 1845 church stands on the site where the first French Church was erected by the Huguenots in the 1680s before being destroyed in the fire that swept through Charleston in 1741. The present church is the last in a series of renovations and reconstructions that have taken place on the site during the last three-and-a-quarter centuries. Rebuilt in 1744 after the fire, it fell into decay during the 1770s and was destroyed by dynamite in 1796 to keep a rampaging fire from Charleston's wharves. During the nineteenth century, it was rebuilt in 1805 and again in 1845.

The Huguenot cemetery, adjoining the Huguenot church has been the final resting place for Huguenot settlers for more than three centuries. Its ancient tombstones are a link to the past, when French refugees helped to build a settlement in what is now one of the loveliest cities in the South.

The Gothic Revival Huguenot church is the oldest surviving Huguenot house of worship in the Western Hemisphere. Designed by Edward Brickell White, it is an impressive edifice with bright white stucco over brick and an unusual ornamentation of iron and carved stonework. Its clear glass windows were part of the original French Church. ©Photos Jane Bernbach

Unlike the English, who generally stayed close to the coastlines and established permanent settlements, the French ventured up the St. Lawrence Valley to the Great Lakes, where they formed alliances with the Huron and Algonquin Indians. Father Jacques Marquette, the young Jesuit priest who spoke several Indian dialects, was the first Frenchman to venture into the heart of North America when he entered the Mississippi River in 1673 and turned south.

More than any other Frenchman, Jean-Baptiste Colbert, Louis XIV's powerful controller general of finance, was responsible for sustaining the French colonies. Colbert, who saw North America as a source of wealth for the home country, tried to organize the fur trade by creating monopolies and issuing licenses to responsible traders. But the trade turned out to be an unruly one. Unlicensed traders, called *coureurs de bois*, operated on their own, often cheated the Indians and sold their furs to the highest bidder.

Colbert also gave support to Robert Cavelier, Sieur de La Salle, the most celebrated of the French explorers. Granted a monopoly of the fur trade at Fort Frontenac, La Salle exceeded his remit by descending the Mississippi to its mouth, creating a string of outposts along the river and claiming all of *Louisiane* for France. Others followed in his wake: the Jesuits and other missionaries set up fur trade entrepôts at St. Ignace and Michilimackinac in the 1680s, Cahokia in 1699 and Kaskaskia in 1718. St. Louis, the northern capital of *Louisiane*, was set up as a fur trading post in 1764.

But *Nouvelle France*, whose government found *Louisiane* to be a financial burden, never experienced the dynamic influx of immigration that the English colonies enjoyed. By 1660, the English had 58,000 colonists in New England and the Chesapeake region compared with just three thousand French at isolated settlements in *Nouvelle France*. Though the French colonial population grew fivefold to fifteen thousand by 1700, it was still too feeble to compete with the steadily increasing number of English colonists, who by then numbered more than 250,000. Despite their small numbers, by 1755 the French had laid claim to a vast domain in *Louisiane* – from the Allegheny Mountains in the East to the Rockies in the West, and from the Gulf of Mexico to the Canadian border.

Early French outposts: the Upper and Middle Mississippi Valley

THE PATHFINDERS: JACQUES MARQUETTE, FIRST FRENCH EXPLORER TO REACH THE MISSISSIPPI

A young Jesuit priest was the first French explorer to enter the Mississippi. Jacques Marquette, born in Laon, France, was only thirty when he first arrived to labor among the Indians in Canada. After joining the Jesuit fathers at Québec, he proceeded to learn six different Indian dialects. In 1671, he established a mission for the Huron and Odawa Indians at St. Ignace, on the north shore of the straits of Michilimackinac (now "Mackinac"). From there in 1673, he set out to find the Mississippi, joined by a young French Canadian named Louis Jolliet and by five other Frenchmen in two simple birch canoes. "The joy that we felt at being selected for This Expedition animated our Courage, and rendered the labor of paddling from morning to night agreeable to us," he wrote in his journal.

The expedition's course took it along the northern shores of Lake Michigan to the River Menomonie, where at a village the local Indians warned Marquette that on the great river he would find murderous tribes who would show no mercy to intruders. Undaunted, the young priest and his men pushed on to Green Bay, where they entered the Fox River, crossed Lake Winnebago and reached the Wisconsin River. On June 17, they spotted the junction with the Mississippi at what is now Prairie du Chien, Wisconsin. This was "a joy which I cannot express", Marquette wrote.

The expedition sailed past the junction with the Missouri River (where St. Louis now stands) and the Ohio River until they reached the junction with the Arkansas River. There Marquette was confirmed in his belief that the great river, which he called "Colbert" after Louis XIV's controller general of finance, flowed into the Gulf of Mexico. He was also convinced, from conversations with the Arkansas Indians, that the Spanish would present a danger if he continued south. Reluctantly, he returned north, this time taking the Illinois River, where near the present town of Utica, he said a mass at a village of the Illinois Indians, which he called Kaskaskia. As the expedition reached Green Bay, exhausted by the trip, he stayed on to rest while Jolliet continued to Québec to report the results of the voyage.

The following spring, Marquette returned to Kaskaskia, where he was greeted with great enthusiasm by the Indians. After laying the groundwork for a mission that he called the Immaculate Conception, he became ill again and turned north, back towards the mission at Michilimackinac. He died peacefully *en route* at the age of thirty-nine. The following year, Indians dug up his remains and bore them back to the mission at Michilimackinac for a proper burial.

<

A devout man who lived to bring the gospel to the Indians, Marquette combined a missionary's spirit with an explorer's natural curiosity. The young Jesuit accomplished much for *Nouvelle France* and gave all of his compatriots, French and Indian alike, a lesson in courage and devotion. This memorial to the explorer is in Utica, Illinois, near Starved Rock.

Colonial Michilimackinac: a strategic French trading post and colonial village

The Straits of Michilimackinac (now called "Mackinac") were strategically important in the establishment of *Nouvelle France*. Jacques Marquette, who was the first to arrive with his band of roving Huron Indians in 1671, established a mission on the north side of the straits at St. Ignace for both the Huron and the resident Odawa. It was at St. Ignace that Marquette linked up with the young merchant, Louis Jolliet, *en route* to becoming the first of the French explorers to reach the Mississippi. La Salle passed through the straits several times in the 1680s, first during his travels on the upper Great Lakes, then on his way to descend the Mississippi to its mouth in 1682.

The straits became a premier fur trading depot in the next few years. In the 1680s, Fort DuBuade was established next to the St. Ignace Mission. In time, though, Michilimackinac on the south side of the straits, became the most important *entrepôt* for the fur trade of the Northwest. From here, canoes stocked with goods from French settlements in the East traveled to the trading posts on Lake Superior, then over to the Illinois River and south to French outposts at Cahokia, Kaskaskia and New Orleans. They returned laden with furs – beaver, otter, muskrat and fox.

In 1715, the French built a fort at Michilimackinac, one in a chain of French forts that extended from Montreal through the Great Lakes and northwest to Winnipeg and beyond. The fort was a support base for the trading post and the center of a French colonial community that grew up within the settlement's palisades. Even though Michilimackinac fell to the British in 1761, the French stayed on, living in the rowhouses and co-existing in relative harmony with the occupiers. They remained until 1781, when the British burned or disassembled most of the buildings, and then moved to Mackinac Island, located high on a bluff and a more defensible site against a potential attack from the Americans.

Archaeological excavations began at Michilimackinac in 1959 and continue to the present day. Using eighteenth-century techniques and meticulously scraping away layers of dirt, historians and architects have excavated more than half of the buildings in the village.

Several of the northwest and southwest row houses, where French settlers made their homes, have been re-created. *Poteaux-en-terre*, with steeply pitched roofs and long stone chimneys, they generally have gardens surrounded by palisaded fences. The Church of Ste. Anne, with its octagonal cupola, was the center of Catholic activities in the settlement. The blacksmith shop, adjacent to the church, is a small vertical log structure with a long stone chimney. Other French structures include the Chevalier House and the Solomon/Levy House, originally a home for French Canadian fur traders.

∧

Chevalier House.
The buildings in colonial Michilimackinac were constructed primarily of pine or white cedar. Several were vertical log, post-in-ground (*poteaux-en-terre*) structures in the same French Colonial Style found in French settlements on the Mississippi.
©Mackinac State Historic Parks

<

In the extensively reconstructed village, restorers have been careful to use the same wood species used in the original buildings.
©Mackinac State Historic Parks

THE KING AND THE COUNCILLOR — LOUIS XIV, COLBERT AND *NOUVELLE FRANCE*

Louis XIV, the Sun King (1638-1715), led France to pre-eminent power during his reign, and his court at Versailles was the most magnificent in Europe. While her traditional rival, England, was developing colonies in North America, France established settlements in *Nouvelle France* and was vying for control of the areas west of the English colonies.

Louis XIV undertook the first measures to ensure the development of *Nouvelle France*. In this he was aided by Jean-Baptiste Colbert (1619-1683), who, as councillor of state, controller general of finance and secretary of state for the navy, personally oversaw the colony's affairs. Colbert, a brilliant political strategist and skillful administrator, envisioned an imperial and modern state.

Apart from the king, he was the most powerful man in France.

France became so powerful that resentful nations allied against her. In 1667, war broke out with the Spanish, followed in 1672 by conflicts with the Dutch. At the same time, England and France were competing for dominance in Europe and establishing rival empires in the Far East. The three countries waged a series of late seventeenth and early eighteenth-century wars that had repercussions in both Europe and North America.

Colbert worked to create a favorable trade balance, increase colonial holdings and develop the French merchant marine to better exploit trade. In *Nouvelle France*, fur trading and fishing were intended to offset the Crown's military expenditures, but revenues from both proved to be disappointing, and the colony's economy had to be heavily subsidized by the Royal Treasury. Moreover, *Nouvelle France* never witnessed the vital surge of immigration that the English colonies enjoyed. After 1632, France prohibited religious dissidents from emigrating to *Nouvelle France*. As a result, numbers of Huguenots crossed the Atlantic to settle in British America instead. After Colbert's death in 1683, this trend intensified with Louis XIV's revocation of the Edict of Nantes.

Nouvelle France also faced strong competition in attracting other new settlers from France, as nearby Spain and the prosperous West Indies proved to be more attractive than the North American colonies. The growing French Army absorbed potential emigrants as well; although Louis XIV built the largest military force in Europe, the vast majority of his men under arms were needed to fight his European battles. The king's near constant wars on the European continent diverted his attention from *Nouvelle France*, leaving France with few men and resources to defend and develop the colonies. In time, this and vacillating government policies led to the weakening of the French foothold in North America. Forty-four years after the death of Louis XIV, the French were defeated by the British at Québec, and lost control of almost all of their territory east of the Mississippi.

<
King Louis XIV by
Claude Lefebvre (1670),
Châteaux de Versailles
et de Trianon.
©Photo RMN - Gérard Blot

∧
Jean-Baptiste Colbert
by Claude Lefebvre,
Châteaux de Versailles
et de Trianon.
©Photo RMN - Gérard Blot

Adventures in the fur trade – Prairie du Chien and Green Bay

Many of the early French in North America were engaged in the fur trade. Beaver pelts furnished by the Indians were in great demand and were shipped by the thousands to eager consumers in the mother country. At the height of the trade, some 140,000 livres' weight of beaver were being shipped from *Nouvelle France* each year.

Despite the drawbacks of cyclical fur markets and wars with the Iroquois and Fox Indians, fur trade *entrepôts* sprang up all over the Louisiana Territory. Two of the more prominent were at Prairie du Chien and Green Bay in present-day Wisconsin.

Founded around 1754-55, Prairie du Chien is located just above the junction of the Wisconsin and Mississippi Rivers, where Marquette first entered the Mississippi in 1673. The settlement was a rendezvous point for French Canadian traders who exchanged trinkets for the valuable furs furnished by local tribes. Even after the French ceded the territory to Britain, the French Canadians continued to run the trade well into the nineteenth century. St. Feriole Island, which sits offshore in the Mississippi, was a fur trade center and later the site of the American Fort Crawford, burned by the British in the War of 1812.

Green Bay is located at the junction of the Fox River and the bay that leads into Lake Michigan. The first

European to visit the site was probably Jean Nicolet, a Norman from Cherbourg, who landed in Green Bay in 1634-35 on his search for a water route to the Orient. Later, the French settlement consisted of a military outpost, a mission and an entrepôt. At the height of the fur trade, fortunes were made at Green Bay, which was an *entrepôt* in the region with the best and richest furs. But in 1741, with the French government showing a serious deficit, licenses for all of the western fur trade were suspended and the posts were auctioned off to the highest bidder. When the lease of Green Bay expired in 1746, no one bid for it, and two private traders took over.

The French fur trade eventually died out, killed off by greed and savage competition. The French of Prairie du Chien and Green Bay stayed in the trade long after it had ceased to be profitable, and their lands were eventually sold off to the great fur companies. But Wisconsin is still marked by towns that were once French fur trade outposts – Fond du Lac, Oshkosh, Sheboygan and Manitowoc.

In *Nouvelle France*, the fur trade was the principal source of revenue, with fur trade *entrepôts* springing up all over the Illinois Territory. One of the more prominent was at Prairie du Chien in present-day Wisconsin, where the Wisconsin Historical Society has established the Fur Trade Museum.
(Villa Louis Historic Site)
©Photo Dale Hall

Fur pelts in the Fur Trade Museum at Prairie du Chien. Beaver was particularly prized by French consumers. But the trade was cyclical and eventually died out because of greed and savage competition. Present-day Wisconsin has a number of cities that were once French fur trading outposts.
(Villa Louis Historic Site)
©Photo Dale Hall

The pathfinders: René Robert Cavelier, Sieur de La Salle claims Louisiane for France

Born in Rouen to wealthy merchants in 1643, La Salle was at first attracted to the Jesuits, but unlike his predecessor, Marquette, rejected them at an early age. His brother, a priest in Canada, encouraged him to voyage to North America. The young explorer arrived there for the first time in 1666.

En route to find the Mississippi, La Salle and his men followed the Kankakee River to its junction with the Illinois River, which flowed into the Mississippi near present-day Prairie du Chien, Wisconsin.

Ambitious to explore the West and to acquire a monopoly of the fur trade, La Salle soon alienated a wide range of powerful adversaries – the Jesuits who saw him as a threat to their own influence with the Indians; the merchants who resented his efforts to control the commerce in fur; and some French governors of Canada who saw in him a rival power to their own. Like Marquette before him, La Salle was first interested in finding a water route to China and Japan, but soon became convinced that the Mississippi, the great river to the west, of which the Indians spoke, flowed instead into the Gulf of Mexico. After 1679, he set out on a series of voyages which would lead him thousands of miles in a single-minded quest to found a *Nouvelle France* in the West. He built the *Griffon*, the first commercial ship to sail on Lake Erie. But the ship, laden with furs for Fort Niagara, disappeared and its cargo was never recovered.

In 1680, La Salle traveled to the Illinois River and built Fort Crèvecoeur near present-day Peoria. But when he returned north for supplies, the men at the fort burned it down and deserted. Undaunted, in 1681 he set out with twenty-three Frenchmen and eighteen Indians for a push to the Mississippi. On the sixth of April 1682, the expedition finally reached the Gulf of Mexico, where La Salle planted a column and claimed all lands from the Allegheny Mountains in the North to the Rocky Mountains in the West, as well as the immense Mississippi basin, for Louis XIV, for whom he named the territory *Louisiane*.

Despite his courage and talent, he was a solitary man, disliked by his men. The rest

René Robert Cavelier, Sieur de La Salle by Francisco Iardella. Rotunda, U. S. Capitol.
©Photo Architect of the Capitol

of his life was a sad spiral downward. Returning from his voyage to the Gulf, he found himself under the control of a new French governor of Canada, Le Febvre de la Barre, who undercut him at every turn. In 1684, La Salle set sail from La Rochelle with around three hundred colonists to establish a French fort at the mouth of the Mississippi. But he overshot and ended up in Texas, where after three difficult years, he was assassinated by his own men and his colony was annihilated by disease and Indian attacks.

A man of extravagant flaws and virtues, La Salle was eventually destroyed by lesser men who resented him. In Francis Parkman's words: "America owes him an enduring memory, for, in this masculine figure, she sees the pioneer who guided her to the possession of her richest heritage."

The first European colony in Illinois – Peoria and Fort Crèvecoeur

Peoria in central Illinois was at one time an important French trading site, because of its strategic location as a port on the Illinois River from which furs could be shipped up or down-river and back to Europe. The Peoria area's old French Trading House, once the property of John Jacob Astor, saw thousands of dollars worth of trade pass through each year.

The French experience began in 1673 when Père Marquette and his men were the first Europeans to see the region where Peoria now stands. La Salle and his ubiquitous lieutenant Tonty followed in 1680 and constructed Fort Crèvecoeur, abandoned and destroyed a few months later. Tonty returned in 1691-92 after the French abandoned Fort St. Louis at Starved Rock to build Fort St. Louis II, on Lake Pimiteoui ("Fat Lake" or "Lake of Great Abundance"), now called Lake Peoria.

Around 1730, a small French village, "the old village", was established in present-day Peoria and remained occupied until the 1790s. Though the Illinois Territory was ceded to the British after the Treaty of Paris in 1763, many citizens of Peoria remained resolutely French. In October 1812, after the American takeover, the U.S. Government, believing the French were in league with the British, sent a raiding party to the town, deported the citizens of the French village to an area nearby, and burned the village to the ground. Though

some French trickled back into the area afterwards, this effectively ended the era of French Peoria.

Fort Crèvecoeur was the first French fort established in Illinois. La Salle, along with Tonty and Father Hennepin had chosen the site as the first in a chain of forts the explorer meant to build along the shores of the Illinois and Mississippi Rivers. Inside the palisades, La Salle built four log cabins, two for the men and one for the priests. Leaving Tonty at the fort, La Salle set off in the spring of 1680. But later the following summer, he learned from Tonty that the men had mutinied and burned down the fort. On one of the charred beams were scratched the words "Nous sommes tous sauvages" (We are all savages). Crèvecoeur had endured only four months. Despite a number of archaeological digs, the remains of the fort have never been conclusively found, and disputes continue to rage over its location.

The Fagotte Cemetery, located on a farm near East Peoria, contains more than twenty gravestones, some in French, others in French and English. Between 135 and 150 people, most of whom were French or of French extraction, are buried in Fagotte. Among them is Jean Pierre Mougeon, a soldier who fought with Napoleon and who suffered frostbite on the French army's retreat from Moscow.

∧

The present reconstruction of Fort Crèvecoeur was built in 1980. Though the original fort was more than twice as large, the reconstruction is in keeping with the original site, with a space for La Salle's and Tonty's tents in the center and cabins for the men, a blacksmith shop and palisades.

< ∨

Once covered by weeds and bramble, the Fagotte Cemetery, resting place for dozens of French settlers, has now been partially restored. The cemetery is all that remains of a large French settlement in the area. Every year Fagotte receives a grant for upkeep from the French Government.

La Salle's "natural fortress" on the Illinois River - Starved Rock

Indian legend has it that in the 1760s, Pontiac, chief of the Ottawa tribe, was assassinated by an Illinois tribesman while attending a tribal council. To avenge his killing, a band of Pottawattamies attacked the Illinois, who took refuge on the summit of a bluff on the Illinois River. Cut off from supplies, the Illinois were eventually destroyed by starvation. Hence the name, "Starved Rock".

In 1680, upon seeing the cliff which he called "The Rock of St. Louis", La Salle resolved to build a fort on its heights. Two years later, he returned to Starved Rock, had the forest at the top of the cliff cleared and a palisaded fort constructed to protect the Illinois Indians in the valley below from their savage enemies, the Iroquois. Eventually, more than twenty thousand Indians lived under French supervision in the surrounding area.

But the success was short-lived. Embroiled in quarrels with the new French governor of Canada, Le Febvre de la Barre, La Salle was soon cut off from supplies while the governor intrigued to deprive him of reinforcements. In March 1683, the Iroquois besieged the rock, and though they were repulsed, the Indians' confidence in their French protectors began to waver. The French abandoned Fort St. Louis and retreated to what is now Peoria. The fort served as a trading center after La Salle's departure, but was abandoned in 1692. By 1720 all traces of it had disappeared.

Archaeological digs in the 1940s confirmed that Starved Rock was indeed the site of Fort St. Louis. Handwrought nails and other items of the period linked it with the fort. Though no vestiges remain, plaques throughout the site, now a state park, commemorate the presence of La Salle, Tonty and the other French explorers who built a fortress on this majestic bluff.

French America

French traces in the oldest town in Illinois - Cahokia

In 1699, only seventeen years after La Salle claimed the Louisiana Territory for France, French Canadian missionaries from Québec traveled down the Mississippi and established an outpost among the Tamaroa and Cahokia Illini Indians in a remote spot near the confluence of the Missouri and Mississippi Rivers. At the time there were around two thousand Native Americans living in the area, and the missionaries built a chapel outpost and went about the job of Christianizing the natives. The settlement, Cahokia, grew up around the mission; its name is derived from the Cahokian Indian tribe and means "wild geese".

The oldest town in the state of Illinois, Cahokia became the first of several forts and villages in the "bottom region" of the "Pays des Illinois" (the Illinois Country). From these modest beginnings, the settlement later became a major trading center and the focal point of political activity in the Northwest Territory. It remained so throughout much of the eighteenth century until the growth of its neighbor, St. Louis, founded in 1764, outstripped it in population and influence.

Cahokia exercised a political and economic influence that belied its modest size. As a trading post, the village served as a way station for goods traveling downriver to New Orleans and upriver to Canada. Its courthouse was an administrative center for justice on the western frontier. And a number of prominent figures in early American history – including Auguste Chouteau, who co-founded St. Louis – made their homes here. From December 1803 to May 1804, Lewis and Clark established their base in Cahokia and trained their recruits for their voyage to the West.

In July 1778, during the Revolutionary War, George Rogers Clark and his Virginians occupied the town, and the Illinois French were drawn into the American Revolution. Even after the war, the French influence remained. In the mid-nineteenth century, one observer wrote: "The lapse of nearly two centuries has not entirely destroyed the original impress upon this people of the manners, customs and language of Old France."

Now a sleepy hamlet across the Mississippi south of St. Louis, Cahokia is notable for having preserved and maintained some of the most remarkable French structures in the continental United States. The Cahokia Courthouse is one of the most impressive. At the height of its influence, around 1801, the court decided cases from as far north as the Canadian border.

Constantly threatened by Mississippi floods, the courthouse saw its influence diminish after the county seat was shifted to Belleville in 1814. After a number of transformations, the building had deteriorated badly and was used only to store farm machinery. Dismantled and then rebuilt, in a reduced form, for an exhibit at the 1904 St. Louis World's Fair, the courthouse was again dismantled before being rebuilt in 1940 at its original site.

A short distance from the Cahokia Courthouse stands one of the most signficant religious buildings in the continental

<

Holy Family Church. This exquisitely carved wooden figure of the Virgin is one of the fine carvings in the church. Tradition has it that the vertical log timbers in the church were harvested from Cahokia's commons.

∨

The Jarrot House, built from 1807-1810, in contrast to the vertical log construction of other Cahokia historic structures, is an imposing two-story brick house in the Federal Style more suited to Baltimore, Jarrot's port of entry to America. The Federal Style was a unique expression of the American identity. It transformed Georgian architecture by stripping it of all embellishments to create a style that was both lean and massive.

≫

The majestic wood-carved staircase would have been the envy of Jarrot's neighbors. It is likely that the large center hall, with doors front and back, had a multi-purpose use — as a reception hall and work space.

United States. The vertical log Church of the Holy Family was dedicated in 1799. Its antecedent dates from 1699 when its first pastor, Father St. Cosme, and two workmen erected a missionary cross, a chapel and a log rectory.

The early chapel of the Holy Family Church was replaced in the 1730s, then again in 1785. In 1913, the building underwent a restoration, at which time the exterior was encased with clapboard siding. In 1950, the siding was removed to expose the original oak timber construction, the *pierrotage* stonework was repaired and the roof of cypress clapboard with sycamore covering was restored. The *oeil-de-boeuf* (bull's eye) window, with frame and hinges intact, a characteristic of early French architecture in the U.S., was rediscovered.

Entrepreneur, landowner, slaveowner, farmer, merchant, philanthropist, Nicholas Jarrot was a man of many parts. Born in the small French village of Vesoul in Franche-Comté, Jarrot came to Baltimore, the center of colonial American Catholicism, in 1791. In 1793, he made his permanent home in Cahokia. Blessed with business acumen, he established a series of businesses in Cahokia, including stores, mills, even a ferry to St. Louis. But the

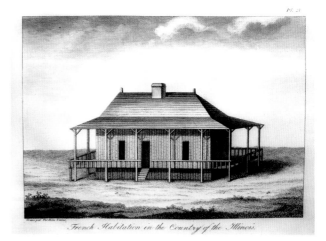

French Habitation in the Country of the Illinois.

real source of his wealth was land speculation. Jarrot sold land he had bought from veterans of the American Revolution for pennies on the dollar. In time, he accumulated a vast domain of more than 25,000 acres.

He first lived in a *poteaux-sur-sole* frame house, but as his wealth grew, so did his aspirations. The Nicholas Jarrot House, Jarrot's brick showplace second house, was first started in 1807. Because it was built by local artisans unfamiliar with brick, it has its share of architectural idiosyncrasies. But it retains almost all of its original features, including plaster, flooring, millwork and even some window sashes.

The Martin-Boismenue House, a remarkable French Creole dwelling, is located in Dupo, adjacent to Cahokia. It was saved in 1980 by the action of the local fire chief who knew how to read old houses and had a passion for preserving them. At that time, after the building had been bought by a local owner, it was a run-down apartment building. The buyer, thinking it useless, wanted to tear it down and put up a car wash. But the fire chief, an avid researcher of old houses, suspected that underneath the siding the house had historic value. After stripping off the siding, he discovered the vertical log timbers beneath. Within twenty-four hours, a group of interested local citizens organized themselves, secured a bank loan, bought the house and obtained grant money to restore it. It has been acquired by the Illinois Historic Preservation Agency and refurbished with attractive rustic period furnishings.

< >
Church of the
Immaculate Conception
in Kaskaskia. The altar
from the early 1700s,
the top part of which is
a tree trunk hollowed out
in the back, hand-carved
from native black walnut
and cottonwood, was
built with wooden pegs.
The brass sanctuary lamp
by the altar dates back
to the mission period.
The altar stone, carried
to the New World by ship
from France, arrived
at Kaskaskia by canoe.

The vanished capital – Kaskaskia

Standing now on the tranquil island of Kaskaskia, accessible only by a small bridge off Missouri Highway 61, it is difficult to imagine that this was the site of a once thriving settlement, the first capital city of the territory and later of the state of Illinois. Father Jacques Marquette established the first Kaskaskia parish in 1675. Soon after, tribal conflicts pushed the local Indians and the Jesuits further down the Mississippi, eventually to a five-mile wide peninsula north of the confluence of the Mississippi and Kaskaskia Rivers, where fur trading posts had already been established.

By 1718 the village of Kaskaskia had been laid out on this spot, and in the style of later French settlements like Cahokia and Ste. Genevieve, had an adjoining commons and commonfield. What started as a French fur trading settlement turned into an agricultural community. Flour mills were in operation, grain was exported up and down the river, and the first cattle were brought to the Midwest.

Kaskaskia reached its pinnacle in the early nineteenth century. In 1800, it became part of the Indiana Territory, and in 1809 the Territory of Illinois was established with Kaskaskia as its capital. At that time the population was between five and seven thousand, and the first newspaper in the state, *The Illinois Herald*, was printed here. Kaskaskia, a center of

Nouvelle France, became known as "the gateway to the West". Sadly, very little remains. The flood of 1844 caused many residents to flee for good. The 1881 flood, which gouged out a new channel leading into the Kaskaskia River bed, caused much of the town to cascade into the Mississippi. Kaskaskia, now an island, has a population of only seventy-five, yet it retains a potent, almost spiritual attraction. Two haunting reminders of Kaskaskia's French heritage remain.

The history of the Church of the Immaculate Conception can be traced back to the early days of the settlement, when a log church was constructed by Jesuit priests. In 1843, a new church, constructed of bricks shipped from Pittsburgh, was completed, and in a tower over the main entrance was placed a bell sent to the community by King Louis XV of France.

∧
The Bell Shrine.
The Kaskaskia bell,
a gift of Louis XV,
was cast in La Rochelle,
France in 1741. On the
bell are inscribed the
words: "Pour l'église
des Illinois par le soins
du Roi d'outre lea"
(For the church of the
Illinois, by gift of the
King across the water).

<
The Church of the
Immaculate Conception
has a number of
remarkable features.
The statues of the Virgin,
child and Joseph
are thought to date
from the 1700s.

>
Pierre Menard House.
The old family Bible
is on display in one
of the front rooms.

<<

Constructed between
1800-1802, the Pierre
Menard House remains
one of finest examples
of French Creole
architecture in the
middle Mississippi Valley.
Built in *poteaux-sur-sole*
style, with a surrounding
galerie, this frame house
was one of the few
Creole free-standing
homes outside a village
center. Native woods —
oak, walnut, ash, cypress
and poplar — were used
in its construction.

∨

Pierre Menard House.
The elegance of the house
reflects the family's
affluence. The mantels
and the three fireplaces
in the house are
originals, as are the
floors in the front three
rooms and the entrance
hall. The pianoforte
in the parlor, made in
Boston, dates to 1820.

>>

Pierre Menard House.
The kitchen is set apart
from the house in
the fashion typical of
the time, because of the
fear of fire. The kitchen
is supported by three
wooden walls and one
in stone, the latter
of which holds the large
fireplace. An original
crane remains, used to
hold pots over the fire.

After the devastating floods of 1881 and 1893, the village moved and rebuilt the old church, brick by brick, and a bell spire was built over the side entrance. The present lofty church spire was added in the early 1900s. Some years after the restoration of the church and her old relics, devastating floods in 1974 and 1993 invaded the building, causing severe damage.

Next to the church stands the Bell Shrine, which now houses Louis XV's Kaskaskia bell. After its arrival at New Orleans, it took almost two years to deliver the 650-pound bell to Kaskaskia. Men walking along the Mississippi pulled the raft that contained it hundreds of miles to its resting place. The bell rang on July 4, 1798 to commemorate the capture of Kaskaskia for the Americans by George Rogers Clark, earning it the description the "Liberty Bell of the West". The bell rang again to celebrate the triumphant visit of Lafayette to Kaskaskia in 1825 and has rung under French, British and American flags.

On a high bluff across the Mississippi from Kaskaskia are the earthwork remains of Fort Kaskaskia. Built in the middle 1750s by French settlers who feared an attack from British troops during the French and Indian War, it was destroyed in 1766 by the townspeople to avoid its falling into the hands of the enemy.

On the far side of the river stands the elegant Pierre Menard House. Menard, the son of a French soldier, was born in 1766 at St. Antoine-sur-Richelieu near Montreal. In 1790, after moving to Kaskaskia, he struck out on his own, amassing a sizeable fortune in the commerce in fur and becoming part of a commercial elite of capitalists engaged in the import/export trade in the Illinois country. But Menard is primarily remembered for his public life and his charitable works. In 1818, he was appointed the first Lieutenant Governor of the new State of Illinois, and helped draft the state constitution. The Pierre Menard House, now a State Historical Site, was the place Menard returned to after his public life was completed. To the left of the property stands a *fumoir* (smokehouse), which has been fully restored. A small museum with Menard's personal effects is on the premises; among other items, it displays a slipper one of his daughters wore to a ball given for Lafayette when he passed through the area on his triumphant final visit to America in 1825.

Creole House, a white frame house believed to have been constructed around 1808, is *poteaux-sur-sole* with an overhanging roof covering a porch (*galerie*). Several rooms and the kitchen were later added to the house, but one original room, the center room with fireplace, has survived and the original log construction is clearly visible.

A resolutely French village - Prairie du Rocher

Clustered below limestone bluffs on the eastern bank of the Mississippi is the small village of Prairie du Rocher (Prairie of the Rocks). One of the first French settlements in the *Pays des Illinois*, the village remained essentially French long after its neighboring villages in the middle Mississippi Valley had succumbed to British and American influence.

The village's rich history can be traced back to around 1722, when Pierre Dugué, Sieur de Boisbriant, a French Canadian and first lieutenant of the king in the government of Illinois, conveyed land where the village now stands. Like other French villages in the Mississippi Valley, Prairie du Rocher developed as a church surrounded by houses. The village had a communal pasture, used for grazing cattle and other livestock, and common fields with elongated farm plots, each with a small section fronting the Mississippi. Though the village was essentially agricultural, some tradesmen – masons, carpenters, tanners, tavern keepers and workers in the wheat mills – also made their homes here.

Early homes were generally of frame constructions, *poteaux-en-terre* (post-in-earth) or *poteaux-sur-sole* (post-on-sill), with thatched roofs and porches (*galeries*), though the occasional stone house could also be found. The frame houses generally had a *bousillage* filling. Now a quiet farming town with a population of around six hundred,

seemingly bypassed by time, Prairie du Rocher still retains some vestiges of its French past.

Creole House, a white frame house, was purchased in 1830 by William Henry, who owned a water-driven gristmill on Prairie du Rocher Creek. A number of his furnishings, including his dishes, remain in the house. Though it has seen considerable alterations over the years, the outline of a French Creole house is distinctly visible.

The Church of St. Joseph is the third church to serve the faithful of Prairie du Rocher. The first church, made of logs, was built as early as 1718; the second, near Fort de Chartres, was constructed in 1731; and the present one, built on higher ground to the north, was completed in 1858. Although the stately stone structure of St. Joseph's has been altered over the years – the front part of the building was added on in the early 1900s – the soft brick on the outside and the windows are thought to be original. At the edge of town, the Cemetery of the Parish of St. Joseph contains several French gravestones, including those of Father Gagnon and Father Luc Collet, two former priests of the church.

∧

The Cemetery of Saint Joseph has a number of plain wooden or metal crosses, a French Canadian tradition. The occasional French name graces the stones, and a large aluminium cross marks the spot where the original Church of St. Joseph stood.

<

St. Joseph's Church. When the church was moved to the village from the area near Fort de Chartres, the stunning gold communion vessels, a gift to the parish from France, came with it.

few years and never made much use of the facility, which they renamed Fort Cavendish. The British finally abandoned it altogether in 1771. The years that followed were marked by flooding and steady deterioration, so that by 1848 the site was virtually a total ruin when the U.S Government sold it. The State of Illinois bought it in 1914 and established a state park. In the 1940s, the old guard house was finally rebuilt. But in the great Mississippi flood of 1993, water submerged the structure. Now largely restored, the fort, along with a museum housing artifacts of the French period, is open to the public.

∧
Fort de Chartres.
On the grounds,
the ancient foundations
of Fort de Chartres
are now clearly visible.
The outlines of the
ancient barracks are
indicated by "ghosting",
with beams representing
the height and shape
of the original structure.

The only French stone fort on the Mississippi - Fort de Chartres

Situated only a mile from the Mississippi, Fort de Chartres is a reconstruction of the first and only stone French fort built on the river. Named after Louis, Duc de Chartres, son of Philippe d'Orléans, the Regent of France during the early years of Louis XV, the stone fort was originally built during the 1750s. Pierre Rigaud de Vaudreuil de Cavagnal, the governor of *Louisiane*, ordered its construction near Kaskaskia, then capital of the Illinois Territory. Abandoned by the French in 1765 after the French and Indian War, the fort was taken over by the British without a shot being fired.

Fort de Chartres played a key role for the French in the Illinois Territory as the seat of government, the military and administrative center of the region and the headquarters of the Provincial Council that conducted the affairs of the French King. Construction was largely completed by 1754.

Following the French and Indian War, British Highlanders arrived to take over the fort in 1765, but they stayed only a

∧
The rebuilt powder
magazine is the only
surviving portion of
the old Fort de Chartres,
whose facilities also
included a storehouse,
a guards' building,
a commandant's
house, east and west
barracks, a chapel
and a government/
officer's building.
©Steve Anderson

>
Fort de Chartres played
a key role for the French
in the Illinois Territory
as the seat of
government, the military
and administrative
center of the region
and the headquarters
of the Provincial Council
conducting the affairs
of the French King.

MISSOURI

It is said that Taille de Noyer, an impressive plantation home with a double-hipped roof, was once a fur trading post. One wing of the house contains remnants of the original log cabin, built around 1790, and one of its rooms has the original hand-hewn, log-studded walls.

Community spirit preserves a historic center – Florissant
French fur trappers and farmers, arriving in the 1770s, called it "Fleurissant" (flowering). Later, during the Spanish period, it was called "San Fernando", which became St. Ferdinand when it came under American control. That name endured until 1939, when reverting to a version of the original French, it became definitively "Florissant". In 1950, this once-quiet Missouri hamlet in the shadow of St. Louis had less than four hundred inhabitants. Then, when St. Louis required more living space, it exploded – with a population that jumped more than 900 per cent, to 38,000, between 1950 and 1960. Now a lively community, it is Missouri's sixth-largest city.

But Florissant is a suburban community with a difference. For thanks to the efforts of local commissions, non-profit organizations and preservation-minded citizens, it has vigorously conserved its historic center, the "old town", which harbors a rich mixture of shrines and eighteenth and nineteenth-century homes. A number of the streets, which were laid out in sixteen even squares with common-fields in the manner of early French towns, are named after Catholic saints – Rue St. François, Rue Ste. Catherine, Rue St. Jacques and Rue St. Pierre.

Though the early settlers were French, Florissant experienced new waves of immigration in the nineteenth century, when the Germans and later the Irish moved in. This mix of cultures still prevails: a German church, Sacred Heart, stands just up the street from the celebrated French Shrine of St. Ferdinand; restored early German and Spanish homes are interspersed among country French and Creole-style dwellings. Florissant is also distinguished by its links to two exceptional European religious figures of the nineteenth century – Rose Philippine Duchesne and Father Pierre Jean DeSmet, both of whom used the city as a base. Mother Duchesne, the indomitable French nun who started up the Academy of the Sacred Heart, also was the inspiration behind the founding of other Sacred Heart academies in Louisiana. She set up the first free Catholic school for Indian girls, and in 1827 established City House in St. Louis. This remarkable woman was canonized as a saint by Pope John Paul II in 1988.

The Old Ferdinand Shrine stands as a vivid reminder of early French Catholic missionary education and a testament to the determination of Florissant's citizens to preserve a threatened heritage. Originally built in 1821, the main building is the oldest Catholic church between the Mississippi River and the Rocky Mountains. Remodeled in 1880 to its present Gothic style, the church suffered a devastating fire in May 1996. But the citizens of Florissant refused to give it up. A non-profit group, originally formed in 1958, bought the building for $1, and within a few months had raised a considerable sum to save it.

Adjoining the church is the convent wing, considered to be one of the finest brick buildings in Missouri. Built in

<

Taille de Noyer. Period
heirlooms furnish the
house – a piano of
rosewood with hand-
carved hickory legs from
the late 1800s; a sewing
cabinet in Eastlake
styling; and an *étagère* of
carved rosewood brought
from France in 1858 and
transported up the
Mississippi from New
Orleans.

<<

Old St. Ferdinand Shrine.
Inside this lovely church
is a painting believed
to be from the School
of Rubens; a sanctuary
lamp, the gift of Penlaver
Cardenas, Bishop
of Louisiana and Florida,
in 1799; and relics of
St. Valentine, believed
to be a gift of the King
of France to Bishop
W. Louis DuBourg
of New Orleans.

1818, it is preserved almost in its original condition. The interior chapel still contains some of the old pews from the church, ravaged by fire in 1836. The convent is also associated with Mother Duchesne, for whom it was built. She arrived in Florissant on Christmas Eve, 1819, remained until 1827, then came back again from 1834 to 1840.

The convent accepted its first American in 1821, and others followed during the remainder of the decade. The school, a flourishing institution, had twenty-one boarders by the following year. Although the Society of the Sacred Heart abandoned the convent and school in 1846, the Sisters of Loretto continued the religious tradition with a new school which remained until 1955.

Despite its French name (which means "clearing in a walnut grove"), Taille de Noyer's background is mainly Irish and American. The house's history is linked to the Mullanphy family, and particularly with John Mullanphy, who bought it around 1805 from Hyacinthe Deshetres, one of the founders of Florissant. Mullanphy, a successful merchant and philanthropist, also gave a significant contribution to build the Church of St. Ferdinand. He gave Taille de Noyer to his daughter on her marriage, and since she had seventeen children, Taille de Noyer had to be considerably enlarged over the years. Descendants of the family remained in the house for nearly a century and a half.

Like the Shrine of St. Ferdinand, Taille de Noyer was threatened with demolition, but local citizens stepped in to save a landmark. Funds were raised to move the house two hundred yards to the west. Though the great fire of 1849 and subsequent urban renewal destroyed virtually all of the French Creole homes in central St. Louis, Florissant, to the northwest, was largely spared. In its historic center, as a consequence, can be found several surviving nineteenth-century houses – all privately owned, some covered in clapboard or whitewash, but with the distinctive outline of their Creole past preserved.

Among these are the Auguste Aubuchon House and the Bellisime House. Gabriel Aubuchon arrived in Florissant from Kaskaskia in the 1790s, and is believed to have built this house circa 1800. One of his descendants, Auguste Aubuchon, purchased the property in 1844.

Bellisime House is a typical French-style home built around 1810. Its original owner, Alexander Bellisime, traveled with Lafayette from France and fought beside him in the Revolutionary War. The story goes that Bellisime, seriously wounded at the Battle of Yorktown, later met Lafayette and the two had a tearful reunion on the General's visit to St. Louis in 1825. The Bellisime House has the *poteaux-sur-sole galerie* and the steep, double-hipped Norman roof. The interior of the one-and-a-half story house contains some Greek Revival details and still has the original fireplace.

<
The Auguste Aubuchon House, which stands on Rue St. Louis, has the characteristic steep, double-hipped French Creole roof and pillars (*poteaux-sur-sole*) lining the *galerie* (porch). Originally of log construction, altered over the years, it is covered in white clapboard. Curiously the house has two front doors, possibly to provide an additional exit in case of fire.

<
A number of other Creole houses survive in "old town" Florissant, some of which maintain their distinctive character despite modern alterations. The hipped French Creole roof and pillars (*poteaux-sur-sole*) lining the *galerie* (porch) are typical Creole features.

From fur trading post to gateway to the West – St. Louis

The French called it "Pain Court" (short of bread), a rueful reflection of hard times on the western frontier. Later named for King Louis XV and his patron saint, Louis IX, St. Louis, like many French settlements, began as a fur trading post. Its founder, Pierre de Laclède Liguest, was the son of a lawyer from the province of Béarn in southwest France.

In New Orleans, the young Laclède entered into a partnership with Gilbert Antoine Maxent, a prominent merchant granted a monopoly of the fur trade among the Indian tribes on the upper Missouri River by the last French governor of Louisiana, Jean-Jacques Blaise d'Abbadie. After a voyage upriver from New Orleans, Laclède and a group of thirty or so colonists, including the fourteen-year-old half-brother of LaClède's children, Auguste Chouteau, finally settled on a site for St. Louis. The site had several advantages: it was elevated, making it less susceptible to flooding; it was heavily forested, which would provide building materials; and it had access to limestone and other minerals from the cliffs along the Mississippi. Clearing of the site began in February 1764.

In the months that followed, Laclède campaigned to have French settlers across the river join the settlement at St. Louis. Since few of them wanted to live under British rule, most readily acquiesced. By 1772, there were 577 inhabitants in Pain Court/St. Louis. Laclède had the village laid out according to a gridiron plan adapted from Spanish colonial towns and the similar layout of New Orleans. The landing became a public market place called "Place d'Armes" or "Place Publique". A long street – La Rue Principale – paralleled the river. Other streets were named Rue de l'Église, Rue des Granges, Rue Missouri, Rue de la Place and Rue de la Tour. The city had a considerable French population well into the nineteenth century.

The gridiron plan provided for standard size house lots. Most of the houses were Creole in style, with French hipped roofs and porches (*galeries*) around the exterior to shelter inhabitants from the blistering heat of summer. The roofs over the porches and the walls were supported by posts in the ground (*poteaux-en-terre*) made of cedar or mulberry, which resisted rot, similar to the few still surviving in Ste. Genevieve. More elaborate houses, such as the one owned by Auguste Chouteau, were considerably larger and constructed of stone. Thatched roofs were common, and palisades and pointed posts surrounded each house and closed off sections of the town to guard against Indian raids and roving animals.

The gridiron plan also called for a commons and a commonfield. The former, based on French Canadian design, was used for grazing cattle, hunting small game and gathering firewood; the latter was divided into lots and used for strip farming. Corn, maize, wheat, rye, tobacco and hemp were among the prominent crops. The early years of St. Louis until the Louisiana Purchase were marked by a thriving fur trade despite the dangers posed by pirates on the Mississippi. What was once a trading post became a village, then a town, then a city.

In 1780, the British and their Indian supporters attacked the settlement. Warned in advance, Lieutenant Governor de Lebya prepared fortifications. Fort San Carlos, erected with the help of local inhabitants, consisted of large stone towers at the four corners of the village. When the British and Indians attacked, they were met by a flurry of musket fire and withdrew. When the Americans triumphed in their struggle for independence, the fortifications fell into ruin. By 1799, they were essentially useless. Not a trace of them remains today, with the exception of a plaque in a downtown office building commemorating their location.

As the "gateway to the West", St. Louis was the jumping-off place for the Lewis and Clark expedition in 1803. On March 10, 1804, with the final ceremony of the Louisiana Purchase, it came under American control. The first steamboat on the Mississippi traveled from St. Louis to Louisville, Kentucky in 1817. Under the Missouri Compromise, the state was admitted to the Union as a slave state in 1821 (Maine had been admitted as a free state the previous year.)

∨
The Old Cathedral. Four Doric columns grace the cathedral's façade, with three doors, each with an inscription in Latin, French and English. To the right, Eero Saarinen's famed Gateway Arch, erected in 1965, is a symbol of St. Louis as the "gateway to the West".

< ∨

The Basilica of St. Louis contains evidence of its French origins. Near the entrance is a painting depicting Louis IX, for whom the city of St. Louis is named. Below is a statue of the same king, which stands on one side of the altar.

>

The elegant Chatillon-DeMenil House is one of the most striking examples of Greek Revival architecture in the Middle Mississippi Valley.

In 1849, the city suffered a devastating fire, which started on a steamboat, then spread to the shore, sweeping through the downtown area and causing an estimated $6,000,000 in damage. After the great fire, followed by twentieth-century urban renewal and massive freeway construction, the French sites, sadly, have largely been obliterated. But there remain tantalizing reminders of the Gallic impact on the city.

From its early days, St. Louis has had a flourishing Roman Catholic population. The first church, built in 1770, was made of logs, a small rectangular building with a clapboard roof. Soon it was in poor repair and the citizens of St. Louis built another, and by 1818, that church too was in need of replacement. The third church on the site was made of brick, but was poorly designed and also had also to be replaced.

The present basilica, the first cathedral west of the Mississippi, partially financed by a contribution from Pope Gregory XVI, was consecrated in 1834. The cathedral was spared from the great fire of 1849 by a brave local citizen, who died saving it by blowing up an adjacent building. The seat of the Archdiocese of St. Louis until 1914, when the new cathedral in the western part of the city was dedicated,

the cathedral became a basilica when it was so designated by Pope John XXIII in 1961. Called by the Pope "a treasure of the universal church", the structure is now officially named the "Basilica of St. Louis the King". But this dignified building in the shadow of the Gateway Arch has remained simply the "Old Cathedral" to citizens of St. Louis.

The elegant Chatillon-DeMenil House is one of the few remaining structures reflective of early St. Louis history. It was originally built by Henri Chatillon, a colorful hunter and fur trader born in one of the French villages near St. Louis. Chatillon's exploits were recounted by Francis Parkman in 1849 in his classic *The Oregon Trail*. Chatillon built the first part of the house in 1848, then later sold it to a wealthy Frenchman, Dr. Nicholas DeMenil, who owned a string of drugstores in St. Louis. DeMenil formed a link with one of the great St. Louis French families by marrying Emilie Sophie Chouteau, a descendant of Auguste Chouteau, who founded St. Louis. DeMenil commissioned an English architect to erect the Greek Revival façade and to add several additional rooms

On the edge of the city, dotted among the rolling green hills of Calvary Cemetery, are the gravesites of many of St. Louis's early French families. The oldest surviving Catholic cemetery in St. Louis, Calvary dates from 1854. It assembled graves from three other cemeteries that were displaced over the years as the city's growth caused crowding. Auguste Chouteau was moved three times before finding his final resting place here.

<

This portrait of Emilie Sophie Chouteau, wife of Nicholas DeMenil, hangs in the Chatillon-DeMenil House. The strong-willed Emilie, a descendant of Auguste Chouteau who co-founded St. Louis, was determined to have a home reflecting the tastes of her wealthy southern cousins.

∧

A number of items from the DeMenil period remain – the ceiling medallions, marble mantelpieces and plaster decorations are all original, as is the inlaid hall floor in five different hardwoods. The DeMenil pieces include a walnut piano, a mahogany bed, dresser and lady's dressing table.

<<

The Chatillon-DeMenil House is elegantly furnished, with a fine collection of nineteenth-century pieces. The flowered window shades were typical of the time.

FRENCH COLONIAL ARCHITECTURE AND ITS ORIGINS

The buildings constructed by the eighteenth-century French colonial *habitants* of Upper Louisiana demonstrated their ability to create durable homes from a variety of local materials: native stone, hewn timbers, wooden pegs and hand-forged nails. Built in a distinctive vertical log style, the timber-framed homes have many features that reflect the progression of settlement from France to French Canada to the mid-Mississippi River Valley. In addition to the wooden elements that framed the exterior walls, the spaces created between the vertical timbers were packed with material to complete the wall systems. This infill, primarily known as *bousillage*, also provides clues to the abundance of local materials and the practices of the local *charpentiers*.

In his 1935 article "Survival of French in the Old District of Sainte Genevieve", Ward Dorrance cites Canadian origins for the word *bousillage*, defining it as "a mixture of mud or clay with straw, twigs, hair, etc.,

for use in the construction of log buildings". A French-English dictionary published in Philadelphia in 1845 defined the verb *bousiller* as "to make a mud-wall", while more modern definitions include references to ruin or destruction or "botching" a job.

Since early written references to *bousillage* are scarce in colonial archives, its authentic composition and origins are not precisely known. Its root word, *la bouse*, refers, however crudely, to cow dung. It has been suggested that the *bousillage* used in colonial-building construction therefore must have contained the commodity in question as a main ingredient, leading us to believe that the *habitants* of *Nouvelle France* were indeed a thrifty lot! More likely, though, is the theory that since a straw binder has been found in historic samples of *bousillage*, the term may simply be derived from the appearance and texture of the substance, rather than any olfactory similarities.

Origins

The roots of vertical log construction, with the resulting variations in the infill materials, can be traced to France, where numerous outstanding examples are found in the timber-frame manor houses of the *Pays d'Auge* of Normandy. In his work *Manor Houses in Normandy*, Yves Lescroart notes: "Some *logis* have retained their nogging of cob – a mixture of clay and vegetable fibers – usually reserved for farm and other outbuildings and more often than not covered with a thin coat of whitewash." This simple infill material found in utilitarian buildings of the *Pays d'Auge*

Bousillage.

In Normandy, the infill between posts is called "torchis".

A Norman truss.

is the most logical connection to the *bousillage* of Upper Louisiana, despite the variety of other infill materials also found in Normandy – brick, pebbles, stone and terra cotta.

As settlement in French Canada began, vertical log construction was to become a part of the cultural landscape. In his book *La Maison Traditionnelle au Québec*, Michel Lessard identifies the common seventeenth-century *pieux-en-terre*, or post-in-ground construction, as his *maison d'etablissement*. When construction in Québec increased during the seventeenth and early eighteenth centuries, builders began to employ two major variants of vertical log construction, both *pieux-en-terre* and *maison de colombage*, the latter of which was built on a foundation. Each method depended on a *mélange* of small stones bound together with a clay mortar to fill the gaps between the vertical logs. While the space between the logs of a *pieux-en-terre* structure generally measured between 7 and 9 inches, this dimension could expand up to several feet in a *maison de colombage*.

Following the initial period of development in Québec, *pieux-en-terre* construction was relegated more commonly to outbuildings and farm structures. *Colombage pierroté* construction further evolved during the eighteenth century and used stone infill bound with clay or more durable lime mortar packed between the vertical timbers.

American variants: Ste. Genevieve

The increasing French presence in the mid-Mississippi River Valley during the early eighteenth century resulted in the formation of a number of villages throughout a region known as the *Pays des Illinois*, or the Illinois Country. The village of Ste. Genevieve was settled on the west bank of the Mississippi River in the late 1740s, with many of its *habitants* tilling the rich alluvial soil of the nearby flood plain. In the years following the disastrous flood of 1785, the village moved to its present location on higher ground on a flat expanse between the forks of the Gabouri Creek. Today, Ste. Genevieve preserves a remarkable number of the vertical log buildings that once were found so commonly throughout these French colonial settlements.

Restoration and preservation work undertaken in Ste. Genevieve during the last fifty years has revealed a broad range of colonial building materials and techniques. The houses of its National Historic Landmark District illustrate the abundance of local stone and timber, while serving as indicators of the progression of the vertical log construction found in Québec and Normandy.

In a number of *poteaux-sur-sole* buildings, including the Louis Bolduc House and the Green Tree Tavern, traditional *bousillage* is found as the infill material between the vertical logs. Straw, used as a binding material in the clay, is still visible in much of the original material. The *bousillage* is tightly packed between the logs and troweled to provide a smooth transition from log to log. With the average vertical log measuring eight inches across, the infill material spanned approximately five inches between the logs.

In many of the vertical log houses in Ste. Genevieve, a hand-hewn depression helps to secure the infill material in position between the logs. This "cupping" technique created a slight depression in the opposing faces of the vertical logs, and would have been hewn into the logs before their assembly into the wall. The *bousillage* or infill material was packed into the cavity formed between the logs, creating a convex cross-section of material. Because of the resulting shape of the infill, even slight shrinkage of the *bousillage* would not allow it to tip out of the wall cavity.

In *Building a House in Eighteenth-Century Ste. Genevieve*, Melburn Thurman notes that small wooden braces were also set diagonally between some of the vertical logs of the Bequette-Ribault House to stabilize the infill material. In several walls of this house, shaved willows of a few inches in diameter were found to have been used as fillers between the vertical logs, with *bousillage* packed around them.

Stone infill in Ste. Genevieve buildings differed from French Canadian *maison pierrotée* in technique and in size of stone. In the St. Gemme-Amoureux House, sizable limestone pieces are wedged between the timbers in a random fashion. They are packed in place with a *bousillage* "mortar," which then appears to have been skimmed over and smoothed, eventually with a coat of whitewash over both *pierrotage* and vertical timbers.

The small, one-room LaSource-Durand cabin illustrates a different method of packing a limestone infill. Limestone pieces, generally measuring two inches thick, were neatly stacked between the timbers on a slight angle, one on top of the other. *Bousillage* mortar may have been used to complete the process, although some of the stones appear to have been stacked dry without mortar.

Construction of vertical log buildings continued in Ste. Genevieve into the nineteenth century, and infill techniques evolved with the increased variety of materials of the period. In the 1809 Dorlac House, handmade bricks were laid in place between the logs with a lime mortar and clay binder. The bricks, used both whole and cut in half, were supplemented by small infill of limestone. The cupping technique described above does not appear to have been used in this nineteenth-century structure.

These remarkable structures demonstrate the progression of the vertical log style of construction throughout the colonial period, tracing French settlement from Canada to Upper Louisiana. The utilitarian *bousillage* infill between the vertical timbers vividly shows the evolution of the style over time, with variations in methods and use of abundant local materials.

James Baker

> The walls of the Louis Bolduc House are constructed of vertical, hand-hewn, white oak logs mortised into a sill. The walls, infilled with *bousillage*, are whitewashed on both the interior and exterior sides.

> The *galerie* of the Louis Bolduc House (1790s), which is broken at the northwest end by a kitchen, was covered by a roof in an 1820 restoration.

A rich store of French colonial homes – Ste. Genevieve

Walking the streets of this small southeast Missouri town – with its ancient homes and the French tricolor planted in flower pots and shop windows – one can imagine oneself transported to a French colonial village. Ste. Genevieve, a town of roughly 4,500 inhabitants, sixty-five miles downriver from St. Louis, was just that: a French enclave on the Mississippi, one which retained its dominant French language and culture well into the nineteenth century and which today has the largest conglomeration of French colonial vertical log structures in the world. Three of the five existing post-in-ground (*poteaux-en-terre*) houses in the U.S. are to be found here.

Founded around 1750 as an agricultural settlement on the alluvial plain bordering the west bank of the Mississippi, Ste. Genevieve (originally nicknamed "Misère") has lived under three flags – French, Spanish and American. Its first French settlers were French Canadians – a smattering of families, seeking unexhausted agricultural land west of the Mississippi. Most had migrated from the east side, taking advantage of land grants from the French colonial authorities at Fort de Chartres.

In time, Spanish garrisons, German settlers and American colonists supplemented the French population and made their mark, but despite the changes in rule and population, for much of the eighteenth and nineteenth

centuries Ste. Genevieve remained resolutely French. The early growth of the town was spurred by several developments: the richness of its arable land, its strategic location downriver on the trade route to St. Louis, the increasing importance of lead mining at Mine La Motte and nearby Potosi, and the unwillingness of settlers to live under British rule on the east side of the Mississippi.

The fortunes of Ste. Genevieve have been tied to the river. "Old Town" Ste. Genevieve, several miles downriver from the present town, was installed near the border of the river until the 1780s. But during that decade a series of devastating floods – capped by the massive inundation of 1785, which came to be called *l'année des grands eaux* (the year of the great flood) – forced a retreat of the town to higher ground over the next several years. The place finally settled on, a mile back from the river, was called "les petites côtes" (the little hills), north of the original town and between the branches of Gabouri Creek. Modern Ste. Genevieve rests here. The move eased, but did not eliminate, the menace of the river. Rampaging waters have covered the New Town on several occasions, the latest during the great flood of 1993.

In the space of fifty years, Ste. Genevieve found itself buffeted by three different changes of regime. In 1762, the French, starved of funds during the French and Indian War (1756-63) and still embroiled in a European war with England, ceded Louisiana, including all of its lands west of the Mississippi, to the Spanish in the secret Treaty of Fontainebleau. Even before the American takeover, an increasing number of American settlers found their way to "New Town" Ste. Genevieve, and in 1804, Jean-Baptiste Vallé,

< In the back, the Louis Bolduc House has formal boxwood gardens and a separate smokehouse/ kitchen similar to one that might have originally been one of the ancillary buildings on the property.

< The garden of the Bolduc-LeMeilleur House, across the way from the Louis Bolduc House, is laid out in a more informal style than that of its neighbor.

<

The massive fireplace of the Louis Bolduc House is adorned with nineteenth-century tools and utensils.

>

The furnishings in the Louis Bolduc House are antiques, many of them dating back to the eighteenth century. Included among them is a trunk covered with animal hide and several pieces of French Canadian furniture of the period.

∧

The elegant interior of the Guibourd-Vallé House is filled with antiques collected by Anne Marie Vallé on her travels worldwide.

a member of one of Ste. Genevieve's most prestigious clans, took over as the first American commandant in the town.

Agriculture was the basis of the economy in both Old and New Town Ste. Genevieve. A commonfield (*les grands champs*) bordered the villages and was surrounded by a fence with stakes in the ground to protect the crops from grazing animals. Each landowner maintained his section of the fence, and trees were used to mark the boundaries of individual lots.

Living conditions in eighteenth-century Ste. Genevieve were basic. Most village houses were simple vertical log structures, with two main rooms and partitioned-off sleeping areas. They were small, with whitewashed interior walls, sometimes paneled and plastered. The roofs were steeply pitched, generally supported by massive trusses pegged into place. Some were covered with thatch, others with wooden shingles. Residential properties were a square arpent (around .85 of an acre) and were surrounded with picket fences to keep animals out.

The *poteaux-en-terre* (post in the ground) houses had upright posts of mulberry or cedar; the *poteaux-sur-sole* (post on a wooden sill) houses generally employed oak or black walnut. A *galerie*, or outside porch, was common in Ste. Genevieve, to enhance the living space in clement weather and to shelter the house from summer heat.

Mining and later manufacturing contributed to the growth of modern Ste. Genevieve, though agriculture continued to underpin the local economy. The salt springs at Saline Creek were exploited by the town's major families – among them the Vallés, Bolducs and Bauvais – whose ancient homes still remain in the town. But agriculture remained the prime source of wealth. Riverboats carried Ste. Genevieve foodstuffs – along with hides and pelts – downriver to New Orleans, Cape Giradeau and New Madrid and upriver to St. Louis. In return, boats from New Orleans often brought European goods – clothing, faïence and wine – back to Ste. Genevieve. In 1807, Frederick Bates, secretary of the Louisiana Territory, wrote that Ste. Genevieve was "the most wealthy village in Louisiana".

Restoration work, begun in the 1930s, continues on a number of key structures, some of which – like the Bequette-Ribault House and Green Tree Tavern – are privately owned. Other restored properties are managed by a mix of public and private operators, among them the Missouri Department of Natural Resources (the St. Gemme Bauvais/Amoureux and the Felix Vallé Houses) and the National Society of Colonial Dames of America in the State of Missouri (Louis Bolduc House, Bolduc/LeMellieur House and Linden House).

Tourism has brought thousands of new visitors to Ste. Genevieve to see some of the more than sixty historic structures. Nowhere in the United States can one find more links to the French heritage than in this small Missouri town.

The historic structures and sites

Louis Bolduc, born in St. Joachim Parish, Canada, in 1734, moved to Ste. Genevieve in the 1760s. He became the richest citizen in the settlement, with interests in planting, lead mining and salt production. Along with the Vallés, the Bauvais and a few others, the Bolducs were one of the powerful ruling families of the town.

Bolduc first built a home in Old Town Ste. Genevieve, then moved up to the New Town when flooding made living in the Old Town unsustainable. The Louis Bolduc House, a *poteaux-sur-sole* construction on a stone foundation, is thought to date from the 1790s. The Bolduc family lived in it continuously until 1949, when it was donated to the National Society of Colonial Dames of America in the State of Missouri. The house was carefully restored in 1956-57 and is now recognized as one of the finest restorations – if not the finest – of a French colonial house in the Mississippi Valley. The double-hipped roof is supported by an impressive king post Norman truss, common to French colonial homes in the Louisiana Territory. The ceilings are

high and the house has an east-west orientation, allowing the air to circulate. Typical features include the surrounding *galerie*, broken at the end by an enclosed kitchen.

The Amoureux House is one of the three *poteaux-en-terre* houses remaining in Ste. Genevieve. Originally built around 1792, it has been altered over the years, but still retains much of its primitive charm and architectural integrity. Built by Jean Baptiste St. Gemme Bauvais, who moved to Ste. Genevieve from Kaskaskia in the late 1780s, then bought by Benjamin Amoureux in 1852, the house remained in the Amoureux family for several generations before being sold in 1923. Today, again in the process of restoration, it is owned and operated by the Missouri Department of Natural Resources. Important restoration work was performed on the house in the 1840s and 1960s. The roof, originally hipped and thatched, was changed to the present gabled form, a *galerie* was added and the total length of the house shortened.

In 1993, the destructive Mississippi flood inundated Amoureux's cellar, requiring bracing to reinforce the original logs. But the rest of the structure was largely undamaged.

<

The Amoureux House is one
of the three post-in-ground
(*poteaux-en-terre*) houses
remaining in Ste. Genevieve.
It is one of Ste. Genevieve's
most authentic, surviving
eighteenth-century houses.

∧

The Amoureux House.
Amoureux's hipped roof
is supported by a massive
Norman truss. The original
framing members are still
in place behind gable end.

In the cellar, original features
include the floor joists,
two hundred-year old logs that
run the width of the house.
The walnut beams on the
ceiling are beaded, a feature
requiring hours of handiwork.

>
The Vital St. Gemme
Bauvais House has
undergone major changes
over the years. In the
nineteenth and early
twentieth centuries,
remodeling lopped
off fourteen feet from
the north end and cut
the apparently rotting
king post trusses.
The ends of the roof
were altered by adding
gables, and a kitchen
addition took up part
of the *galerie*.

<

The door latch and some of the shutters on the Bequette-Ribault House are original and date back more than two hundred years.

>>

Exceptional care was taken in the restoration of the Bequette-Ribault House. The same species of wood used by the original builders was employed to replace rotting timbers, and restoration craftsmen worked with the same kind of tools used by the original builders. A U.S. Interior Department survey noted: "The building is the only Illinois *poteaux-en-terre* building known to survive almost complete with its truss system, ceiling and floor framing basically intact."

The Guibourd-Vallé House, built around 1806, is one of the most elegantly furnished of Ste. Genevieve's ancient houses. Anne Marie Vallé, wife of Jules Vallé, was an avid antique collector and filled the house with objects gathered in her travels worldwide. The original builder of the house, Jacques Guibourd, was born in France. After spending some years as a wealthy planter in St. Domingue, he fled to Ste. Genevieve following the slave rebellion in that country. Though the haste of his flight left him with few resources, his pedigree enabled him to receive a land grant from François Vallé II, Ste. Genevieve's commandant. After Guibourd died, his wife, Anne Marie, remained in the house. She was clearly a woman of some taste. The elegant antiques in the house include oriental ceramics, serpentine Queen Anne chairs, Venetian mirrors and blue-bird lamps by Daum – a far cry from the spare furnishings in other Ste. Genevieve restored homes.

One of the three *poteaux-en-terre* structures in Ste. Genevieve, the Vital St. Gemme Bauvais House has an illustrious history. Dating from 1792, it was the home of one of Ste. Genevieve's wealthiest citizens, a brother of Jean-Baptiste St. Gemme Bauvais, who built the Amoureux house. Previous generations of the family hailed from St. Martin, Perche, in France. In the nineteenth century, the Vital St. Gemme Bauvais House was home to a number of celebrated figures: Henry Brackenridge, author of *Recollections of Persons and Places in the West* (1834), lived here for a time as a child, and Louis Menard, son of the first Lieutenant Governor of Illinois, Pierre Menard, did as well.

The house, though altered, is still of historic significance. Unlike the *bousillage* filling found in other old Ste. Genevieve homes, the fillings between the wall logs is *pierrotage*, a mixture of rocks and mortar. The joists in the cellar are original. The present owners have exposed the massive ceiling beams still present in the main *salle*. For their work in restoring the house, they received the 2001 Preserve Missouri Award.

The Bequette-Ribault House is of interest, not only because so much of it is original, but also because it is one of the few remaining French colonial homes that was owned by a free woman of color. Clarise Ribault, born in Virginia, was the companion, if not the wife, of a widowed Frenchman, John Ribault, who came to Ste. Genevieve in the early nineteenth century. Clarise purchased the house in the late 1830s, and her descendants lived in it for more than 130 years, until the last great-grandson died in 1969.

THE ART OF PRESERVATION CARPENTRY

When I was a student in historic preservation, I had the good fortune to work on restoring one of the five remaining post-in-the-ground (*poteaux-en-terre*) houses left in the United States. That experience caused me to fall in love with vertical log construction.

To authentically reconstruct an old house, it is necessary to use the same type of lumber cut to the same size, and using the original building techniques – namely hand-hewing the joists and sills.

The hands-on restoration of these buildings is of considerable interest for several reasons. First, it is fascinating to learn about the builder and the building. Second, the tools used by men working two hundred years before I was born allows the builder to speak to me. Third, I am always impressed by workmanship that has stood the test of time, and is in better condition than much of what has been built in the last fifty years. This is a graphic illustration of the pride the original builder took in his work.

To find old buildings to restore, one should first look for any available ancient maps. These can pinpoint the locations of the buildings and can provide valuable clues as to the early owner, as well as information concerning when the site was occupied. This, in turn, can help place the structure in a time period and/or construction style, and can indicate, for example, whether it is a French-style building of the mid-eighteenth to nineteenth century in the Midwest. Court records, such as land grants and wills, are other valuable sources of information. But perhaps the most informative method is to go out and ask people directly. This is much more stimulating than sitting in a dusty courthouse.

I travel the back roads of the Midwest, looking for old buildings. When I find a house that looks as though it could be a French vertical log home, I first look at the foundation. If it is brick, I lose interest, as I have never found one with a brick foundation. The next place I look is the roof. If it has that wonderful double-pitched roofline, my heart rate increases, and if the fireplace is intact, I become more excited still. The next thing

to consider is the construction style of the windows and doors. If that falls into place, the real challenge begins. This involves going up to the door and asking a complete stranger about his or her house. I have been very lucky in my road research in that owners have often directed me to other houses in the area.

The quality of the builder can often be gauged by the quality of the workmanship on his building. The vertical logs have different levels of quality, depending on the builder and the period during which the construction occurred.

The size of the logs used depended upon how they were used: larger logs were needed for the bottom sills, and averaged about 10 x 12 inches. The logs were selected to be as close as possible to the size required, in order

> America's preservation architects often make use of eighteenth and nineteenth-century tools to lend authenticity to their work.

to eliminate unnecessary work in hewing them to the finished dimensions. The logs were hauled to the site, and the bark was removed by using a chisel, drawknife or bark spud. Following the removal of the bark, the builder squared the log. To do so, he marked it by using a string line, which had been soaked in berry juice for color. The next step was to "score" the log by cutting slits into it at the intervals marked. Next, a broad axe or foot adze was used to cut away the wood between the slits and to create the final smoothing.

The logs were generally hewed on two sides, the interior and the exterior. They were then cut with a gutter adze to form a cupped area to hold the *bousillage*, usually made of mud and straw or limestone and mortar. After the logs were finished, the next step was to lay out the wall openings for any doors and windows, and to mark on the logs the location and size of mortises and tenons. This was usually done using a scribe.

Then each mortise was roughly cleaned out with a boring auger brace or a mortise axe, and finished with a mortising chisel. The tenon was usually made using a hand saw for the rough shape, and was finished with a chisel. The bottom post-on-sill

(*poteaux-sur-sole*) buildings are usually held together with a wooden peg called a tree nail. The sections of the top plate were generally joined using the same method, or sometimes they were lapped and spiked together to keep them from coming apart.

The materials used in the building depend on the type of building it was and what materials were available. The existing *poteaux-en-terre* buildings were made using eastern cedar, which is commonly found

in Missouri. A cedar post is a good choice, because it is highly resistant to rot and no insects appear to be attracted to it. Materials, such as oak, mulberry and different wood species, have been used, but no complete examples remain today. All the verticals that touch the ground were made of cedar, while the top plate was generally of oak, usually white oak. The roof truss system was of oak, and the rafters were often made of lighter wood, such as pine or river willow.

Preservation architecture is a special discipline offering rich rewards to those who pursue it. Unlike the repetitive work required on many modern buildings, preservation architecture is full of surprises – from the discovery of long-ignored historical properties to the opportunity to work with ancient materials and restore them to their original use.

Jesse Francis

> To connect an ancient *galerie's* posts to the sills, preservation architects use mortise, tenon and wooden peg fastening techniques.

Felix Vallé House.
The restorers of the Felix
Vallé House located
account books for the
store located on the
ground floor of the house
and have an inventory
of the items stocked here
– an imposing range
that included hardware,
dry goods, foodstuffs,
fabric, pins, needles,
thread and ribbons.

< ∨

      >

Felix Vallé House.
The restorers of the Felix
Vallé House located
account books for the
store located on the
ground floor of the house
and have an inventory
of the items stocked here
– an imposing range
that included hardware,
dry goods, foodstuffs,
fabric, pins, needles,
thread and ribbons.

The Felix Vallé House.
A limestone Federal-Style
building with Anglo
features, the Felix Vallé
House is a symmetrical
one-and-a-half story,
gable-roofed building,
with outside stone
chimneys. A back-porch
stairway leads to the
second-floor bedrooms.
There is a charming
garden and nineteenth-
century outbuildings
believed to have been
built by the owner.

The Bequette connection dates back to the earliest days of the house, either in the late 1700s or the early 1800s. It is known that Jean Baptiste Bequette II owned the lot and that either he or his descendants built the house. His family lived in Bequette-Ribault until 1837. The surviving house has important original features. One of the three *poteaux-en-terre* houses in Ste. Genevieve, the logs of its walls are nearly two hundred years old. The remarkable Norman trusses on the upper level, with their original pegs, are essentially intact except for some pieces that were damaged by fire and replaced during the restoration. The interior door, with its iron work and three sets of shutters, is original as well.

One of five Ste. Genevieve houses inhabited by members of one of Ste. Genevieve's most powerful families – the Vallés – the Felix Vallé House is notable for being a transition dwelling, incorporating a blend of French elements with the American Federal Style of architecture that came to Ste. Genevieve following the American takeover. It was also a dual-purpose dwelling, part of it being the site of a thriving business. The Felix Vallé House was built in 1818 by Jacob Philipson, an American merchant from Philadelphia. Sold to Jean-Baptiste

Vallé, the house was deeded to his son Felix, who lived there with his wife, Odile Pratte Vallé, until his death in 1877. Odile, one of Ste. Genevieve's wealthiest and most generous citizens, lived in the house until she died in 1894.

The house links two of the most celebrated names in the Illinois Country: Vallé and Menard. In 1817, Jean Baptiste Vallé went into business with Pierre Menard, who in 1818 became the first Lieutenant Governor of the new state of Illinois. The firm, first called B. L. Vallé and Company, was later named Menard & Vallé.

The Felix Vallé House was both a living quarters and a mercantile store. The store has been carefully re-created to look as it might have done around 1830. While the store was operating, steamboats brought the goods from St. Louis and New Orleans, and local citizens could buy some of the same items available in larger cities all over the U.S.

Research on the Felix Vallé House has yielded clues as to the configuration of the general store, whose ceiling and floor are original. Marks on the original paint of the ceiling helped restorers re-create the shelves, and the wear pattern in the floor helped re-create the counters.

The undulating burial ground of Memorial Cemetery is the final resting place for many of Ste. Genevieve's pioneer families. With few exceptions, it has been closed to new graves since 1882, so that the cemetery has retained its original character. Buried here are Jean Baptiste and Jeanne Vallé, Vital St. Gemme Bauvais, Jacques Guibourd, Louis Bolduc and Felix and Odile Pratte Vallé.

>>

Furnishings in the Felix Vallé House reflect a blend of styles used by the Vallé family. The furniture in the dining room is generally American Empire style, dating from 1820-1840. The dining room chairs are mahogany with sabre legs. The portrait above the mantel is Felix's father, Jean-Baptiste Vallé, Civil Commandant of the Post of Ste. Genevieve in the early 1800s. In the living room, the marble-top table is American Empire, dating to the 1830s. The couch, American Empire from the 1820s, has beautifully carved lion's paw feet with an acanthus leaf motif, very much in style during the period.

<

The graves in the Ste. Genevieve Memorial Cemetery are often topped with columns or marble slabs, though these are only decorative features. The early citizens of Ste. Genevieve are buried six feet under.

RESTORING THE GREEN TREE TAVERN: A PERSONAL HISTORY

My project was to restore a French Creole vertical log, *poteaux-sur-sole* (post-on-sill) house built between 1790-91 in Ste. Genevieve, Missouri, officially called the Nicolas Janis House, but popularly known as the Green Tree Tavern, or just the Green Tree.

To restore a building as accurately as possible is to recover the form and details of that building and its setting as they appeared at a particular time in the past. This is done by removing any alterations made to the building not authentic to the period to which the building is being restored, and by reconstructing as accurately as possible any original features now missing.

Before deciding to do anything to a historic building, one should thoroughly research it. Fortunately, the Green Tree is prominent enough that there was a sizable body of documentation on it going back to the 1830s. There are also oral traditions about the Green Tree which I was able to glean from local residents.

The next step is to decide to which historic period one should restore the building. I decided to take the Green Tree back to 1791, the year its construction was completed. When I purchased the house, there was a *galerie* on three sides. I asked a local contractor to remove the siding and interior walls on the northwest side of the building in order to expose the original *galerie*. But when the siding and interior walls were removed, I was in for a shock. Instead of exposing chamfered red cedar posts supporting the roof, as was the case for the *galerie* on the other three sides of the building, willow studs were revealed instead. This implied, contrary to what I had read and heard, that the northwest side of the building never had a *galerie*, but had always been an enclosed part of the building.

If one wants to restore a building as authentically as possible, it is imperative to seek the help of an expert. In my case, finding this expert was not as easy as one might think. I do not think there are fifty eighteenth-century vertical log French Creole buildings still standing in all of North America. I interviewed various restoration architects before choosing one, Jack Luer, who had worked for many years restoring French colonial houses. Luer said that he first had to "read the building". That would take time and would include, among other things, carefully taking some of the building apart. When we did so, there were many clues that the original stairs to the attic had been moved from the southeast wall of the large central room, which was probably the trade room, to the southwest wall of that room, called the parlor in early architectural drawings.

Luer speculated there must have been a turnaround at the lower end of the stairs that would have provided extra steps

<<
The architect's plans for restoring the Green Tree.

<
The *bousillage* filling between the Green Tree's vertical log exterior walls.

necessary to allow the risers to be comfortably used. That insight gave him the confidence to pull the plaster off the southeast wall where the turnaround must have been. Indeed, when the plaster was removed, it revealed that new machine lathing had been used to cover the spot where the turnaround originally had been before the stairs were moved to the southwest wall. The remaining original hand-cut laths showed a perfect profile of the original turnaround.

Since most of the original *galerie* no longer existed, this part of the building could not be restored; it had to be reconstructed. To reconstruct it, we had to use the same type of lumber cut to the same size, and use original building techniques – namely hand hewing of the joists and sills. Mortise, tenon and wooden peg-fastening techniques connected the posts to the *galerie's* sills and plates.

Working with typical general contractors on a restoration project can have its problems – the biggest one being their professional mindset, which seems to dictate that their finished work be straight and square and looking new. In one case, I decided to recycle the bricks from a chimney built for the house during the 1860 remodeling and which was no longer needed. I did this because with their rounded edges, chipped surfaces, and worn appearance they would more closely

resemble the missing 1791 bricks than new ones would. Though I instructed the contractor's bricklayers to reconstruct the fireplace using the 1860 bricks, I was shocked to see they had reconstructed – but with new bricks! Using old bricks to build a new fireplace simply was not in their mindset.

Attempting to do an authentic restoration on an historic building is not for the faint of heart. It is fraught with frustrations, including

criticism from those who see your mistakes and are confident they could do a better job. Nonetheless, I believe restoring the Green Tree was worthwhile. When I put my hand on a piece of its original fabric, I still get a thrill, thinking that it was worked on and put into place during George Washington's first Administration and that I have had the privilege of restoring it for future generations.

Hilliard J. Goldman

>
Craftsmen familiar with eighteenth-century building techniques restore old homes using ancient tools such as the foot adze, the auger brace and the mortise axe.

While French explorers and French Canadian settlers were settling the Louisiana Territory from the north, another set of Frenchmen approached it from the south. Once again, the reasons were political rather than economic. If France could control the mouth of the Mississippi, it could dominate the two great North American rivers – the St. Lawrence in the north and the Mississippi in the center and south. The aim was to keep the British and Spanish from overrunning the continent.

But efforts to set up sustainable settlements in the south met with frustration. France, engaged in continental wars, could afford few men and resources to defend and develop the colony. Disease and starvation were rampant, and the humid climate did not easily lend itself to food production. Geography also worked against the southern colonies: the coastline was low and lacked a good harbor. The result was a series of setbacks: efforts to set up a French capital at Biloxi and Mobile ended in failure. By 1712, Louis XIV was giving serious thought to giving up Louisiana altogether.

Only New Orleans, which was accessible to deep draft vessels via the Mississippi, proved to be a sustainable capital. But it too had difficulty attracting settlers. Several schemes were tried to populate the area. John Law's Company of the Indies brought six thousand slaves (mainly from Senegal and Benin) to Louisiana, but despite shameless advertising, few French volunteered to migrate to the swampy and humid colony. The Company was forced to rely on military conscripts, prostitutes and convicts.

Surprisingly, Louisiana survived, though it continued to be a drain on the French treasury. During the Seven Years War (1756-63), Louis XV, to prevent England from seizing control over half of North America, ceded Louisiana to his cousin, the Bourbon King Charles III of Spain. For the next forty years, under Spanish rule, the colony grew more diverse with immigrants from the Canary Islands, Anglo-Protestants, Irish, Acadians from Novia Scotia, former slaves fleeing revolutions in Haiti and St. Domingue and Americans in search of opportunities after the American Revolution. The 1800 Treaty of San Ildefonso retroceded Louisiana back to France, setting the stage for the Louisiana Purchase in 1803. Napoleon, faced with war in Europe and seeing the United States as a bulwark against English expansion, sold the territory to the Americans for $15 million. The era of French dominance in the Louisiana Territory was over.

Taking Root:
the Lower Mississippi Valley and the Gulf Coast

ARKANSAS

First European settlement on the lower Mississippi – Arkansas Post

The small settlement of Arkansas Post along the Arkansas River was the first European settlement in the lower Mississippi Valley. First started by Henri de Tonty, based on a grant from his commander, La Salle, it struggled, was abandoned, was devastated by several floods, was attacked by Indians and later by Union soldiers, was relocated, thrived briefly and died out. But the Post is of considerable historical interest, for it helped establish the claim of France to the greatest waterway on the continent and stands out as a reflection of the struggle among the French, British and Spanish to control the Louisiana Territory.

Tonty, La Salle's most trusted lieutenant, established the Post's first site in 1686 at the Quapaw village of Osotouy, around thirty miles from the mouth of the Arkansas River. It was to be an Indian trading station, an *entrepôt*, and an intermediate stop for French traders sending furs and other goods from the Illinois Territory to the Gulf of Mexico. There were also plans for a fort, a chapel, a resident priest and land grants for settlers.

Alas, the Post never lived up to the aims of its founders. The original site was abandoned by 1699. It was re-established more than twenty years later, when Frenchmen, drawn by extravagant claims of silver mines and untold riches – inspired by John Law's *Compagnie d'Occident* and published in a Paris newspaper – were drawn to this isolated place on the Arkansas River. In 1721, around eighty settlers moved in, along with a small military detachment. But there

were no riches, agriculture did not flourish, the population soon declined and the military post was abandoned four years later. It was not to be re-established until 1731.

In 1749, a band of Chickasaw Indians attacked the Post, killing some settlers and taking others as slaves. Shortly after, the Post was moved some miles upstream to a site called Écores Rouges (Red Bluffs). The present Memorial stands on this site. This time, the French built a stockade using the familiar *poteaux-en-terre* construction, with a *bousillage* filling between the posts. A more elaborate structure, it contained an officers' quarters, a soldiers' barracks, a storehouse for supplies and a powder magazine. But in 1756, the French authorities thought the new site was too far from the Mississippi and moved it to a location nearer the mouth of the Arkansas River. In 1779, the Spanish, who had taken it over in the meantime, moved it yet again, back to the relatively high ground of Écores Rouges.

With the American population growing in the early 1800s, the Post became increasingly an agricultural settlement. On March 2, 1819, reflecting its new importance, it became the capital of the new Arkansas Territory. Its reign, however, was brief. In 1821, the capital was moved to Little Rock, and the Post began to decline once more.

The co-existence of French, Spanish and later American settlers created social tensions. The Americans tended to regard the French as lazy and frivolous, and the French

∨

A replica of an ancient cannon at Arkansas Post. The French fortified the Post in the mid-eighteenth century. When the Americans took over, they again fortified the site, and during the American Civil War the settlement was caught in a major battle between Confederate and Union forces. The Confederate troops at the Post numbered several thousand, but they were overwhelmed by the Union army, who bombarded the southern troops from the river and forced its surrender.

A replica of Tonty's cross, used to signal traffic on the Arkansas River, has been erected at Arkansas Post. Tonty, who had been granted a seignory on the lower Arkansas River by La Salle, had great plans for the village, which was the first of several locations that later became Arkansas Post. But the isolated settlement languished for some decades.

resented new customs and legal systems being foisted upon them. An American Presbyterian missionary, writing in 1773, said: "The French people generally came to the place of worship arrayed in their ball dresses, and went directly from worship to the ball. A billiard room was near, and parts of my audience sometimes came in for a moment, and after listening to a few sentences, returned to their billiards."

During the American Civil War, with the fort a threat to Union Army supply lines, Union troops traveled upriver and, in January 1863, attacked the Confederate forces stationed there. Virtually all of the houses were destroyed by cannon fire, and nearly five thousand Confederate troops surrendered to the Union forces.

The Post never recovered from the battle. In 1903, the river changed course, and in 1927 a particularly vicious flood submerged the entire site, drowning the remaining buildings. In February of that same year, a bill establishing Arkansas Post as a unit of the state park system was approved, and in 1960 President Eisenhower signed into law legislation establishing the site as a National Memorial.

Now administered by the National Park Service, the Post's three hundred-plus acres – complete with an informative visitors' center and a replica of the cross Tonty had erected to signal boats traveling the river – encompass some of the nineteenth-century town and the approximate site of two of the eighteenth-century trading and military posts. Largely a peaceful recreation and picnic area, some seven miles south of Gillett, Arkansas, the Post allows the visitor to stroll on land where the settlers of three nations – France, Spain and the young United States – vied to carve out a sustainable settlement near the intersection of the Arkansas and Mississippi Rivers.

∧

The flooding of the Arkansas River devastated Arkansas Post on several occasions after its establishment in 1686. Though the Post was moved to the relatively high ground of Écores Rouges in 1779, it continued to suffer from the elements. In 1788, the fort at the settlement fell into the river; in 1903, the river changed course around a mile south; and in 1927 a particularly vicious flood submerged the entire site.

TEXAS

>

In 1684, La Salle left
La Rochelle with four
ships and two hundred
men and women to settle
near the mouth of
the Mississippi. But the
expedition overshot by
four hundred miles and
sailed on to Matagorda
Bay, in Texas. One of the
ships was lost *en route*
to Spanish buccaneers
and another, the *Aimable*,
was wrecked as it tried
to land. A third ship,
La Belle, was lost as
it explored the coast.
The loss of *La Belle*,
which was loaded
with vital supplies,
was a devastating blow
to La Salle's Texas colony.
(La Salle's Expedition in 1684
by Jean-Antoine Théodore
de Gudin, Château de Versailles
et de Trianon) ©Photo RMN

La Salle's tragic colony in Texas – *La Belle* and Fort St. Louis

La Salle's ill-fated voyage to Texas was the last tragic act in the explorer's remarkable career. In 1684, La Salle left La Rochelle with four ships and around three hundred colonists, some of them marriageable women and girls from Paris, to establish a French colony at the mouth of the Mississippi and to protect the area from Spanish incursions. Plagued by inaccurate maps, and unable to differentiate features on the low-lying coast, the expedition overshot by four hundred miles and ended up in Matagorda Bay off the Texas coast. A landing was made near Matagorda Island.

The months that followed were excruciating for the colony. One of the ships' captains, Tanguy le Gallois de Beaujeu, who resented La Salle, returned to France with his ship, the *Joly*. Another ship, the *Aimable*, was lost when it ran aground on a reef. Scorched by the Texas sun, sick with nausea and dysentery, several colonists died each day. Undaunted, the determined La Salle pushed inland, heading up what is now called Garcitas Creek to a site near present-day Victoria, Texas. He then selected a low bluff as the site to build his fort, which he named Fort St. Louis. It was here that some months later the colonists learned that his supply frigate, *La Belle* – with its vital stores, ammunition and tools – had been swept onto a sand bar and abandoned by its crew, only a few of whom escaped in a raft. The Texas colonists found themselves stranded, hundreds of miles from the Mississippi.

After fruitless excursions to find the river, La Salle returned to Fort St. Louis and resolved to travel north to French Canada to find help for the colony. On that overland trek, in 1687, he was murdered by his own men near present-day Navasota, Texas. A statue in his memory now overlooks Matagorda Bay at Indianola.

The wreck of *La Belle* remained undiscovered for more than three hundred years. Not until 1995 did searchers find it in Matagorda Bay. The following year, a seawater cofferdam – a watertight structure to keep water out of an

enclosed area – was built around the ship and the water pumped out, allowing archaeologists to do a dry-land excavation in the middle of the bay. In an operation that attracted attention worldwide, the ship was extracted and reassembled. More than one million artifacts were retrieved from the wreck. A sailor's remains were also found, and he was buried with full honors in the presence of the French ambassador to the United States and Texas state officials.

By 1689, most of La Salle's Texas colonists had died of disease or had been massacred by the Karankawa Indians. The remains of several were buried by the Spanish when they reached the spot in 1689. Three centuries later, in 1997, a ranch foreman accidentally dug up the cannons of Fort St. Louis, which had been buried in neat rows by the Spanish. During recent excavations, traces of the fort itself were found nearby. Thousands of artifacts – including French ceramics, gunflints, musket balls, fragments of wine glasses, jewelry and religious medallions – have been excavated in the vicinity, vivid reminders of the tragic fate of the earliest European settlers in Texas.

The Ursuline nuns in Texas – San Antonio

Founded in 1535 in Brescia, Italy by St. Angela Merici, the Ursuline Order was named after the legendary St. Ursula, a Christian princess revered as a virgin martyr and as the patron saint of learning. The Brescia Order, reflecting the Ursulines' respect for education, established the first institute dedicated exclusively to the education of young girls. In time, the Ursuline Order spread throughout Europe. In Paris, one of its most illustrious pupils was Françoise Scarron, called Madame de Maintenon, the second wife of King Louis XIV, who, in 1686, founded an educational institution for impoverished young women of the nobility at Saint-Cyr, near Paris.

The first voyage of the Ursuline nuns to the Louisiana Territory was in 1727, when twelve arrived in New Orleans after a turbulent voyage from Rouen. Through the years, they performed selfless work educating the children of poor blacks and Indians and caring for the sick and disadvantaged.

In the nineteenth century, the Ursuline tradition was carried over to Texas. Pope Pius IX created a Catholic diocese for the state in 1847, and the bishop, Jean-Marie Odin, asked the Ursulines to establish a school and convent in the growing city of San Antonio. François Giraud, a French-trained architect, was asked to design a school for a ten-acre site in the city. Assisted by Jules Poinsard, another French architect, Giraud began work on the project in 1848, using a process called *pisé de terre*, in which rock, straw and native clay were compressed by hand and used as infilling between the stones.

Three years later, seven Ursuline sisters from Galveston, Texas and New Orleans arrived by stagecoach in San Antonio to set up the school and convent. The Ursuline Academy "for the education of young ladies of refinement" was opened in the still-unfinished building. Through the years, other buildings were added – a dormitory and a Gothic style chapel in the 1860s and a priest's house in the 1880s. By 1900, there were three hundred students in the academy. In keeping with their tradition of religious tolerance, the Ursulines opened their premises to other congregations of women as these other groups waited to establish their own institutions: the Sisters of Charity of the Incarnate Word, the Carmelites and the Presentation Sisters were welcomed successively over a period spanning nearly a century.

The Ursulines remained at the old site for 120 years before moving their academy to northwest San Antonio. In 1965, the last group of resident nuns moved away, and the property fell into ruin. But six years later, in 1971, the Southwest School of Art and Craft moved to the old site and raised funds to restore it, while respecting the architectural integrity of the Ursuline buildings. Now, visitors to the carefully restored structures can view fine examples of French Gothic Revival architecture, a rarity in this part of the United States.

<

The original Ursuline Convent, built in 1851 on the San Antonio River, is believed to be the oldest surviving example of *pisé de terre* work in Texas. Its design is attributed to the French architect Jules Poinsard.
©Photo Richard Q. Kroninger

<

Construction on the first Ursuline Academy building, which has been preserved in San Antonio, was begun in 1848 by the French-trained architect François Giraud and was completed in 1851.
©Photo Richard Q. Kroninger

MISSISSIPPI

>

The Old Biloxi Cemetery
has graves that date from
the 1700s. Among the
French names scattered
here are those of other
immigrants – Italian,
German, English – who
settled in this part
of the Gulf Coast.

∨

Fort Maurepas was built
at the site of the first
French settlement
in *Nouvelle France*.
The recreated, palisaded
fort, close to the Bay of
Biloxi, is presently used
as a tourist attraction
and as a setting for
historical reenactments
of Biloxi's French past.

The first French settlement in the Mississippi Valley – Biloxi

There are few traces of the French heritage in Biloxi on the south Mississippi Gulf Coast, but for a time in the late seventeenth, early eighteenth centuries, this was the site of the first French settlement and the first French capital of Louisiana.

As early as 1699, sixteen years after La Salle claimed the Louisiana Territory for France, and twenty years before the founding of New Orleans, around sixty French settlers, under the command of Pierre LeMoyne, Sieur d'Iberville, left La Rochelle, France to find the mouth of the Mississippi that La Salle had vainly sought to find years before. The aim was to secure the river against the claims of England and Spain. After going upriver as far as present day Baton Rouge, Iberville and his men returned south to establish a fort and settlement. They selected a spot near what is now Ocean Springs, Mississippi to erect their fort, which they named Fort Maurepas after the French minister of the navy. The small settlement of Biloxi (first named "Bilocchey" and "Biloxéy" after the Indian tribe, the Biloxis) grew up around the fort.

The new colony suffered from benign neglect by the mother country, which was preoccupied with continental wars, and its population never increased in substantial numbers during the eighteenth century. There were not many eligible women to build up the settlement – except for local Indians and some black women brought from Haiti, along with a smattering of "cassette girls" from orphanages in France. Biloxi was nevertheless the capital of the Louisiana Territory for two years before the capital was moved to Mobile.

In 1723, Jean Baptiste Le Moyne, Sieur de Bienville moved the French capital once again to present-day New Orleans, which was accessible to deep draft vessels via the Mississippi River, and Biloxi was virtually abandoned. In 1810, it became part of the short-lived Republic of West Florida. In the nineteenth century, the town gained new immigrants from throughout Europe, and also became a refuge for wealthy people from New Orleans, fleeing from yellow fever epidemics, who built stately mansions along the coast.

There is no agreement about where the first French fort, Fort Maurepas, was located other than that it was either in or near present day Ocean Springs, a small town just east of Biloxi. Completed in 1699, the original palisaded fort was built Vauban style, as were several other French forts in the Louisiana Territory, with four bastions at the corners to provide an unimpeded field of fire. Sixteen cannons and a store of munitions protected the small French contingent who lived here. In 1702, the fort was abandoned when the French capital was moved to Mobile. Whether washed away by hurricanes or otherwise destroyed, its remnants have never been found.

>

In 1699, Jean-Baptiste
le Moyne, Sieur de
Bienville, along with
a small French contingent,
set foot on a peninsula
some sixteen miles west
of present-day Biloxi,
which he named Bay
St. Louis. A statue of
Bienville has been erected
in one of the squares
of this picturesque town.

∧

The LaPointe-Krebs
House, a galleried home
with double-pitched roof
in the French Canadian/
Creole Style, has been
restored to its 1820s
appearance. The house
has one story and an attic,
walls framed of cypress
and cedar (*colombage*)
and a one-story porch.
The wall coverings
between the vertical
timbers are called "tabby"
and are a mixture of sand,
oyster shells and water,
combined with animal
bones and pottery.

One of the five *poteaux-en-terre* houses in the U.S. – Pascagoula

Said to be the oldest standing structure in the state of Mississippi, the LaPointe-Krebs House, popularly known as Old Spanish Fort, most likely dates from 1721-26 (though the remaining structure probably dates from around 1772). It is one of the only five post-in-the-ground (*poteaux-en-terre*) houses remaining in the continental United States.

The house takes its name from the union of a French woman, Marie Joseph Simon de la Pointe, with Hugo Ernestus Krebs, a German from Alsace. In 1715, Marie's father, Joseph Simon de la Pointe, a French Canadian who arrived in the Louisiana Territory with Bienville in 1700, petitioned the King of France for a small strip of land in what is now the northern section of the coastal city of Pascagoula.

Joseph de la Pointe built an estate containing several buildings surrounded by a stockade, but the only one that survived is the carpenter shop, which evolved into the Old Spanish Fort. It is thought this name derives from the Spanish period of the late eighteenth century when the building was supposedly used as a fortified residence by an officer of the Spanish army. In 1751, on the death of Marie, Hugo Krebs inherited the property, and for almost two hundred years it remained in the family.

Although it has been through several alterations, the house is still of historical interest. The earliest renovation probably dates around 1775. In 1820, the western room was constructed, the roof expanded and shingled, some of the floors covered with shell concrete and double fireplaces were cut into the walls. Other major renovations took place in 1940 and in 1995. The LaPointe-Krebs cemetery, said to be the oldest family cemetery in the U.S., rests nearby.

The massacre at Fort Rosalie – Natchez

The view of the Mississippi from the bluff at Natchez is one of the great panoromas along the entire river's length. From here, the river flows under the bridge that lies below the former site of the French Fort Rosalie and curves gently left into the distance *en route* to Vicksburg. Across the river, the buildings of the small town of Vidalia, Louisiana can be seen in the distance.

Natchez, in southwestern Mississippi, is a town of gracious southern charm, with a store of nineteenth-century antebellum homes and historic parks. But the French history in this southwest Mississippi town is dominated by a single melancholy event, the massacre by the Natchez Indians of more than 250 French settlers at Fort Rosalie in November 1729.

French incursions to the Natchez area began as early as 1682, when Réne Robert Cavelier, Sieur de La Salle, on his

V

The elegant mansion, Rosalie, built from 1820-1823 by Peter Little, sits near the site of the original Fort Rosalie and the French settlement that surrounded it. The house is a fine example of the Federal Style of architecture.

∧
The Grand Village
of the Natchez Indians,
where the tribe lived
from around 1200 A.D.
until 1730, has been
recreated outside
of Natchez.

>>
The Mississippi River
as seen from the bluff
at Natchez. The bluff
offers one of the most
striking views of
the river to be found
in the United States.

descent of the Mississippi, visited the Natchez Indian village near Emerald Mound, close to present day Natchez. In 1716, two years before the founding of New Orleans, Bienville, in response to attacks on French traders by the Natchez Indians, ordered the construction of a fort near the Natchez villages. The fort, named Rosalie for wife of the Comte de Pontchartrain, was the center of a French village of a few hundred settlers that grew up around it.

Relations between the Natchez Indians and the French were delicate and complicated. But in the early period of French settlement, the two nations were generally friendly, with French soldiers taking Natchez women as concubines and wives. In the 1720s, however, matters deteriorated. In 1728, the then Natchez chief, called the Great Sun, who was friendly to the French, died and pro-English elements took over the tribe. The situation was

exacerbated when the French commander, Sieur de Chopart, an arrogant and insensitive man, attempted to expropriate some Natchez lands.

The Natchez, incensed by French incursions, insinuated themselves into Fort Rosalie and massacred all but around fifteen of the settlers and soldiers inside. The French population never again reached its previous level. Revenge was swift as French soldiers pursued the tribe, and by 1731 wiped most of it out, sending some of the survivors to the West Indies as slaves. The Natchez were never again reconstituted as a nation.

Though a second fort was built on the site, it was manned by only a small garrison of no more than fifty French soldiers. In 1763, following the Treaty of Paris, the French definitively abandoned Fort Rosalie, later named Fort Panmure by the British who had taken it over.

ALABAMA

Ancient French capital of the Louisiana Territory – Mobile

In 1702, sixteen years before the founding of New Orleans, a young French Canadian naval officer, Pierre le Moyne, Sieur d'Iberville, established the first formally planned European-style community on the northern Gulf Coast. Blocked by the Spanish from entering the port of Pensacola, now in Florida, Iberville sailed on to Mobile Bay, where he landed on a small island, which he named Massacre Island because of the discovery of a pile of bones, possibly from an Indian burial ground, sitting on the soil. The name was later changed to Dauphin Island to honor Louis XIV's eldest son.

Dauphin Island, later under the charge of d'Iberville's brother, Bienville, was not the main settlement, only a way station for goods traveling to the main colony, located on the right bank of the Mobile River. Called Twenty-Seven Mile Bluff, the settlement was near the present town of Axis, Alabama. For nine years, this colony, named after the Mobilian Indians in the region, served as the capital of French Louisiana. It became known as *Vieux Mobile* (Old Mobile).

But Bienville's choice of location was not a fortuitous one. Because of the marshy nature of the land, heavy rains saturated the ground and flooded the streets. The fort, called *Fort St. Louis de la Mobile*, suffered from water seeping into the *magasin*, ruining the supply of gunpowder. In 1711, the colonists finally abandoned the settlement and moved to the present site on Mobile Bay. In doing so, they apparently torched the remaining buildings of *Vieux Mobile*.

A strategic Gulf Coast port, Mobile changed hands several times during the eighteenth and nineteenth centuries as France, Britain and Spain battled for empire in North America. Present-day Mobile has only random traces of the early French presence. But its place names – Old Dauphin Way, Bienville Square, DeTonti Square – are reminders of the first French colonists who claimed this port for the Crown.

The first Fort Condé was built by the French in the early 1700s and became the administrative and military center of the Louisiana Territory. France held the fort and Mobile until the 1760s. But in 1762, the English blockaded Mobile Bay and menaced the city. The Treaty of Paris in 1763 organized Mobile as a part of British West Florida, and shortly thereafter the French commandant, Pierre De Ville, delivered Fort Condé to the English, who renamed it Fort Charlotte. It later fell to the Spanish Governor of Louisiana, Bernardo de Galvez, in 1780.

Strategic Fort Toulouse, first built in 1717, was a French outpost at the eastern frontier of French Louisiana that served to guard against English incursions into the area. The reconstructed fort, one of the most faithful recreations of a French fort in the U.S., has been built of similar materials that made up the original. The rustic furnishings of the buildings are based on information found in eighteenth-century archives.

After the Americans took over the city in 1813, the fort was demolished and the materials used for new construction and for fill along the river. The present reconstruction, begun during the American bicentennial celebration, is now a visitors' center for the city. The ramparts overlook the important port of Mobile.

In 1829, Pope Paul IX issued a Papal Bull establishing the diocese of Mobile covering a vast territory that included the entire states of Alabama and Florida. The first bishop, Michael Portier, was from Lyon, France. The cornerstone for the present Cathedral of the Immaculate Conception was laid in 1835, and the building was consecrated in 1850. Sitting on one of the highest points in downtown Mobile, it is solidly built, with inverted archways in the basement, enabling it to resist the floods and hurricanes that frequently batter this part of the Gulf Coast.

A stategic French outpost in eastern Louisiana – Fort Toulouse

Fort Toulouse, also known as "Post aux Alibamons" (Post of the Alabamas), was named after Louis Alexandre de Bourbon, the Count of Toulouse. First constructed in 1717 as a strategic French outpost at the easternmost edge of French Louisiana, it served for nearly five decades to limit the growing English expansion in the Louisiana Territory. Located on a bluff near the junction of the Coosa and Alabama rivers near present-day Wetumpka, Alabama, the fort was successful in establishing friendly relations and fostering trade with the local Indians and limiting the British presence in the region.

To counter the British, the Grand Chief of the Alabamas invited the French to build a fort in his village and at his expense, perhaps the only time the Indians invited colonial powers to settle on their territory. The French contingent,

<
In the 1970s, excavations uncovered nearly the entire plan of Fort Toulouse: the trench foundation of the powder magazine and indications of its stockade fence with remnants of its quartered upright posts. Using evidence from historical archives and archaeological excavations, the Alabama Historical Commission has reconstructed the old fort in the same dimensions as the original.

under Lieutenant de La Tour Vitral, arrived in July 1717. The fort they built was a palisaded one, Vauban-style, with a moat surrounding the stockade. The palisades were largely *poteaux-en-terre*, a mixture of hard and soft woods, which rotted after only a few years.

The fort was enlarged in 1725, repaired a decade later and finally rebuilt in 1751 just south of the first fort. The new fort (presently called Fort Toulouse II) was constructed under the direction of the engineer François Saucier, who also designed Fort de Chartres in Illinois. Also built in Vauban style, with bastions at the four corners as in other French colonial forts, the second fort was larger and contained several structures, including an officers' quarters, a barracks and a powder magazine.

At the edge of the frontier, life at Fort Toulouse was often tedious and difficult. Ships with supplies only arrived sporadically from Mobile, and at times the soldiers were compelled to ask the Alabamas for food. There were a number of desertions, and in 1721 a full-fledged mutiny took place. The mutineers were later captured and some of them executed. Despite these hardships and the harassments from the British, the fort, with between twenty and fifty French marines, continued to function reasonably well, and matters improved when women from France and from Mobile arrived to marry some of the soldiers. In 1758, forty-eight officers and men and some 160 civilians lived in or near the settlement.

The French defeat in the French and Indian War spelled the end of Fort Toulouse. When the last French soldiers and settlers evacuated it in 1763, the English declined to take possession. In 1814, following the Creek Indian War, Andrew Jackson ordered an American fort built on the old French ruins. But after a few years, the residents of that fort and nearby settlements moved downstream to Montgomery, and the area was abandoned and reverted to farmland. Excavations in the 1970s led to the faithful reconstruction of the fort, and the palisaded posts and bastions were implanted in the same dimensions that were used in the 1700s.

>>
Once part of the Red River, the lovely Cane River Lake was formed when the river changed course and left the lake as an isolated body of water near Natchitoches.

LOUISIANA

>

A statue of Louis
Juchereau de St. Denis,
the founder of
Natchitoches, sits
in a park near Cane River
Lake. St. Denis was
one of the most
prominent figures
in French Louisiana.
In 1713, he was sent
up the Red River to
establish a French fort.
He chose Natchitoches
because the local Indians
were friendly and
because a log jam
prevented boat travel
further up the river.

Creole charm in north Louisiana – Natchitoches

In 1714, four years before Bienville founded New Orleans, a young French Canadian officer, Louis Juchereau de St. Denis, led a small party two hundred miles up the Red River to establish a settlement in a village inhabited by the friendly Natchitoches Indians. The aim was to establish trade with the Spanish in the West while preventing them from advancing further into French Louisiana.

In time, the settlement thrived and became the second busiest port in the Louisiana Territory after New Orleans. Steamboats plied the Red River and exported Indian furs and products from Natchitoches to ports worldwide. The town, a crossroads for overland highways leading to the West, became one of the country's most important trading posts and later a bustling cotton market, with elegant cotton plantations springing up along the Cane River.

But the town's destiny was molded by the river that served it. Between 1830 and 1850, the Red River deserted Natchitoches and carved out a new course five miles to the east. Steamboat traffic, and with it Natchitoches's commercial importance, dwindled away. What remained was the lovely, though isolated, Cane River Lake.

Visiting Natchitoches today, it is difficult to visualize the vibrant commercial centre that once lay here. The town, off the beaten track from other French settlements, has a tranquil Creole charm, a host of French historic structures and plantations downtown and in neighboring Cane River Country and natural surroundings that include a national forest and serene, crystal lakes.

<

Natchitoches as seen
from Cane River Lake.
Once the second busiest
port in the Louisiana
Territory after New
Orleans, Natchitoches's
commercial importance
dwindled after the
Red River changed
course. The tranquil
lake which remained
behind is bordered
by historic plantations
and serves as a recreation
area for the town.

>

Built in the early 1700s
in Vauban style, with
palisaded walls and four
corner towers, Fort
St. Jean-Baptiste once
housed marines sent
by the French ministry
of the navy. Constructed
largely of pine, using
bousillage and *poteaux-
en-terre* construction, the
recreated fort contains
the same kind of double
palisaded walls that were
implanted in the original.

Completed in 1979, the reconstruction of the French Fort St. Jean Baptiste is a composite of various images of the fort and partially based on drawings made by the French engineer Broutin in 1733. The first fort, built in 1716, was at the same time a trading center and a military outpost. A second fort was built after the first one suffered damage from the river.

Louis Juchereau de St. Denis was named commandant in 1722 and remained until his death in 1744. In 1731, the Natchez Indians came up the Red River to the Natchitoches village and laid siege to the site. The French repulsed the attacks, though there are reports that one of the palisaded walls was burned. Abandoned by the French at the end of the French and Indian War, the fort was later used briefly by the Spanish, then definitively abandoned after the Americans took over following the Louisiana Purchase. Based on extensive research, the reconstructed fort, a short distance from the original (which has never been definitively located), contains the same double palisaded walls

>>

The rustic furniture in the recreated Fort St. Jean Baptiste is modeled after furniture of early eighteenth-century forts. Fort St. Jean Baptiste contained, among other structures, an officers' quarters and a powder magazine.

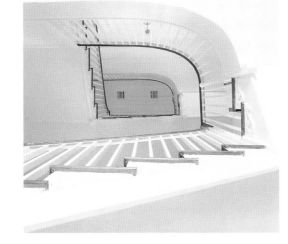

The elegant curved staircase in the Prudhomme-Roquier House mounts from the first to the third floor.

v

The Prudhomme-Roquier House has been furnished with Louisiana Empire Style pieces from the 1840s. In the parlor, where guests were entertained, the restorers have placed a flowered couch with carved claw feet and a flip-top gaming table of the period.

>

The galleried façade of the Prudhomme-Roquier House in Natchitoches, one of the few remaining two-story *bousillage* houses in the United States. The three prominent dormers (windows) are set vertically in a small gable that projects from the slope of the roof.

that St. Denis had erected in the 1700s. Constructed largely of pine, using *bousillage* and *poteaux-en-terre* infillings, the fort contains a general store, a chapel, the house of the commandant, a powder magazine and a bread oven.

One of the more meticulously restored structures in Natchitoches, the Prudhomme-Roquier House is one of the few remaining two-story *bousillage* houses in the United States. Built in the early nineteenth century, the house was originally given by Jean-Baptiste Prudhomme to his daughter, Marie Louise, as part of her marriage dowry. Marie Louise married François Roquier, born of

French parents and one of the largest land grant owners in Natchitoches. The Roquiers retained control of the house for several decades. In 1811, Marie Josephine Henrietta Roquier married John C. Carr, a wealthy plantation owner, and the Carrs added Greek Revival architectural embellishments to the house before they ceded control of it in 1834. A succession of owners followed, and in 1948 the structure was divided into apartments. Fortunately, the Service League of Natchitoches, Inc. purchased the property in 1976 and has been restoring the house to its 1825-1840 appearance.

<

The rustic furniture in the *galerie* of the Wells House in Natchitoches is typical of that found in Creole structures in Louisiana. The *galerie* had a social function as a place to meet and talk while one was sheltered from the blistering heat of the Louisiana summer. It also served to keep the interior of the house cool by distancing the sunlight from the living quarters.

∨

The Wells House in Natchitoches is a *poteaux-sur-sole* Creole house, with *bousillage* walls, hand-hewn timbers and cypress post and beam construction. Furnished with period furniture by the present owner, the house boasts a collection of faïence and other ancient artifacts found on the property.

Built around 1776, the Wells House is one of the oldest structures in the Mississippi Valley. Although the roof line and other features have been modified over the years, the house has been restored with a keen sense of its historical importance. The Roque House (not to be confused with the Badin-Roque House) sits in a park in downtown Natchitoches, and belonged to Madame Aubert Roque, the granddaughter of Augustin Metoyer.

The Chamard-Dunahoe House, of French colonial construction with American features, takes its name from André Chamard, a French descendant of the Bourbon family who was knighted by Louis XVI. In the nineteenth and twentieth centuries, the house passed through several owners and was threatened with demolition in 1977 before being saved by the Historic Commission of Natchitoches. The house has hand-hewn cypress rafters held together by wooden pegs and square nails, *bousillage* walls, and unlike many local houses, two fireplaces in the interior of the rooms. The present owners have modernized the interior but have respected the house's historic framework.

<
The façade of the
Chamard-Dunahoe
House in Natchitoches.
Of considerable historic
interest, the house
is named for André
Chamard, a French
descendant of the
Bourbon family who
was knighted by
Louis XVI. Threatened
with demolition,
it was saved by the
Historic Commission
of Natchitoches
in the late 1970s.

<
The Roque House
in Natchitoches,
which dates from the
early 1800s, was moved
to Natchitoches from
its original location
in Bermuda, several miles
down the Cane River.
Another classic French
Creole cottage, it has
a hipped roof, gallery,
central chimney
and a double fireplace
with some of the
original bricks.

>

Located near the Cane
River in Natchitoches,
the Badin-Roque House is
one of the few remaining
poteaux-en-terre bousillage
houses in the United
States and the only
one in Louisiana. Dating
from the mid-nineteenth
century, the house
was once owned by
Jean-Baptiste Metoyer,
the grandson of Marie
Thérèse Coincoin and
Claude Metoyer of Melrose
Plantation. Badin-Roque
is a classic Creole cottage
with a central chimney
and a dirt floor.

In Natchitoches Parish, south of Natchitoches proper, lies the Cane River National Heritage Area, 116,000 acres of rural Louisiana containing a rich mix of Creole-style plantations with their unique blend of cultures that include French, African, American Indian, Spanish and Creole. The Cane River plantations – Cherokee, Magnolia and Oaklawn – reflect Creole architecture and were built before the cotton boom of the 1850s, when the Greek Revival style became predominant in Louisiana plantation architecture.

Melrose Plantation is a living monument to three formidable women – Marie Thérèse Coincoin, Cammie Garrett Henry and Clementine Hunter. It is also one of the most historically rich plantations in the American South. Born in 1742, Marie Thérèse Coincoin was first a slave, then a free woman of color, then finally an enterprising landowner who

had slaves of her own. Her period of servitude lasted forty-four years, first in the household of Louis Juchereau St. Denis, the founder of Natchitoches, then under the beneficent protection of Claude Thomas Pierre Metoyer, a prosperous Frenchman from La Rochelle. Taken with her beauty and force of character, he took her as his mistress and fathered ten of her children. Because of social taboos, the two could never marry. Metoyer eventually set Marie Thérèse free with a gift of sixty-eight acres of land and married the widow of a friend.

From her small legacy, the fiercely determined Marie Thérèse, growing indigo and tobacco and raising cattle, built up a substantial inheritance for her children, all of

<

The Lemee House
in Natchitoches has
a fountain and patio at
the rear, erected in a mix
of French and Spanish
architectural styles. The
fountain was originally
erected on the riverbank;
the lower section held
water for mules, horses
and oxen; the upper
was used by people for
drinking purposes. The
house has a rare cradle
roof, with an upswing
at the eaves to divide
the force of the wind.

>

The main house
at Melrose Plantation
dates from the 1830s.
Of simple construction,
the house has every
timber notched
and pegged in place.
The wall fillings are
bousillage, composed
of mud and Spanish
moss. The *galeries* were
lengthened and closed
in by the Henry family
to create space
for bathrooms.

Inside Melrose
Plantation, much of the
Henry family furniture
is preserved – the dining
room table; the chairs,
re-upholstered with
handwoven material;
a three-sectioned armoire;
and a hundred-year-old
patchwork quilt, woven
by Cammie Henry.
The large four-poster bed
in Miss Cammie's bedroom
is also a family piece.

whom she bought out of slavery. In time, her descendants became the wealthiest family of free Negroes in the United States. At her death in 1817 at the age of seventy-five, she and her children owned hundreds of acres of plantation land – most of which they would retain until after the Civil War – and nearly one hundred slaves. Today there are said to be more than ten thousand surviving Coincoin family descendants, spread all over the U.S.

At Melrose, Claude Thomas Pierre Metoyer's successor was Cammie Garrett Henry, known affectionately as "Miss Cammie". After purchasing Melrose in 1898, Miss Cammie set about restoring the outbuildings and preserving essential features of the big house. But she will also be remembered as a major patron of the arts. Several renowned writers came to reflect and write at Melrose, including François Mignon,

author of *Plantation Memo*, who stayed for thirty-two years; Lyle Saxon, author of *Children of Strangers*, John Steinbeck and William Faulkner. The writers tended to stay in Yucca House, the original colonial residence, which dates from 1796.

Unlike other plantations, the outbuildings at Melrose are of as much interest as the main house. Apart from Yucca House, there is the African House, dating from around 1800, a slave fort and provision house made of bricks baked at Melrose and hand-hewn cypress slabs; the Weaving House, restored in 1973; the Bindery; the Writer's Cabin; and Clementine's house. Clementine Hunter, a Melrose field hand and cook for the Henry family, began painting primitive scenes of plantation life when she was in her fifties. By the time of her death in 1988 at the age of 101, her paintings were – and are – fetching enormous prices. A number of them hang at Melrose.

<<

Several Creole plantations can be found along Natchitoches' Cane River. Beau Fort Plantation dates back to the early nineteenth century. The one-and-a-half story structure is of *bousillage-entre-poteaux* construction, with a frame constructed of cypress timbers that are mortised, tenoned and pegged in place.

<

Oakland Plantation on Cane River is a fine example of a Creole raised cottage. The main house was completed in 1821 and is made of *bousillage* between posts. There are several outbuildings on the property, among them two *pigeonniers*, an overseers' house, a massive roofed log corn crib, a carriage house, a mule barn that was originally a smokehouse, a carpenter's shop and cabins.

<

Magnolia Plantation, between Melrose and Cloutierville, was established in 1835. The main house was burned by Union troops during the Civil War. The present house is a reconstruction of the original.

Inside Destrehan Plantation, a remarkable double staircase leads to the upper floors. A central parlor on the lower level, part of the nineteenth-century remodeling, spans the full depth of the house The River Road Historical Society has filled Destrehan with a fine collection of early to mid-nineteenth-century furnishings and decorative arts. They have also managed to retrieve a number of items that once belonged to the Destrehan family.

THE RIVER ROAD AND FALSE RIVER PLANTATIONS

The earliest surviving Creole plantation – Destrehan

On the east bank of the Mississippi not far from New Orleans stands Destrehan Plantation, the oldest documented plantation home in the lower Mississippi Valley. The house, once part of a plantation of some six thousand acres, has survived with many of its features intact, despite being occupied during the Civil War and later despoiled by vandals. It has also been the home of some of Louisiana's most prominent political figures.

Its first owner, Robin de Logny, was the son of Laurent Robin de Logny, who hailed from the Champagne region of France. Robin, a commandant of the parish, signed a contract to build a large house with wide *galeries* surrounding

while living in the house. To make room for his expanding family, he added two *garçonnière* wings and replaced de Logny's indigo crops with sugar cane.

At Jean Noel's death, the house was bought at auction by his son-in-law, Stephen Henderson, a Scot who built up a considerable fortune. The next owner, Pierre Rost, a native of France, was a judge on the Louisiana Supreme Court. Enamored of the Greek Revival style that became the rage in Louisiana in the 1840s, Rost replaced the wood colonettes supporting the gallery with massive Doric columns of brick and enclosed the back gallery.

Occupied by the Union Army and run as a sugar plantation, Destrehan was later restored to the Rost family. It

>>

Destrehan Plantation has a generous double-pitched roof, part of which covers the surrounding *galerie*. The top floor infillings are *bousillage*, the ground floor is in the original brick.

the entire structure. In 1790, after three years of work by the architect, a free person of color, the house was finished.

Robin died two years later and the house was purchased by Jean Noel Destrehan, a native of New Orleans, for $21,750. Jean Noel, who became Speaker of the Louisiana Territorial House of Representatives and later a United States Senator, had seven of his fourteen children

passed through several hands before being taken over and restored by the River Road Historical Society in 1971. A masterpiece of Creole architecture, Destrehan has a generous double-pitched roof, part of which covers the surrounding *galerie*. It is now filled with a fine collection of early to mid-nineteenth century furnishings and decorative arts and items that once belonged to the Destrehan family.

< The façade of Houmas House is one of the loveliest among Louisiana plantations, with massive plastered brick Tuscan columns, federal arched dormers, a cupola and moveable louvered shutters. Two graceful hexagonal brick *garçonnières* sit on the sides of the house, and centuries-old live oak trees shade the grounds.

> Houmas House has superb gardens containing camellias, magnolia grandiflora, larkspur, lady banksia roses and fragrant sweet olive. A wistaria arbor, more than 180-feet long, complements the flower beds. An ancient *pigeonnier*, recently restored, stands on one side of the house.

Elegant remnants of a sugar plantation – Houmas House

Houmas House, on the southern section of Louisiana's River Road, was the main house of a plantation once consisting of twenty thousand acres, at the time the largest sugar plantation in Louisiana. Named after the Houmas Indians, from whom its first owner, Alexandre Latil, purchased it in the late eighteenth century, it was at first a simple Creole house of four rooms, nothing like the elegant Greek Revival house that now faces the Mississippi. The restored older house was incorporated into the rear of the main house, and is now attached to it by an arched carriageway.

The first house was bought in 1812 by a Revolutionary War general, Wade Hampton, a Carolinian, whose son-in-law John Smith Preston came to take over the Hampton properties in Louisiana. It was during the decade 1830-1840 that Preston, it is thought, constructed the main house in its present form before selling it to a wealthy Irish immi-

grant, John Burnside, who owned a large mansion in New Orleans. Burnside's ancestry may have saved the house: when the Civil War broke out, Burnside faced down the Union General Ben Butler by insisting that as a citizen of the Crown, an occupation would have violated his immunity.

With the house spared, the sugar crop flourished and the plantation continued to produce tons of sugar when William Porcher Miles took it over in 1881. At its peak, more than eight hundred slaves worked the property. But the end of slavery in the 1860s and a sugar mosaic virus in the 1920s fed the decline. Large parcels of the land were sold off; and today only twenty-seven of the twenty thousand acres remain.

Houmas was revived in 1940 when Dr. George B. Crozat, a wealthy orthodontist, bought the property and filled it with fine antiques from his New Orleans home. Most of these, however, were sold at auction when the house passed to another owner in 2003.

< The interior of Houmas House features a helix spiral staircase, one of the finest in Louisiana. It has been recently opened up so that one feels the full effect of the spiral. Dr. George B. Crozat, one of the recent owners, also added a palladian window on the landing, replaced the fireplaces and mantels and installed closets and cupboards in the house.

The dining room at Oak Alley features a magnificent, sixteen-foot long mahogany table and an equisitely carved medallion on the ceiling. Suspended from the ceiling is a punka or "shoe-fly" fan, which had a double purpose: to enhance the comfort of dinner guests in humid Louisiana by circulating air over the table, and to keep flies and other insects off the food.

∧

Oak Alley is lavishly furnished. In the master bedroom stands an imposing four-poster bed adorned with pineapples, the symbol of southern hospitality. The bedroom also contains a child's cradle, the only piece of original furniture in the house. The house has been restored to its 1838-1848 appearance.

<<

The celebrated façade of Oak Alley, a marriage of Creole and Greek Revival features, is dominated by the massive twenty-eight, two-story Tuscan columns (an echo of the twenty-eight giant oaks fronting the property). Eight feet in circumference, the columns support the slate-covered hipped roof. The *galeries* on both floors are several feet deep.

An icon among Louisiana plantations – Oak Alley

The giant oaks were here a hundred years before the house. They were planted by a person unknown, probably during the early years of the seventeenth century. Now, more than three hundred years later, they grace the covers of magazines and books, symbolizing the romance that is Louisiana.

The oaks, in two rows of fourteen trees each, stretch from the house a quarter of a mile towards the levee that borders the Mississippi. Majestic at all times, they are perhaps best seen at dusk with a mist, when the giant Tuscan columns of the plantation seem to float between the extended branches. The oaks have been denuded of moss, since the Stewart family, the last private owners, decided it would detract from their beauty. Seen from the house, they are one of the South's most stunning sights.

The house was built in around two years starting in 1836. It was the concept of Jacques Télésphore and Celina Pilié Roman, both from prosperous New Orleans Creole families. Jacques, it is said, engaged Celina's father, Gilbert Joseph Pilié, as the architect of Oak Alley and George Swainey, a master builder, to bring the house to completion. The property, when Jacques purchased it, was already a thriving sugar plantation, with a principal house and several outbuildings – a plantation store, *garçonnières*, slave quarters and an overseer's house. Of these, only the reconstructed overseer's house remains.

The imposing dimensions of Oak Alley are evident when stepping into its central hall, eleven feet wide and forty-eight feet long, the largest among Louisiana plantations. The floor plan is symmetrical, with both floors containing two rooms at the front and two others at the rear.

Only one piece of original furniture – the child's cradle in the master bedroom – remains of the furniture owned by the Roman family. But the decorator took great pains to research inventories of the plantation and of the Roman's house in New Orleans, as well as those of similar houses in Louisiana during the early to mid-1800s. Oak Alley today is lavishly furnished with Louisiana and French furniture of the period that has brought the house back to its 1838-1848 appearance. The lavender bedroom has been left exactly as it was when Josephine Stewart, wife of the last private owner, died here in 1972. The clock in the room is fixed at 7:30, the time of her death.

Like most Louisiana plantations, Oak Alley fell on hard times. In the early 1920s, it was abandoned and lapsed into a dilapidated state, with cattle roaming through its rooms and bats nesting in the eaves. Fortunately, in 1925 Andrew and Josephine Stewart bought it and spent years bringing it back to elegance. Before Josephine died, at ninety-three, she set up a non-profit foundation to run this magnificent property.

The search for Laura Locoul Gore – Laura Plantation

Laura Plantation, some fifty miles upriver from New Orleans, is one of the most meticulously restored Creole plantations in Louisiana. The present owners sifted through thousands of documents and letters and traveled widely in the U.S. and Europe to recover the original furniture and artifacts to place in the house. Their search was spurred by their discovery in 1993 of the diary of one of the formidable women who managed the property, Laura Locoul Gore, for whom the plantation was named.

The first owner of Laura, Guillaume Duparc, was from Normandy. A dashing naval officer with a questionable past, he was banished by his father and joined the French navy. He distinguished himself during the American Revolution, fighting alongside Washington, Rochambeau and de Grasse at Yorktown. Awarded a land grant in 1804 by the American government, he moved to St. James Parish with his wife, Nanette Prud'Homme, daughter of an aristocratic family from Natchitoches. Her father, Jean-Baptiste Prud'Homme, was once a court physician for Louis XV.

V

Laura Plantation's raised Creole house (sometimes called the "Big House") is essentially constructed of brick and cypress. The hand-made bricks of Mississippi mud were fabricated on the property by slaves. Of classic brick-between-post construction, the Big House is built on a series of subterranean pyramids to support the structure in the spongy Louisiana soil.

> Detail of the pantry in Laura Plantation. Used as a storeroom which opened directly into the dining room, the pantry was never painted or wallpapered. The gray ceiling is not painted but is covered with soot from thousands of candles and lamps. Now stocked with period baskets and other food containers, the pantry is a vivid reminder of the Creole lifestyle that flourished at Laura.

∧ ∧

The pantry at Laura Plantation is the oldest intact room in the house. One part of the wall has been left open to expose the original brick infill. In Laura's bedroom, dominated by a four-poster bed, the owners have placed artifacts from her early years, including a Parisian mother-of-pearl fan that was an engagement gift from Laura's father to her mother.

>

The colorful front *galerie* at Laura Plantation. Before nineteenth-century modifications, the house was U-shaped, with *galeries* all the way around. In 1820, the sides of the porches were enclosed to provide space for bedrooms.

On Guillaume's death four years later, Nanette took over the plantation and ran it for twenty-one years, the first in a long line of women to take the reins at Laura. One of Nanette's daughters, Elisabeth, married Raymond Locoul, a Frenchman from Bordeaux, and soon operated, from the plantation, the largest wine distribution center in Louisiana. The Locoul's son, Emile, in turn, married Désirée Archinard, a fourth-generation Creole from Alexandria, Louisiana. Laura Locoul was born to the couple in 1861, the year the American Civil War began. When she was thirteen, Laura's father named the plantation for her.

When Laura was twenty-nine, she left the plantation to live in St. Louis. Determined to live as an emancipated American woman, she married Charles Gore in 1891 and lived her last seventy-two years in Missouri. Her diary of plantation life, composed after she left Louisiana, is a clear-eyed, unsentimental view of the hardships and pleasures of running a Creole plantation. In it she describes the living conditions of the slaves (there were almost two hundred at Laura); the cholera that ravaged the plantation; and the grueling task of harvesting and grinding the sugar cane, the plantation's main crop. In the Creole tradition, the plantation was a family centered business and a self-contained unit, with main house, slave cabins, blacksmith shop and sugar refining facilities all on the property.

In time, when the price of sugar fell, it became necessary to sell Laura. In 1891, an Alsatian family, the Waguespacks, bought the property and their heirs lived on it for ninety years. In 1993, it was sold to a sugar cooperative, which, in turn, leased it, in a ruined state, to the present managers.

Originally built around 1805, Laura, like most Louisiana plantations, was once a vast domain, some twelve thousand acres with a narrow front on the Mississippi. When it was sold in 1993, it contained 1,500 acres, thirteen of which comprise the historic site today. But what remained was significant: a number of historic structures, including four of the sixty-nine slave cabins that once stood on the property; a French-style dowager's house (built 1829); and a main house

(called the "Big House") that provided clues as to the layout, wood composition and colors of its various rooms. Years of arduous work in restoration have resulted in an authentic representation of the French Creole lifestyle that prevailed in this part of Louisiana for over two hundred years.

Inside the main house, there was a strict gender division: the men's rooms were located on the downriver side, the women's upriver. This carries over into the parlors; with each sex having its own.

Many of the architectural features of the Big House are original, including the cypress mantel in the men's parlor, the open beam ceilings and the Norman truss in the attic. The owners have collected more than seven hundred photos, over three hundred family artifacts and five thousand pages of documents found in the French *Archives Nationales*.

FROM LAURA'S DIARY

"When the cholera raged one summer and negroes were dropping in the fields, they were brought to their cabins to die. George and I watched all this by climbing into an old apple tree to munch green apples or persimmons or anything that came our way. Mother was too busy looking after the sick and thought we were safe at play. There were frequent outbreaks of cholera and yellow fever and I now often wonder how we ever escaped. But we were the sturdiest bunch of roughnecks that anybody seemed to know.

"On another occasion in the middle of the night, I heard someone call and tell Mother that the overseer's old mother was dying and, please, to come over at once. This seemed to be an opportunity I could not miss! I rushed to the overseer's house across the yard and entered the bedroom on tip-toe for all

the family were on their knees, weeping. Mother was wiping the forehead of the woman and reading the litany of the dying and I stood peering over the foot of the bed.

"Then the poor, old lady gave one last dying gasp and with it, she spit out stuff from her mouth called 'black vomit', the surest sign of yellow fever. Some of the vomit splashed on me and Mother, in the midst of her prayers, glanced up and saw me!

Well, down went the prayer book. Mother tore after me and I slid down the steps until I was caught by someone before I got to the house. Poor Mother was horrified! I was rushed to the wash house, a small building in the yard, washed, bathed and dressed in fresh clothes while my old clothes remained to be disinfected before I returned to the house."

– *Memories of the Old Plantation Home*
by Laura Locoul Gore

> The four remaining
original slave cabins
at Laura are poignant
reminders of the
hardships slaves endured
while working on
Louisiana plantations.

The oldest Greek Revival plantation in Louisiana – L'Hermitage

Once an indigo and sugar plantation comprising a thousand acres, L'Hermitage, built between 1812-1814, is the oldest Greek Revival plantation remaining in Louisiana. Admirably proportioned, with twenty-four massive Doric columns that encircle the exterior, it has been carefully restored by its present owners.

The house's history is linked to important figures in American history. The first owner was a Creole, Michel Douradou Bringier, whose father came from Aubagne, France. Michel fought with General Andrew Jackson at the Battle of New Orleans during the War of 1812 and named the house after Jackson's home in Tennessee. His wife, Louise Elizabeth Aglae DuBourg, was a Creole whose family had a coffee plantation in St. Domingue. Her uncle was the

Bishop of New Orleans, Louis DuBourg, who was instrumental in persuading the Catholic Church to set up Sacred Heart academies in the Louisiana Territory.

During the Civil War, L'Hermitage suffered more severely than most Louisiana plantations. Union soldiers ransacked the house, stealing some articles of furniture, tableware and paintings along with farm equipment, livestock, sugar and 25,000 pounds of snuff tobacco. After passing through a succession of owners, L'Hermitage was abandoned in the 1940s and finally rescued by its present owners in 1959.

To restore L'Hermitage to its original 1812-14 floor plan, the owners pored over court records and their own personal collection of hundreds of original documents and some three thousand handwritten notes and letters pertaining to the family. They also replanted the double row of oaks leading to the house.

∧

L'Hermitage, whose Greek Revival Style preceded the heyday of Greek Revival planation architecture in Louisiana, has been called the most perfectly proportioned plantation home on Louisiana's River Road. It was abandoned in the 1930s and finally rescued at the end of the 1950s. The present owners have replaced and renumbered the original floor joists, refurbished the floors of cypress and pine and replanted the double line of oaks that approach the house.

The miracle of the Sacred Heart – Grand Coteau

A tranquil central Louisiana town of two thousand inhabitants, Grand Coteau contains more than seventy historic structures – among them the Academy of the Sacred Heart, the St. Charles Borromeo Catholic Church and St. Charles College, the first Jesuit college established in Louisiana. It also contains a fine collection of historic homes reflecting a variety of architectural styles – Creole, French, Acadian, Anglo-American and Victorian. The town also claims to be the site of the only verified miracle on the North American continent.

Established by a land grant in 1776, Grand Coteau developed into an educational and religious center in the early nineteenth century. Bishop Louis William Dubourg, the patron of Sister Philippine Duchesne, established St. Charles Church here in 1818. Three years later, the Academy of the Sacred Heart was founded, and in 1837 St. Charles College was started by a Jesuit educator, Father Nicholas Point. The town – fed by an influx of French and German merchants – grew up around these institutions.

In 1821, two Sacred Heart nuns, Mother Eugenie Aude and Sister Mary Layton, traveled down the Mississippi from St. Louis to set up the Sacred Heart Academy in a building donated by the widow of a local planter. Mother Aude had been a member of the Napoleonic Court in France, and Sister Layton was the first American to serve as a lay sister under Mother (later Saint) Philippine Duchesne in Missouri during the first trying days of the Sacred Heart in the Louisiana Territory.

In 1866, Mary Wilson, a young postulant at the Academy of the Sacred Heart, became critically ill. Physicians attending her pronounced her situation hopeless, and the townspeople of Grand Coteau prayed to the Blessed John Berchmans, a Jesuit priest from what is now Belgium, noted for his piety, to spare her. Berchmans, who died in 1621, was said to have appeared at Mary's side a few days later and told her she would recover, as she did, much to the astonishment of attending physicians, who could find no medical reason for the turnaround. This is the so-called Miracle of the Sacred Heart. Berchmans was eventually canonized in 1888, and the infirmary where Mary lay ill has been transformed into a shrine, where thousands of pilgrims come each year to pay homage to St. John Berchmans.

The striking St. Charles Borromeo Catholic Church, with its mansard Renaissance Revival roof and elaborate rear belfry, is an architectural rarity in Louisiana. It was built in 1879, following approval of the plans by Pope Pius IX. The Religious of the Sacred Heart raised about a third of the cost of building the church, the Jesuits another third and the parishioners the rest. It was built of cypress wood harvested from the property. The ornate belfry was added several years later. The wife of a local doctor donated the three-thousand-pound bell, which was too large for the front steeple, and required a new belfry to house it. This bell, named "Eleanor" after the doctor's wife, is still rung today.

∧

Grand Coteau's St. Charles Borromeo Church, built in 1879, has an ornate belfry at the rear, which was added in 1886. The belfry houses a three-thousand-pound bell which was too large for the front steeple.

<

The Shrine of John Berchmans at the Academy of the Sacred Heart commemorates the Belgian-born saint said to have appeared to one of the Sacred Heart nuns and to have cured her of what was thought to be an incurable illness. This has been called the "Miracle of the Sacred Heart".

<<

Founded in 1821 by French and American nuns, the Academy of the Sacred Heart in Grand Coteau is one of twenty-one Sacred Heart academies in the United States.

Λ

The graceful façade
of Evergreen Plantation
features two free-
standing spiral staircases
that rise to the second
floor. Other features
include a hipped roof,
a pedimented portico
and a roof deck with
balustrades, all exquisitely
proportioned. Still
a functioning sugar
plantation, Evergreen
has been family owned
for 250 years.
©Evergreen Plantation

Planters and artists – Evergreen and Oakley

One of the last eight surviving Greek Revival plantations on Louisiana's River Road, Evergreen is unique in being a complete plantation complex. The main house replaced a raised Creole cottage that was erected here in the 1790s. The transformation took place in the 1830s when Pierre Becnel, a descendant of French and German immigrants, took it over and refashioned it into a symmetrical Greek Revival mansion with eight stuccoed-brick Doric columns that extend from the ground to the roof. The house, with its hipped roof and graceful curved double stairways leading to the first floor *galerie*, is both imposing and pleasing to contemplate.

Perhaps the most distinguishing feature of the plantation complex is the line of slave cabins, set in a double row at right angles to the river. The cabins, which housed sugar workers as late as 1947, have become exceedingly rare in Louisiana. Though there have been alterations, some of their original features – chimneys, shutters and doors – remain.

Of the other structures on the grounds, the Greek Revival privy, the only one in Louisiana, has a special charm. The two *garçonnières*, which flank the house, add to the overall symmetry, and the *pigeonniers*, set slightly back and to the side, complete the harmonious front line of structures.

Evergreen, like other plantations, fell on hard times in the 1920s, when the sugar virus, the great flood of 1927 and the stock market crash caused its decline. It was rescued in 1944 by Matilda Gray, who furnished it with antebellum antiques and resuscitated the exteriors. Her niece still maintains Evergreen today in grand style, and it remains a functioning sugar plantation.

Oakley Plantation in West Feliciana Parish has links with the French through John James Audubon, the celebrated wildlife artist, who arrived here in June 1821 and remained for four months. Audubon, born in St. Domingue of a French sea captain and plantation owner and his French mistress, was raised by his stepmother in Nantes, France. After studying with the famous neoclassical artist Jacques-Louis David in Paris, he came to North America in 1803.

Audubon's fascination with birds led him to spend time in the wild, where he created drawings of a range of bird species. Down on his luck, he took a job as a tutor at Oakley, teaching French and drawing to Eliza Pirrie, daughter of the plantation owner. Here Audubon was able to wander in the forest and paint the rich variety of bird life – woodpeckers, cardinals, house wrens, kingfishers and hawks – that passed through. During his time at Oakley, he completed thirty-two of his famous bird paintings, collected later in *Birds of America*, which was printed in England and became an instant success.

>

Audubon's room at Oakley Plantation has been preserved much as he left it. The bed, the art kit and the spectacles on the desk were Audubon possessions given to the plantation by the artist's descendants. A first edition of one of his prints adorns the wall.

French colonial simplicity and elegance – Parlange

If Oak Alley is the model of a massive Greek Revival plantation, Parlange, which faces False River, impresses with its French colonial simplicity and elegance. The plantation has changed little over two centuries.

Tapering brick columns below and slender cypress columns above encircle the *galeries*, and delicate hand-carved cypress fan-shaped windows decorate the entrances and are above every window. Between the house and the entrance gates are a pair of octagonal two-story brick dovecotes or *pigeonniers*. The upper floor of each was used to raise squab; the lower story of one housed the tutor for the children, while the other provided quarters for the French gardener, who was imported from *le Jardin des Plantes* in Paris.

An asymmetrical house, Parlange's lower level is divided into seven rooms, each opening directly onto the *galeries*. The upper level, divided into four rooms at the front, has a central salon that opens onto the front and rear *galeries*. The original ceiling of the parlor is of hand-hewn cypress logs, so finely placed that they resemble plaster.

The dramatic history of Parlange is strongly linked with the fortunes of a formidable woman, Virginie de Ternant, whose imposing portrait by the court artist Dubufe hangs in

the salon. Virginie was the second wife of the plantation's first owner, Vincent, Marquis de Ternant. Their union produced a number of children, some of whom died tragically. One son who strayed away from his nurse was drowned. Another, unruly and undisciplined, died as a young man. A daughter, after an arranged marriage to an older gentleman from France, committed suicide on her wedding day and was buried in her wedding gown.

After the Marquis died in 1842, Virginie married a second time to another Frenchman, Colonel Charles Parlange of the French army. In time, the plantation took his name. During the Civil War, Virginie was able to save Parlange from destruction by being hospitable and gracious to the Union officer, General Banks, whose troops were camped on the property. She hosted banquets in the evenings and had the servants prepare barbecues in the garden for the occupiers, using her considerable charm to calm what could have been a tense confrontation.

Before the Civil War, there were formal gardens at Parlange. Today, though less formal, the gardens are still lovely. Still a working plantation, with cattle and sugar cane, Parlange is operated by relatives of the original builder. Because of its historical significance, it has been designated as a National Historic Landmark.

∧ ∧
The enchanting perfumed garden at Parlange has winding paths, statuary and a riot of different flowers. Two plaster brick *pigeonniers*, the only octagonal-shaped *pigeonniers* in Louisiana, add a highly decorative touch to the front lawn.

<
The *galeries* at Parlange are open and airy, and most of the doors are aligned, ensuring that air circulates freely throughout the house.

<<
Parlange, which dates from the 1750s, is a two-story raised cottage, with ten brick pillars on the ground floor to support the veranda, and exquisite thin colonettes on the second floor to support the steeply hipped roof.

Alexandre Mouton, whose forebears came from Alsace, became the first Democratic governor of Louisiana. The Alexandre Mouton House, dating from around 1800, is now the Lafayette Museum. Alexandre added three rooms, and subsequent owners built a second and third floor, a cupola and the Greek Revival façade.

The Cajun capital – Lafayette

One of more than forty American towns and cities named after the Marquis de Lafayette, the oil center of Lafayette is the hub and unofficial capital of Cajun Louisiana. Settled in the 1770s by Acadians, who moved to the area after disputes with their European Creole neighbors in nearby St. Martinville, the city, with more than 100,000 inhabitants, has far outstripped its neighbor in size and influence.

In 1812, Jean Mouton, a wealthy Acadian landholder, donated the land on which a church and courthouse were built. Christened Vermilionville in 1836, it profited from steamboat traffic along the Vermilion River and exported its main crop, rice, south to Morgan City. In the 1880s, when the railroad arrived, the town flourished, with new commerce and a more educated Cajun population moving in. In the same period, it was renamed "Lafayette" after New Orleans annexed a town nearby having the same name.

The early 1890s saw the discovery of oil at Jennings, forty miles to the west, and by mid-century Lafayette, now the administrative center of Louisiana's offshore oil industry, was booming. But in the 1980s, the oil price collapsed. To lessen its reliance on the oil industry, the city

> Lafayette's Alexandre Mouton House, Anglo-American in design and construction, is filled with souvenirs of the Mouton family and other families that have lived in the house through the years. The restorers have collected important pieces of nineteenth-century furniture and placed them in the rooms.

diversified its economy in the 1990s, and benefited from an upsurge in tourism, much of which was attracted by the new interest in Cajun culture.

Lafayette now hosts a range of cultural events linked to its French and Cajun roots. The most important are the April *Festival International de la Louisiane* – a showplace of music, film and crafts from French speaking nations – and the September *Festivals Acadiens*, which attracts over 100,000 people. Lafayette also holds the second largest Mardi Gras festival in the country.

The name Mouton looms large in the history of Lafayette and Louisiana. One of the Mouton forebears, Jean, was born in Marseille, France, and came to Acadia (Nova Scotia) in 1708. His grandson, also named Jean, was expelled by the British from Acadia during *le Grand Dérangement*. He was displaced to Louisiana, where he accumulated considerable wealth and land and received legislative approval to create the town of Vermilionville. In around 1800, Jean decided to construct a house in the town, which he used when he and his family traveled from their main house in the country to attend church on Sundays. These *maisons dimanche* (Sunday houses) were common among the more affluent planters. Jean's sixth son, Alexandre, lived in the house, now called the

Alexandre Mouton House, for ten years from 1826, and went on to become the first Democratic governor of Louisiana.

Sitting among a grove of ancient oaks on a gentle rise in the outskirts of Lafayette, the Alexandre Latiolais House is a highly successful restoration of a Creole home. Based on evidence found in the front chambers and one of the rear cabinets, the house is believed to date from the late 1700s.

The house was named for Louis Alexandre Latiolais, who married the grandaughter of Lafayette's founder, Jean Mouton. Later it was owned by the Gilbert and Dominique families before being restored to its 1820s appearance by the present owners.

∧

One curiosity in the Alexandre Mouton House is the staircase, a *trompe l'œil*. When viewed from below, it appears to be curved, though when viewed from above, it clearly is not.

<

The carefully restored interior of the Alexandre Latiolais House in Lafayette, believed to date from the late 1700s. In the restoration, the owners, using courthouse records, have taken considerable care to use the original materials. The mantels still have some of the original paint, and some of the *faux marbre* panels with blue veining were clearly visible after the paint was cleaned. One room, the cabinet room, still has the original flooring.

"Le Petit Paris" – St. Martinville

If Lafayette is the hub of Cajun country, St. Martinville and neighboring Breaux Bridge – along with Eunice and other towns in "Acadiana" – are its heart. French is still widely spoken in this part of central Louisiana, at least by the old. Cajun restaurants and music abound, and the Acadian heritage is still very much alive.

St. Martinville, standing on a levee of the Bayou Teche, is one of Louisiana's oldest towns, founded just after Natchitoches and New Orleans. First called "Poste des Attakapas", the town was settled in the mid-1750s. Its character was molded by an eclectic mix of Acadian immigrants, wealthy planters fleeing the slave uprisings in St. Domingue, and French aristocrats seeking refuge from the excesses of the French Revolution. Because so many of the latter settled in the region – and tried to emulate a Parisian lifestyle – the town was once known at "Le Petit Paris".

But Paris could not be easily transplanted to humid central Louisiana. Though the aristocrats tried their best – staging elaborate balls and importing a French opera company – they were ill-suited to a life of farming or trade. Their descendants, less imbued with memories of France, were forced to adapt, which some of them did quite well, becoming prosperous farmers.

The first Acadian settlers arrived in St. Martinville in the mid-1760s. Refugees from *le Grand Dérangement*, which expelled them from their native *Acadie*, they were essentially homeless and penniless. Aided by local cattlemen and planters, many became small farmers and tradesmen.

Born in the fourth century, St. Martin de Tours, a priest and then Bishop of Tours, was widely known for his many acts of charity. The Church of St. Martin de Tours, honoring his memory, is situated at the heart of picturesque St. Martin's Square in St. Martinville. One of the oldest in Louisiana, the church was started in 1837 and completed five years later. It succeeded and incorporated the village's first chapel, established as early as 1765 by French missionaries. The French painter Jean François Mouchet created the painting of St. Martin de Tours that hangs over the altar.

The Evangeline myth still has potent force in Louisiana. The 1847 poem by Henry Wadsworth Longfellow, based on private conversations and a search of dubious historical

<
The statue of Evangeline, which stands beside the Church of St. Martin de Tours, is modeled after the screen actress Dolores Del Rio, who starred in the movie based on the Evangeline legend and who donated the funds to create the statue.

∧
The interior of the Church of St. Martin de Tours is one of Louisiana's loveliest. It contains gifts from the court of France during the reign of Louis XVI – including the sanctuary lamp and the baptismal font. Also found here are imposing statues of Joan of Arc, St. Louis, St. Jude, St. Roch and Ste. Thérèse of Lisieux.

<<
Dominating St. Martin's Square in St. Martinville is the Church of St. Martin de Tours, started in 1837 and completed five years later.

THE FORMATION OF THE CAJUN PEOPLE

When Samuel de Champlain led the first attempts of the Kingdom of France to colonize North America, the initial settlements were not in Québec and the St. Lawrence Valley, but in a peripheral area known today as the "Maritime Provinces" of Canada. Settling in 1604 at a small island in the river that now forms the boundary between Maine and New Brunswick, French colonizers, led by Pierre Duguay, Sieur de Monts and Champlain, were able to survive a first winter in the land that became known as Acadia, perhaps derived from the Greek name for a paradisiacal land called Arcadia. The following year the site of the settlement was moved to present-day Port Royal, Nova Scotia, which remained the focus of the Acadian colonization.

The development of the settlements was not straightforward. Port Royal was abandoned from 1607-1610, destroyed by an English privateer in 1613 and occupied by Scottish settlers (whence the origin of the name "Nova Scotia") from 1628-1629. In 1632, in the Treaty of St. Germain-en-Laye, Acadia was recognized as being French. At that time, a relatively large number of settlers (about three hundred) arrived to form the genesis of the Acadian

∧

A typical Cajun cottage of the nineteenth century.

people. Many of these and subsequent settlers came from the Poitou area of western France.

Early years

The years from 1632-1650 were marked by conflict (sometimes armed) between fur traders engaged by two rival seigneurs, Isaac de Razilly and Charles de la Tour. In 1654 the young colony was occupied once again by the British – this time until 1670. French Acadia grew to have a population of around two thousand by the dawn of the new century. However, in 1710 during the War of the Spanish Succession, Port Royal was occupied once more by the British, and was awarded to England by the Treaty of Utrecht in 1713. The terms of the treaty were quite vague as to the territorial limits of the two rival European powers in the Maritimes, a situation that led to considerable conflict during the next half century.

Tensions and *le Grand Dérangement*

After 1713, some Acadians moved across the Bay of Fundy to what is now New Brunswick, still considered to be French territory. Those that remained were allowed by the British to practice their Catholic religion and to keep title to their lands and possessions. However, succeeding British governors called on the Acadians to swear an oath of allegiance to the British crown, though this was only sporadically enforced. When Franco-British hostilities led to the Seven Years War in 1756, the inherent instability of the situation became intolerable. This war was the ultimate conflict that decided French or British supremacy in North America, and the British, determined to prevail, were less disposed to turn a blind eye to the ambiguous loyalties of the Acadians.

Under the ruthless General Monckton, the Acadians were told to swear an oath of allegiance to the British monarch or suffer exile.

They were given only a few days to decide, and when they hesitated, British soldiers ruthlessly loaded them on storeships or drove them out of their fertile lands into the wilderness. Many families were separated in this act of what later would be called "ethnic cleansing".

This cataclysm, known in Acadian history as *le Grand Dérangement* ("the Great Removal"), gave rise to stories, legends and myths that continue to this day. The most well-known is the epic poem "Evangeline" by Henry Wadsworth Longfellow. His sentimental fictional character, who was separated from her betrothed, spent years searching for him only to find him on his deathbed, has become a kind of patron saint of Acadians everywhere.

Wanderers

The Acadians suffered terribly during the initial evacuation and their subsequent years of wandering as international refugees. Sent in all directions of the compass, some went to the west of France, to the Poitou region, the land of their ancestors. Others sojourned in England and the Channel Islands until the war was over. Still others were dispatched to Québec, where there is a county named after them and where many prominent Québécois have characteristic Acadian names. A few even escaped into the woods of unsettled parts of Nova Scotia and New Brunswick where they eventually formed more organized settlements.

But the vast majority were dispersed by the British to their colonies on the east coast of North America. In some, such as Quaker Pennsylvania, they were well received and lodged with sympathetic households; in others, such as South Carolina, they were thrown into prison; while in some, like New York, they were refused admittance. In all cases, they were considered to be "enemy aliens" and never formed proper roots.

< Cajun musicians,
the Romero brothers,
at the Evangeline Oak
in St. Martinville.
V
A chef prepares cracklin,
a typical Cajun dish.

When the Treaty of Paris was signed in 1763, the dispersed Acadians could not return to their homeland, which now had new owners. Some in the British North American colonies joined compatriots in Canada and France. Some returned to the Maritimes, but since they were not allowed back into their fertile valleys, they settled in fishing communities on the rocky shores of what would become New Brunswick and Nova Scotia, or began pioneer farming in the southeastern part of New Brunswick around the present-day town of Moncton.

Louisiana

In the Treaty of Paris, the French territories in the Mississippi Valley had been divided and ceded to other powers – the east bank of the Mississippi to Great Britain, the west bank to Spain. The new Spanish sovereigns, who had small settlements in nearby Texas, realized they were threatened by the demographic superiority of the British North Americans. The Spanish desperately wanted to increase their population and economic self-sufficiency to fend off future British expansion. Through various agents, the Spanish began a policy of encouraging dispersed Acadian refugees to move to the Louisiana frontier. The first ship arrived in 1765, and by 1786 a total of about three thousand former residents of Acadia had settled in Spanish Louisiana.

Some of the Acadian migrants settled along the banks of the Mississippi River (the "Acadian coast") upstream from New Orleans, where they were more exposed to a wider world and began to lose their distinctive culture. But many were granted lands in the bayous and plains west of New Orleans, since the Spanish governors wanted to use them as buffers against Indian attacks. This area was known as the Opelousas and Attakapas districts (now Lafayette, St. Martin, St. Mary and Iberia parishes, later spreading north and westward to St. Landry, Avoyelles, Evangeline, Acadia and Vermilion parishes – or "Acadiana"). There the new settlers formed a unique frontier society based on small farming, trapping, fishing and livestock raising, totally unlike the plantation culture based on sugar cane cultivation that developed in Creole Louisiana in the Mississippi Valley proper.

Acadians into Cajuns

This economic and cultural difference led to the formation of a society different from those found in the rest of Louisiana. These "Cajuns" (a corruption of the French "Acadiens") developed a language, culture, social organization, cuisine and music that set them apart from their neighbors. Although one of the main themes of Cajun history is their relative isolation and their cultural distinctiveness, they did have increasing contacts with the other peoples of Louisiana – witnessed by the widening number of Cajun family names – and participated in its political life: two Acadians served as governor of the state and one as lieutenant governor before the Civil War.

In the end, however, the remarkable cultural resilience of the Acadians who settled in Louisiana and those who returned to the Maritimes is one of the most interesting sidebars in North American history. In the case of the Cajuns of Louisiana, this was partially a reflection of their inability or unwillingness to participate in an increasingly English-language education system.

During the twentieth century, the Cajuns began to be assimilated into the mainstream of American culture. At the same time, the wider American culture became more aware of this cultural treasure, with its distinctive cuisine (dishes such as "gumbo"), festivals

(Mardi Gras – celebrated very differently from its New Orleans counterpart), traditions (the "fais do do", or communal Sunday dance) and music (including such offshoots as zydeco, a combination of African-American and Cajun traditions). Cajun society is now increasingly studied and written about, while it is still possible to capture the memories of people who remember many fading traditions. Institutional steps have also been taken to preserve the culture, whose unique aspects have achieved a newfound respect and resonance in the wider world.

Daniel Baker

<

The restoration of
the Alexandre Latiolais
House, a Creole cottage
on the outskirts
of Lafayette, added
lightness and some
modern touches to
the house's appearance.
The façade now has nine
delicate columns rather
than the six massive
ones that graced the
front of the Victorian
house that stood here
before the restoration.
A walkway and a fence
made of cypress have
been added to enhance
the setting.

∨

Acadian Village is
a collection of original
old Creole houses moved
from various locations
in Louisiana and placed
in an attractive setting on
the outskirts of Lafayette.
The houses, each with
a colorful history,
together constitute
a veritable laboratory
of Acadian lifestyles in
the nineteenth century.

>

The New Hope Chapel
in the Acadian Village
is a replica of a simple
1850 Acadian chapel.
It contains exquisite
wooden Stations of the
Cross carved by a local
sculptor. The building
is often used for religious
services and weddings.

On the fringes of Lafayette two theme parks celebrate the
Acadian heritage. The newest, Vermilionville, set on twenty-
two acres beside the Vermillion River, accentuates Acadian
life and crafts, with both original and reconstructed buildings, including an overseer's cottage, plantation home,
cotton gin, chapel and schoolhouse.

Acadian Village is a pleasant conglomeration of several
authentic Acadian-style buildings that were moved here from
other locations in south Louisiana. The Thibodeaux House
(also called Cormier-Thibodeaux), dating from around 1800-
1820, was moved to its present location from the Breaux
Bridge area. The LeBlanc House is notable for its style, which
is of a typical Creole farmhouse, and its links with a colorful
personality in Louisiana history. Moved to its present site from
Youngsville, the house, dating from around 1840, was the
birthplace of Acadian Senator Dudley LeBlanc, spokesman for
the Acadian population and inventor of the tonic Hadacol, a
vitamin mixture which was all the rage in the 1940s.

A grandfather's chair in Maison Olivier. The oldest member of the family stored his books in a compartment in the bottom of the chair, which was built so that if a child sat in it, his feet would not reach the floor, and the chair would topple over. This was meant to teach respect for the head of the family.

∨

The Longfellow-Evangeline State Historic Site, a short distance from St. Martinville, was once the site of a large plantation. The site now includes several Creole structures that were part of the original plantation, including this Acadian farmstead and Maison Olivier, the main plantation house.

sources, became a staple of American public school education. The poem recounts the history of Evangeline Bellefontaine and Gabriel Lajeunesse, exiled from *Acadie* (Nova Scotia) and compelled to travel separately to new settlements in Louisiana. On arriving, Evangeline finds that Gabriel has already departed for the Ozarks. She finds him years later on his deathbed in Philadelphia, where they embrace just as Gabriel dies. Evangeline dies soon after and they are buried together in nameless Philadelphia graves.

Some forty years after "Evangeline" was published, a French Creole educator, Madame Sidonie de la Houssaye, published a new version of the story in her novel *Pouponne et Balthazar*, in which Evangeline and Gabriel became upper-class French Creoles who looked down on their Acadian neighbors. Seeking to correct this distortion of the original story, St. Martinville playwright Felix Voorhies in 1907 wrote *Acadian Reminiscences: The True Story of the Acadians*, in which Evangeline and Gabriel were renamed Emmeline Labiche and Louis Arceneaux, and the story was centered in St. Martinville and Louisiana. Hollywood followed with film versions of the story in 1922 and 1929. The Evangeline

statue sits beside the Church of St. Martin de Tours in St. Martinville, the village where Longfellow set his poem, one verse of which reads: "On the banks of the Têche, are the towns of St. Maur and St. Martin/There the long-wandering bride shall be given again to her bridegroom."

Created in 1991, the Acadian Memorial is a vivid reminder of the expulsion of the Acadians from Nova Scotia and New Brunswick more than two centuries ago. The memorial contains a large wall mural depicting the Acadian refugees who arrived in Louisiana from 1764 to 1788. Painted by Robert Dafford, the mural is twinned with one by the same artist in Nantes, France, which portrays the departure of the Acadians from Nantes in 1785.

Just outside of St. Martinville, the Longfellow-Evangeline State Historic Site hosts several Creole structures – an Acadian farmstead, an Acadian cabin, an old barn built in the 1820s and Maison Olivier, a Creole plantation. The park, established in 1934, was the first in the Louisiana State Parks system. Maison Olivier, constructed around 1815, is indigenous to the site. The plantation house was built by Charles DuClozel Olivier, who married Marie Bienvenue, a Frenchwoman from New Orleans, in 1801. The Olivier family remained in the house until 1927. Though the inside of the house has none of the original furniture, which was taken away in 1863 by Union soldiers, there are a number of period nineteenth-century pieces collected carefully over the years.

A fine example of a raised Creole cottage, Maison Olivier near St. Martinville was once a cattle ranch, then an indigo plantation, then a prosperous sugar plantation. The main house was constructed around 1815.

<
Lake Martin in Breaux
Bridge is the kind of
setting many people
imagine when they think
of Louisiana. Located
just across the St. Martin
Parish line from Lafayette,
the lake, with its
submerged, moss-laden
cypress trees and multiple
varieties of wildlife,
is blissfully undeveloped.
The thousands of nesting
birds that arrive here
in spring make this
one of Louisiana's most
unforgettable sights.

>
The Henri Penne House
was moved more than
thirty miles to its present
site in Breaux Bridge.
Originally owned
by a Frenchman from
Nantes, the house dates
from around 1821.
Other buildings, also
moved to the same
property, include
a *pigeonnier* dating from
around 1827, a *magasin*
used to store food,
and a *maison dimanche*
(Sunday house), where
a planter often stayed
when coming to town
for the weekend.

Crawfish, swamps and *joie de vivre* – Breaux Bridge

A few miles west of St. Martinville sits the small town of Breaux Bridge, termed the "Crawfish Capital of the World", noted also for historic homes and for Lake Martin, a largely unspoiled scenic area with an extraordinary migratory bird population.

Breaux Bridge owes its founding to a formidable Acadian woman with the colorful name of Scholastique Breaux, born Scholastique Melanie Picou in 1796. Scholastique was the widow of Agricole Breaux, the son of Acadian pioneer Firmin Breaux who, in 1771, bought the land where the town sits from Jean-François Ledee, a wealthy New Orleans merchant, who had acquired it under a French land grant.

Breaux Bridge – with its Cajun restaurants, yearly crawfish festival, Creole dwellings and swampy surroundings of the Bayou Teche and Lake Martin – has a special *joie de vivre* that sets it apart from other towns in the South.

The Cypress Island Preserve on Lake Martin is owned and maintained by the Nature Conservancy and has few if any equals in North America. Supporting thirty thousand or more nesting birds each year, it is particularly impressive in spring, when the tree branches are crowded with fowl – ibis, blue and green heron and roseate spoonbills. No less imposing are the amphibians and reptiles, among them alligators that nest in mounds of dirt and leaves and that can often be seen, heads visible, above the green carpet of weeds that cover part of the lake. The trees – old growth live oaks, cypress and tupelo gum – can best be seen from shore. The beauty of the sunset, in this still primeval wilderness, is unforgettable.

>>
The salon of the *maison dimanche* in Breaux Bridge is furnished with late eighteenth-century Louisiana and continental French furnishings and decorative arts.

Maison Madeleine,
a nineteenth-century
Creole cabin near Lake
Martin in Breaux Bridge,
was moved fifty miles
to its current location.
At the time, it had been
abandoned for more than
half a century and had
no electricity, no running
water, no window glass,
a fragment of the current
galerie and only half of
the *bousillage* that serves
as the outside insulation.
A large sugar kettle now
sits in the garden.

dating from around 1827, a *magasin* used to store food, and a *maison dimanche* (Sunday house), where a planter often stayed when coming to town for the weekend.

On a side road leading into Lake Martin sits Maison Madeleine, a one-and-a-half story Creole cottage that once stood in the middle of a sugar cane field. Moved by its owner some fifty miles to its present site, it is notable for having been restored to conserve the essence of its original features. The origins of the house are unclear. There is a theory that it was constructed as an overseer's house. Because there are circular saw marks on the wood, the indications are that Maison Madeleine was constructed after 1840.

Abandoned around 1918, the house had no amenities, a fragment of the current *galerie* and only half of the *bousillage* insulation. To replace these, moss was mixed with mud, and pressed into place upon and around the horizontal bars, then scored to receive the first coat of plaster. Several nineteenth-century hand-hewn beams from a log cabin in Natchitoches were utilized in the "new" outside kitchen behind the house.

∧

View of the *parterre garden* of the Henri Penne House. The garden, with shaped beds of herats, diamonds and stars, is based on research of early Louisiana gardens.

Born in Nantes, France in 1767, Henri Penne moved with his brother to St. Martin's Parish, Louisiana in the late eighteenth century, where he was probably a sugar planter near Jeanerette. Around 1821, Penne, though a Frenchman, built a house of mainly Anglo-American features, including the cross-and-bible doors, the center hall floor plan and the placement of the chimneys on the exterior walls.

The Henri Penne House was moved thirty-eight miles from Jeanerette to its present location. Carefully restored, it is now a salesroom for fine French antiques. Other buildings, also moved to the same property, include a *pigeonnier*

>

Both the *maison dimanche* (left) and Maison Madeleine (right) have bedrooms furnished with elegant four-poster beds. The bed in the *maison dimanche* is a rare inlaid mahogany, eighteenth-century Louisiana piece.

<<

Salon of Maison Madeleine furnished with continental furniture and decorative arts appropriate to this early Louisiana restoration. The mantel is in the *Directoire* style.

< Magnolia Mound in Baton Rouge is a striking blend of federal and Creole design. Located on a natural bluff one mile from the Mississippi River, it was built off the ground so that the air could circulate under it. Other buildings on the property include an overseer's house, a slave cabin, a Creole barn and an outdoor open hearth kitchen.

Iberville's "red stick" upriver from New Orleans – Baton Rouge

The name of the town is said to have originated with Iberville, the French explorer, who, sailing up the Mississippi in 1699 to look for a place to establish a settlement, came upon a red pole with fish and bear remains stuck on it, supposedly used by the Indians to mark off the boundary of hunting territories. The red stick or "baton rouge", as Iberville called it, evolved into the name of the town.

As early as 1718, the French are alleged to have constructed a fort near the area to protect travelers from New Orleans to northern outposts. Following the transfer to England by the Treaty of Paris in 1763, the settlement was renamed New Richmond. In September 1779, the Spanish defeated the English at Fort Butte on Bayou Manchac and then captured Baton Rouge, so that by 1781 West Florida, including East Baton Rouge, was under Spanish influence. In 1810, when the Spanish were overthrown by local settlers, around a thousand persons resided in Baton Rouge. The people declared themselves independent and renamed the area the West Florida Republic. In a few months, the territory was annexed by Louisiana and divided. Louisiana was admitted into the Union in 1812, and Baton Rouge became the state capital in 1849.

At the turn of the twentieth century, the town began to develop industrially because of its strategic location on the first bluff along the Mississippi River north of the Gulf of Mexico. Now a university and petroleum center, present-day Baton Rouge has a population in excess of 225,000.

Once part of a nine-hundred-acre plantation complex, the restored plantation house of Magnolia Mound rests on a bluff in Baton Rouge, a mile back from the Mississippi. Built around 1791, it is surrounded by cypress and majestic live oak trees, some more than 250 years old.

Magnolia Mound had a long succession of owners, the most important of whom was Armand Duplantier, a native of Voisin, France, who came to America to serve with Lafayette during the American Revolution. He acquired Magnolia Mound in 1802 after marrying Constance Rochon, a Creole whose family had also immigrated from France. The widow of the previous owner, John Joyce, Constance brought with her two children from her previous marriage. Duplantier, a widower, had four of his own, and

∧ ∧ At Magnolia Mound, the dining room, originally part of the *galerie*, was also used as an education room, where the mother would do the schooling of the children. In the parlor, Armand Duplantier, the native of France who acquired the house in 1802, had the ceiling raised and installed the Federal Style mantels. The wallpaper in this room was reproduced from scraps of the original found under the paint, and the handsome cove ceiling has been attractively restored.

< The *galerie* at Magnolia Mound. Armand Duplantier, the French owner, had the *galerie* extended during the early nineteenth century.

<
Chêne Vert in Baton
Rouge is an old Creole
house transported across
the Mississippi to
its present location.
The house retains all
of its original features,
including the millwork,
the interior doors, the
mantelpieces and the
pine floors. The dining
room on the ground floor
of the house, now
elegantly furnished,
contains a long table
originally built for
a doctor in New Orleans.

∨
The living room/parlor
on the ground floor
of Chêne Vert in Baton
Rouge. The mantelpiece
is original to the house,
and many of the
Louisiana antiques were
purchased at auction.
The *armoire*, an old
Louisiana piece, has
a side cabinet, unusual
for *armoires* of the period.

together the couple, following the custom of the time, had an additional five children, which called for a major expansion of the house. The Duplantiers added a dining room, two rooms on the south side and extended the front *galerie*.

In the 1960s, the Foundation for Historical Louisiana fought and won a bitter battle with developers, who wanted to destroy the house and build multi-story apartments. Suffucent records remained so that Magnolia Mound could be accurately and successfully restored in the style of the Federal period from 1800-1830. The elegant yellow wallpaper in the parlor was imported from France; thanks to a faded scrap uncovered in the restoration, and is a replica of the original wallpaper put in place by Armand Duplantier. The symmetrical central hall reflects the Federal influence on Creole architecture. The floors are the original cypress; the mantelpieces are Creole.

Meticulous research has also been instrumental in choosing the furnishings, a blend of local furniture and pieces from the Northeast U.S. and from France. The *armoires* in the main rooms are of the period; the chandeliers and clock were imported from France; the Empire square pianoforte was manufactured in New York in the 1820s/1830s. The authenticity of the restoration carries over to other structures on the property. The slave quarter house was moved to the site from

the River Lake Plantation across the river; the outdoor open hearth kitchen has been reconstructed on its original site; and the old overseer's house, based on 1880 survey maps, was moved to the property from a nearby neighborhood.

Chêne Vert, in a quiet residential area of Baton Rouge, is a testament to the owners' determination to acquire a Creole home and to transfer it, despite daunting obstacles, to a new location. The present owners moved it on a flatbed truck from a large plantation seventy-five miles away. Now, elegantly refurbished, it sits on a sloping plot of land, surrounded by ancient live oak trees, and appears to have always belonged where it stands.

A typical two-story Creole plantation, probably built between 1824 and 1834, the house has a Creole floor plan, Federal wraparound mantels, casement windows and glazed French doors. The ground floor has brick walls; the second floor is a frame construction with brick infill between posts (*briquette-entre-poteaux*). The ground floor has a large central room, used for dining. The same floor plan is repeated on the second floor. Court documents indicate Chêne Vert was lived in by one Caroline Fontenot, the daughter of Grand Louis Fontenot, one of the largest landowners in the Opelousas area. The story goes that Louis married off several daughters to Napoleonic officers.

∧

Chêne Vert, located in a quiet corner of Baton Rouge, is a typical two-story Creole plantation. Outside on the impeccably landscaped grounds is a formal elongated *parterre* garden, inspired by gardens found in the New Orleans Notarial Archives.

A multi-ethnic city under three flags – New Orleans

Within an hour of arriving, the visitor to New Orleans senses that this is an American city like no other. With the narrow streets and wrought iron adornments of the *Vieux Carré*, the sumptuous Anglo-American houses of the Garden District, the ambience of easy charm and easy virtue, New Orleans stands out as the most exotic and original metropolis in the continental United States.

Part of the city's originality flows from the mix of nationalities who settled here and around the city – the French Creoles, the emigrés from St. Domingue, the Isleños from the Canary Islands, the Scottish and Irish, the free people of color and slaves from Africa and the later waves of Hondurans, Germans and Italians. Each national group made its imprint on the city's culture, architecture and cuisine. Home of Dixieland jazz and Creole cooking, of Louis Armstrong and Mardi Gras, the "Big Easy", as some writers have called it, is an irresistible draw for visitors worldwide.

The Crescent City takes its name from its location on a bend of the Mississippi, some ninety miles from the Gulf of Mexico. In 1718, its founder, Jean-Baptiste le Moyne, Sieur de Bienville, then Governor of the Louisiana Territory, set sail with around fifty men from Dauphin Island near present-day Mobile to seek a site for a new French capital on the lower Mississippi. Fighting his way upstream, Bienville fell upon a spot that seemed acceptable: it was on higher ground, therefore thought to be less vulnerable to hurricanes and floods;

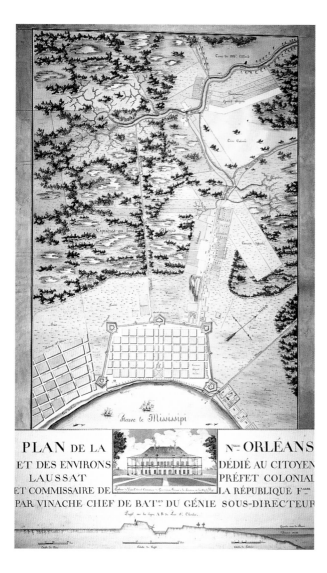

> A nineteenth-century
engraving of the New
Orleans waterfront,
showing steamboats
plying the Mississippi and
planters on the shore.

and it was accessible by alternate routes from the Gulf, either by Lakes Borgne and Ponchartrain, or by the river. Bienville disembarked his men, who set about clearing the site which he named after the Duc d'Orleans, Regent of France after the death of Louis XIV. The early going was painfully slow. Infested with mosquitoes, thick with canebrakes and stubborn vegetation, the new settlement took its toll on the builders, some of whom deserted or died. But by 1719, some primitive houses and huts had been constructed, and the French administration began moving troops and supplies to the town.

In 1720, the French engineer Le Blond de La Tour, assisted by Adrien de Pauger, arrived to draw up plans for the development of New Orleans. They laid out a plan that encompasses the present Jackson Square (called by the French the *Place d'Armes*) and the rectangular grid that is now the French

Quarter (*Vieux Carré*). Envisioned were sixty-six squares with the Place d'Armes at the center, containing a church, rectory and guardhouse. Though a savage hurricane struck in 1723, destroying the embryonic church and most of the houses, most were rapidly rebuilt, and in that same year one Father Pierre Charlevoix was moved to write that "this savage and desolate place … will one day be an opulent city, and the Metropolis of a great and rich colony."

Early efforts to populate the lower Louisiana Territory had met with mixed success. In 1712, a wealthy Paris merchant, Antoine Crozat, received a monopoly from the French Crown to develop it, but after quarrels with Governor Antoine de la Mothe Cadillac and financial reverses, Crozat

dragooning orphans from convents, patients from hospitals, prostitutes and other unfortunates to undertake the perilous voyage to the New World. Many died *en route*, and most of the others were unfit for life in Louisiana. The company then used gentler tactics, selling shares on margin in Louisiana to "concessionaires" who were responsible for locating workers to sail on company ships to the new colony. The workers, called "engagés", were promised land, supplies and clothing in exchange for a three-year indenture.

Law's "Mississippi bubble" burst in 1720, bankrupting thousands of investors, but for all its flaws the Company of the Indies did succeed in establishing the city of New Orleans. The period from the collapse of Law's Company to

abandoned his concession after only five years. The French Crown then turned to a Scot, John Law, who, in 1717, was granted a twenty-five-year monopoly on the commerce and trade of the new colony. Law's infamous Company of the West (later Company of the Indies) engaged in shameless marketing to sell the new territory to reluctant French settlers. Promising untold mineral riches, friendly Indians and a temperate climate, Law's minions first used rough tactics,

the Spanish takeover in 1762 saw a slow increase in population as the city grew in commercial importance, with trade flowing downriver from other French settlements. Indigo and other agricultural products from farms and plantations made their way downriver, and trade with Europe, still limited, began to develop. Most buildings, however, remained wooden and rudimentary, and the city had no paved roads, and no effective system of drainage and sanitation. The

French Government had few resources and devoted little time and attention to developing the city.

In 1762, in the Treaty of Fontainebleau, Louis XV, hoping to keep Louisiana from falling into the hands of the British, ceded all of the colony west of the Mississippi to Spain. But the Spanish contingent under Don Antonio de Ulloa did not arrive in New Orleans until four years later, bringing with it government workers, customs officials and *notaires*. The locals, who had been largely unaware of the transfer, were not pleased, and Ulloa did not make himself popular when, among other gestures, he insisted that only Spanish wine be imported. On October 27, 1768, the local population revolted and Ulloa fled to Cuba.

The following year, a new commander, Alejandro O'Reilly, arrived with a more imposing force of two thousand men. O'Reilly abolished the French Superior Council and replaced it with the *Cabildo*, or town council, and insisted that legal documents be translated into Spanish. He proceeded to execute the leaders of the 1768 rebellion, which earned him the nickname "Bloody O'Reilly". Despite these steps, O'Reilly was,

in the main, a fair and efficient administrator who appointed French officials to important posts and signed treaties with the Indians. He departed after seven months, leaving Louisiana and New Orleans in far better shape than when he arrived.

The Spanish period was marked by three natural disasters that occurred within the space of fifteen years and that changed the face of New Orleans forever. In 1779, a violent hurricane leveled much of the city. As it slowly recovered, the great fire of 1788 struck, burning more than 850 houses. In 1794, another conflagration destroyed the northwest quadrant of the city. As a result, the Governor, Baron de Carondelet, ordered that future buildings be constructed of brick or plastered and roofed with tile. The architecture that one now sees in the French Quarter, with its wrought iron balconies and walled courtyards, is predominantly Spanish, though with strong French influences.

Louisiana was returned to French control in the secret Treaty of San Ildefonso, but no French official appeared in New Orleans for three years until Pierre Clement de Laussat, Napoleon's emissary, arrived in March 1803. President Thomas Jefferson, aware of the transfer, determined to buy New Orleans and ordered his Minister to France, Robert Livingston, to begin negotiations with the French. Livingston, later joined by James Monroe, began a series of tedious negotiations with French officials. To the Americans' astonishment, Napoleon, on the brink of war with England and wanting to establish the Americans as a counterpoint to the British, instructed his Minister of the Treasury, François Barbé-Marbois, to sell all of the Louisiana Territory. The price finally agreed was $15 million, which Jefferson, lacking Congress's approval, had to borrow from Dutch and British banks.

With the sale, called "the greatest real estate deal in history", the United States virtually doubled its size, adding enough territory to form thirteen future states. The Louisiana Purchase also marked an important turning point for the young republic: while it had previously looked to Europe for its trade and sustenance, it began, for the first time, to turn to the West and to focus on enlarging its continental presence.

Some twenty days of balls and parties in November/December 1803 preceded the handover from French to American control, and at noon on December 20, American troops marched into Jackson Square, the French tricolor was lowered and the stars and stripes raised over American-controlled New Orleans. The French were no happier to see the Americans arrive than they had been to see the Spanish forty years before. But the newly appointed Governor, W.C.C. Claiborne, only twenty-six years old, eventually succeeded in convincing the Catholic population that their freedom of religion would not be compromised. Claiborne, who later married a French Creole and learned French, ruled for thirteen years, bringing a level of stability to the city and the Territory. Louisiana joined the Union as a state in April 1812.

The peace was shattered in late 1814 when a British force, sailing from Jamaica, attempted to take New Orleans. On January 8, 1815, Andrew Jackson, commanding a small American force, defeated the British at Chalmette, south of the city. The decisive American victory established once and for all the credibility of the American republic.

The period from the Battle of New Orleans to the Civil War saw New Orleans' population swell to 170,000 and its commercial importance as a port and *entrepôt* make it the nation's leading port and its greatest slave market. But this period of dynamism came rudely to an end with the outbreak of hostilities between North and South. In April 1862, the Union Admiral David Farragut sailed past the guns of the protecting Mississippi forts, and on May 1 the Federal forces occupied New Orleans. The occupation was to last fifteen years.

After the occupation, New Orleans slowly recovered, the Mississippi was reopened and agricultural trade was re-estab-

<

Cession of Louisiana by Constantino Brumidi. The Marquis Barbé-Marbois, the representative of the French government, is standing and showing a map to Robert Livingston, who coordinated the negotiations, and James Monroe, the new Minister to France. The Americans, under orders to only buy New Orleans, were astonished when Barbé-Marbois, under orders from Napoleon, offered to sell the Americans the entire Louisiana Territory, which currently comprises thirteen states. The handover of southern Louisiana, including New Orleans, took place on December 20, 1803. (Senate wing, U.S. Capitol) ©Architect of the Capitol

>

The Ursuline Convent in New Orleans is the only French colonial building to survive the great fire. It has a hipped roof with six prominent dormers. At the rear, there are marble statues of important religious figures – including Saint Rose Philippine Duchesne, who established schools and convents for the Society of the Sacred Heart; and Henriette Delille, a free woman of color who ministered to slaves in the ante-bellum period.

∧

Inside the Ursuline Convent in New Orleans, built in 1752-53, there are a number of original features, including the old cypress stairway that was moved to the building from the 1734 convent.

>

The statue of Our Lady of Prompt Succor in the shrine of the Ursuline Academy in New Orleans. Brought from France by Mother St. Michel Gensoul in 1810, the statue was so named because Mother St. Michel prayed to it to receive quick permission to come to Louisiana. Her prayers were answered promptly. The Ursulines prayed again to the statue during the great fire of 1812 and during the Battle of New Orleans; both times their prayers were answered.

lished. But hard times persisted until the end of the century and beyond. The discovery of petroleum in the early twentieth century and the production of natural gas brought new sources of revenue to the state. In New Orleans, the French Quarter, which had declined at the beginning of the century, was substantially restored beginning in the 1920s. The *Vieux Carré* Commission, established in 1936, fortunately blocked efforts to tear down most historic buildings. Modern New Orleans, now the second largest port in the U.S., still retains the considerable charm of its French past.

Architectural highlights

The second Ursuline Convent on Chartres Street, completed in 1752-53, is the only French colonial building to survive the two fires that swept through New Orleans in the late eighteenth century. Its designer, Ignace François Broutin (who also designed Fort St. Jean-Baptiste in Natchitoches), and the builder, Claude Joseph Dubreuil Villars, were responsible for its solid stucco and brick masonry construction. It replaces the first convent, also designed by Broutin, which was completed around 1734.

The story of the Ursuline nuns is one of the great narratives of courage and faith in early Louisiana. In response to a call from Governor Bienville, who requested a community of nuns to serve as nurses in the military hospital and provide education to the young women and girls in the fledgling colony, twelve Ursuline nuns and novices set sail from Rouen, France in February 1727. Their voyage to New Orleans was a turbulent one, with most of them falling violently ill with seasickness.

The Ursulines were pioneers, establishing the first school for girls and also the first free school and the first orphanage in Louisiana. Over the centuries, they sheltered and educated the children of Indians and blacks, opened the first home for battered women and performed outstanding work in the military hospital of the new colony. The sisters remained in the Chartres Street building until 1824, when they moved to a new location on Dauphine Street. Since 1912, they have been headquartered at the Ursuline Academy on State Street, outside of the French Quarter.

The church on the convent grounds dates from 1845; it has its original ceiling with alternating slats of cypress and pine, and a celebrated window showing the Battle of New Orleans. At the rear of the convent are white marble statues of prominent religious figures – including Rose Philippine Duchesne, who established schools and convents for the Society of the Sacred Heart; and Henriette Delille, a free woman of color who ministered to slaves in the antebellum period.

Dominating Jackson Square stands the white façade of the Basilica of St. Louis, King of France, popularly known as

Facing New Orleans' Jackson Square, the façade of Saint Louis Cathedral is painted white to look like marble. The structure is simple and stately, with a central tower containing two arched windows, flanked by two hexagonal smaller towers. Inside, the cathedral is heavily ornamented, with a white marble baroque altar centerpiece dating from 1852; a mural representing St. Louis, King of France, announcing the Seventh Crusade; and a large painting on the vaulted nave of Christ surrounded by the Apostles bestowing supremacy on Peter.

St. Louis Cathedral. The present church is the second one on the site. The first, dedicated in 1727, was a small church of brick-between-post construction. It was destroyed in the great fire of 1788 along with much of the *Vieux Carré*. The second, completed in 1794 and later designated as a cathedral, was larger than the first and was a low, flat-roofed building, flanked by hexagonal towers, but without a central spire. Less than three months after it was completed, a second devastating fire struck New Orleans, but remarkably spared the building. In 1819, Benjamin Latrobe, architect of the U.S. Capitol, was engaged to add a central tower, but unfortunately died of yellow fever before it was completed.

Between 1849-1851, the cathedral was almost completely rebuilt based on a design of the French architect, J.N.B. DePouilly. The present cathedral, though restored several times since, is essentially the 1851 reconstruction.

In 1964, the St. Louis Cathedral was designed as a Minor Basilica by Pope Paul VI. In part, the Pope's message read: "The Cathedral Church of New Orleans, dedicated to Saint Louis King [of France] is well deserving of acclaim since it is renowned for the spaciousness and splendor of the edifice, and the remembrance of historical events [occurring in it]."

The *Cabildo*, the *Presbytère* and the Pontalba Apartments round out the harmonious group of buildings that comprise

The Pontalba Apartments on Jackson Square were planned by James Gallier, who was later replaced by Henry Howard. They were designed as row houses rather than apartments. The buildings are now, as they were then, of mixed use, with commercial properties below and living quarters above, a typical Creole feature.

The Baroness Pontalba, a remarkable nineteenth-century woman, vigorously supervised the work on the Pontalba Apartments. She insisted on the installation of the cast iron *galeries*, probably the first of their kind in New Orleans. Construction of the Upper Pontalba Building was completed in the fall of 1850.

The red brick Pontalba Apartments were built in 1851 by the Baroness Micaela Pontalba, an extraordinary nineteenth-century woman. Daughter of a Spanish grandee, Micaela was married off because of her wealth to a French aristocrat, whose family was extremely abusive to her. Her father-in-law, outraged when she left her husband, shot her, destroying some of her fingers, but she recovered to return to New Orleans, not only to build the Pontalba buildings, but to talk the city administration into changing the appearance of the *Presbytère* and the *Cabildo* to give them more of a French appearance.

The richness of New Orleans architecture derives from the multiple influences that played upon it. A city which lived under three flags – French, Spanish and American – was bound to reflect a blend of the styles of all three, adjusted for differences in climate, building materials and New World culture. Some French influences include the *porte-cochère* garden houses of eighteenth-century Paris, which have echoes in French Quarter townhouses; hipped roofs, that reflect houses in the French Caribbean

>
A typical New Orleans street scene. Wrought iron balconies, first introduced by the Spanish, are supported by iron posts. Transoms over the doors are segmented, and the façade is colorful and vivid.

Jackson Square. Though the first two were constructed in the Spanish period, and the Pontalba Apartments after the American takeover, there are strong French links to all three. French architecture, taste and sentiment held fast during the Spanish period and French colonial architectural styles continued long after the Louisiana Purchase

The *Cabildo*, built between 1795 and 1799, served as the Spanish seat of government. Designed by the French architect Don Gilberto Guillemard, the Louisiana Purchase was signed in the monumental *Salle Capitulaire*.

The *Presbytère*, built between 1795 and 1813, flanks the cathedral on the right. Also designed by Guillemard, it was originally meant to be a rectory of the cathedral, but was home to the Louisiana State Courts. It too had a mansard roof, added in 1847. The *Presbytère* is also part of the Louisiana State Museum.

∧∧

New Orleans Creole buildings in the *Vieux Carré* display a rich variety of architectural styles. One is the simple Creole cottage, squarish in shape and built close to the street, with no surrounding *galerie*. The cottages often have side gables and a steep, dormered half-story for children's bedrooms. Their floor plan is characterized by the lack of a central hall, with free movement from room-to-room. The Creole townhouses, on the other hand, tend to be two or three stories, sometimes narrow or rectilinear in appearance, often with an upper *galerie* bordered with a wrought iron balcony. They are also set directly on the sidewalk (*banquette*) and may have a passageway leading to a loggia in the rear. The more elaborate townhouses were characterized by a *porte-cochère*, wide enough for carriages to pass through to a rear courtyard.

(Architectural drawings courtesy of the New Orleans Notarial Archives)

∨ ∨

The simple square-shaped Creole cottage in New Orleans often had two front entrances. The Creole features of Madame John's Legacy (below right) include the steep double-pitched roof with arched dormers at the front and rear, the *galerie* running across the front supported by thin colonettes, the raised basement, the large trusses and the *colombage* construction with brick-between-post filling on the second floor. Now used for special exhibits, it is one of the oldest houses in the Mississippi Valley and part of the Louisiana State Museum.

<

The elegant interior of a restored Creole cottage in New Orleans' *Vieux Carré*. The antique furniture is of Louisiana origin; the diamond-shaped design on the mantelpiece is typically Creole.

colonies as well as some structures along the St. Lawrence River. From the Spanish came the use of wrought iron for balconies and tiled roofs (of which only a few remain). From the Americans came the Federal Style characterized by center halls, double parlors, red brick façades and white trim, louvered shutters. The *galerie*, native not only to some houses in New Orleans, but also to structures in the Middle Mississippi Valley, appears to have been an innovation native to the New World, to ward off the blistering sun and humidity that mark the climate in the central and southern American states.

Two New Orleans architectural styles are worth noting. The first is the Creole cottage, examples of which can be found in the *Vieux Carré* and in the neighboring Faubourg

Marigny. The typical New Orleans one-story Creole cottage consisted of a simple square or rectilinear floor plan, with two rooms in front and two in the rear. It was without a central hall, with movement being from room to room. The wall fillings of the timber frames were first of *bousillage*, later of brick between posts. There are often two chimneys, one to serve the back-to-back fireplaces of the two front rooms and another for the two rear rooms. The cottages sat directly on the *banquette* (sidewalk) and were entered through transomed French doors. An overhang on the roof, called an *abat-vent*, protected the passerby from the elements.

The Creole townhouses, which date from the Spanish colonial period after the fire of 1794, were more elaborate affairs. They consisted of two or more stories, French doors throughout, a raised basement, a galleried pavilion above and a rear courtyard. The ground floor was frequently a commercial space, the upper floor(s) living quarters. In back were the service buildings, with sloping roofs to direct the rain into cisterns. Entrance to the rear courtyard/patio was through a narrow passage between

> The courtyard of the historic Merieult House in the New Orleans' *Vieux Carré* – which now houses the Historic New Orleans Collection – features a wrought iron balcony railing, a galleried service quarters on the side and the Williams residence at the rear. Dating from 1792, the Merieult House is the oldest building on New Orleans' Royal Street.

buildings or a *porte-cochère*, a large entrance in the building itself, wide enough for carriages to pass through. The entire structure, with service buildings attached to one side of the townhouse, assumed an L-shaped form.

At 632 Dumaine Street in the *Vieux Carré* stands Madame John's Legacy, a raised cottage and the only building of its kind to have survived in the quarter. It takes its curious name from a story written by George Washington Cable in the 1880s, in which Madame John, the mistress of a man named John, is willed the house and sells it immediately.

The current house was built by an American, Robert Jones, for a Spanish officer, Don Mañuel Lanzos. The original structure, dating from 1726, was gutted in the fire of 1788, but was reconstructed on the original plan and using some of the surviving materials.

The Merieult House, which now hosts the Historic New Orleans Collection, was one of the few structures to survive the great fire of 1794. Built in 1792 by Jean François Merieult, a wealthy export-import merchant, the original house was of timber frame construction. A mixed-use Creole building, it had Merieult's business offices on the first floor and the family's living quarters on the upper floor.

The Merieult House has been restored on several occasions. In the 1830s, the arched doorways were changed into granite pilasters and the house was restored in the Greek Revival Style by General and Mrs. Kemper Williams, who donated their vast collection of historic documents, paintings, books and photographs to what became The Historic New Orleans Collection.

The weathered-looking building called the Laffitte Blacksmith Shop at the corner of Bourbon and St. Philip Streets is named after the Louisiana pirate who smuggled slaves and contraband into New Orleans. But informed opinion is that the building was neither a blacksmith shop nor associated with Laffitte. Probably constructed in the latter quarter of the eighteenth century, the structure has architectural interest as an example of a simple Creole cottage.

∨

The Lafitte Blacksmith Shop is a simple Creole cottage with no central hall. The house, with a heavy timber frame and brick-between-post construction, has a hipped roof with dormers and double chimneys separating the rooms at front and back.

< The Pitot House in Bayou St. John has a delightfully airy appearance. Its upper *galerie*, supported by thin colonettes, has six open bays that circulate air throughout the rooms. The lower floor, also with a *galerie*, is fronted by eight brick Doric columns. In the front garden, ginger, Chinese paper plants and maidenhair fern are among the plants that were common in early Louisiana gardens.

> The colorful rear galerie of the Pitot House. At the rear of the home is a loggia, common to Creole dwellings, with two small cabinets flanking it. An elegant curved stairway in back leads to the upper level.

The Pitot House, named for James Pitot, a native of Normandy and the first mayor of the incorporated city of New Orleans, sits in Bayou St. John outside of the French Quarter. Once a principal artery of commerce, Bayou St. John, named after Jean-Baptiste le Moyne, Sieur de Bienville, connected New Orleans to the Mississippi and served as an alternate route during times of flooding.

The Pitot House is arguably the most faithful restoration of an eighteenth-century colonial home in New Orleans. Originally constructed near the end of the eighteenth century by Bartolemé Bosque, it was later sold to Madame Vincent Rillieux, whose husband did much of the work on the house. Sold to James Pitot in 1810, it was later acquired by the Ducayet family, who, in the mid-nineteenth century, altered its appearance by replacing the double-pitched roof with a higher hipped one. It was later returned to its original appearance by conservationists working with the

Louisiana Landmarks Society. The structure did not always sit on its present site; it was cut in two and removed in sections before being placed here in the 1960s.

The St. Louis cemeteries, located outside of the French Quarter, are notable for their massive sculptured tombs, some designed by famous architects, and for their burial-above-ground layouts that were introduced during the Spanish regime. St. Louis Cemetery No. 1 on Basin Street is the oldest cemetery in the city, dating from 1788; it was moved to its present site in 1796. Cemetery No. 2, on North Claiborne Avenue, was established in the 1820s by the wardens of St. Louis Cathedral. A third cemetery, St. Louis III, is located on Esplanade near Bayou St. Jean. A number of local luminaries are buried in the cemeteries, including, among others, Louisiana's first American governor, W.C.C. Claiborne.

< The above-ground tombs in St. Louis Cemetery No. 2 are frequently surrounded by a wrought iron fence. Some of the tombs were designed by the celebrated French architect, Jacques Nicholas Bussière de Pouilly.

>> The summer bedroom and the parlor in the Pitot House. The bedspread and blanket in the bedroom are of Acadian origin; rare paired game tables in the parlor date from the late 1820s.

For more than seventy years, Great Britain and France fought four major wars for predominance in Europe, mastery of the colonies and control over the shipping lanes. The wars were fought mainly in Europe, but as the colonies became more important to the overall balance of power between the two nations, the struggle engulfed North America as well.

In King William's War (1689-1697), the conflict centered on control of the fur trade. In North America, hostilities began with attacks against English outposts in upper New York and New England. A short-lived peace with the Treaty of Ryswick in 1697 upheld French claims on the Mississippi Valley and Canada. But the fighting was renewed in Queen Anne's War (1702-1713) over the succession to the Spanish throne. In North America, the conflict drew in the British and French in the north and the British and the Spanish in the south. The Treaty of Utrecht in 1713 ended the hostilities, with the British receiving Acadia, renamed Nova Scotia, and fur trading posts in the Hudson Bay area. France retained several islands in the Saint Lawrence River and Cape Breton Island off of Nova Scotia.

In King George's War (1740-1748) – also known as the War of the Austrian Succession – France, Prussia and Spain took up arms against the British. Fighting spread to the North American colonies in 1744 with a French attack on a British position at Canso, Nova Scotia. In the Treaty of Aix-la-Chapelle in 1748, the British returned Louisbourg to the French and acquired Madras in India.

These were preliminaries to the more ambitious British aim to kill off French authority in North America altogether. The French and Indian War, the American phase of which was known in Europe as the Seven Years War (1756-63), was the first true world war. The French first aimed to block British expansion into the rich, disputed territory in the Ohio Valley, and built a chain of forts from Lake Erie to the headwaters of the Ohio. For the first four years, the French troops won important victories at Fort Niagara, Fort Duquesne and Fort Oswego. But the British decision to concentrate huge sums of money and men on North America definitively turned the tide. After the French defeat at Québec in 1759, the next major encounter in North America would see the French side with the American insurgents against the British and result in the birth of a nation.

CONTINENTAL STRUGGLES IN COLONIAL AMERICA: THE SEVEN YEARS WAR AND THE AMERICAN REVOLUTION

THE SEVEN YEARS WAR

> George Washington
was only twenty-two
years old when he fought
and lost a battle to the
French at Fort Necessity.
(Portrait by Jean-Baptiste
Le Paon (1779)) ©Mount Vernon
Ladies' Association)

∨

George Washington's
hastily built, palisaded
fort, which he called
Fort Necessity, was
raised in 1754 at Great
Meadows in southwest
Pennsylvania. It afforded
little protection against
a superior French force.
The recreated fort
has been erected
at the Fort Necessity
National Battlefield.
©Photo National Park Service

**Where George Washington surrendered to the French –
Fort Necessity**

The French and Indian War (the American phase of what
was called the Seven Years War in France) had both political and commercial roots. In their small, exposed and
widely dispersed trading stations, the French and their
Indian allies feared the expansion of the English settlements. The British, led by William Pitt, saw a commercial
advantage in weakening France as a competitor in world
markets and in securing British control of the fur trade and
agricultural products from North America.

The Seven Years War was the culmination of a battle for
empire that raged for nearly a century on the European
continent, with France, Austria, Saxony, Sweden and Russia
aligned against Prussia, Hanover and Great Britain. In North
America, the French and the British were the antagonists,
with each seeking to control rich lands claimed by the
other. For the first four years of the war, the French enjoyed
considerable success, routing the English at Fort Oswego on
Lake Ontario and at Fort William Henry. But in 1758, the
tide turned. Under William Pitt's leadership, the British

devoted more men and resources to the fight, winning
victories at Louisbourg, Fort Frontenac, Fort Carillon (in a
second attack), Fort Duquesne and Fort Niagara. The decisive battle came at Québec in 1759, when General James
Wolfe defeated the Marquis de Montcalm on the Plains of
Abraham. Four years later, in the Treaty of Paris of 1763,
France was forced to cede all of its territory east of the
Mississippi (except New Orleans) to the British. French
power and influence in North America never recovered.

Though France and many of the British colonists in
America were to become steadfast allies during the
American Revolution, there was a period during the 1750s
when they were adversaries. A young Virginia colonel,
George Washington, then only twenty-two, undertook to
secure the Ohio River Valley against French incursions. At
stake was control of a vast territory along the Ohio River
between the Appalachian Mountains and the Mississippi
River, an area claimed by both France and England. The
Battle of Fort Necessity, Washington's first major battle –
and his only surrender to a foreign foe – took place in a
meadow in southwest Pennsylvania, not far from present-
day Uniontown. It was the first skirmish in the French and
Indian War, which started in earnest in 1756.

In January 1754, Washington tried to persuade the French to withdraw from two forts they had built in the Ohio country, Fort Presque Isle and Fort Le Boeuf. The French refused and Washington returned to Williamsburg to report the news to Governor Robert Dinwiddie of Virginia. In April 1754, Washington returned with a force of 132 men with orders to defend a fort being built by the Virginia regiment. Because the French had already destroyed the fort, Washington pressed on to build his own. In May, he arrived at a point he named the Great Meadows and set up camp. Hearing the French were nearby, Washington surprised them at Jumonville Glen, killing ten, among them the French commander, Joseph Coulon de Villiers, Sieur de Jumonville, and capturing twenty-one men.

The victory was short lived. On July 3, a force of six hundred Frenchmen and one hundred Indians, led by Jumonville's brother, Captain Louis Coulon de Villiers, attacked Washington's forces, now reinforced with British army troops, at Great Meadows. In the interim, to protect his position, Washington had built a palisaded fort, which he called Fort Necessity, and dug a series of trenches outside the stockade.

In the long battle, both sides suffered casualties, but Washington was outmanned. Negotiations led to the surrender of Washington and Captain James Mackay of the British army, leaving Fort Necessity to be burned by the French. Washington, with a greatly diminished force, returned to Virginia. The defeat was a low point in his career. Twenty-seven years later, however, he redeemed himself brilliantly at Yorktown, this time against his former allies, the British, and fighting side by side with the French.

The Fort Necessity National Battlefield features a reconstructed Fort Necessity in the middle of the Great Meadow. On the grounds of the Fort Necessity National Battlefield, Mount Washington Tavern, a restored stagecoach stop, sits near the modern visitors' center. A short distance away, the British General Edward Braddock, commander in chief of all British forces in America, is buried on the grounds where he was killed in 1755, trying once again to drive the French from the Ohio territory.

<

In January 1755, General Edward Braddock was dispatched from Ireland, with two regiments of infantry, to link up with the Virginian forces in an attempt to recover the Ohio Valley. He and his British regulars, with George Washington as his aide-de-camp, were ambushed by a French and Indian force near Fort Duquesne. Braddock, fatally wounded, was buried at this spot near Fort Necessity.
©Photo National Park Service

∧

Fort Ticonderoga has
a museum with more
than thirty thousand
artifacts, a research
collection of twelve
thousand rare books
and manuscripts and
the largest collection
of eighteenth-century
cannon in the Western
Hemisphere.

>

Restored in 1909,
Fort Ticonderoga is
surrounded by two
thousand acres of hilly,
unspoiled land. When
built by the French,
it controlled the route
between the Hudson
River Valley and Canada
in the wars of the
eighteenth century.
The area was the center
of battles between the
Indians, French, British
and Americans.

A stunning French victory in the French and Indian War – Fort Ticonderoga

Fort Carillon (now called Ticonderoga, perhaps from the Iroquois word *Cheonderoga*, meaning "place between two rivers"), was the site of the greatest French victory of the French and Indian War. Here on July 8, 1758, a force of four thousand French troops under the command of General Louis-Joseph, Marquis de Montcalm defeated a British force four times its size under Commander James Abercromby. The victory was the high point in France's ultimately unsuccessful struggle to protect its outposts in Canada and to contain the British within their colonies in the northeast United States.

To protect its settlements in Canada, France built a string of forts, including Fort Chambly and Fort Saint-Frédéric, along the river routes to Canada. They also forged alliances with the Indians in the region, notably with the warlike Iroquois, the most powerful of the tribes.

As a further bulwark against invasion, and as a base to harass the British in the south, the French strategy was to build a forward fort at the southern tip of Lake Champlain, to interdict an invasion route between the St. Lawrence River in Canada and the Hudson River to the south. Here a young French engineer, Michel Chartier de Lotbinière, designed Fort Carillon (the name apparently chosen because waterfalls nearby made the sound of a carillon).

Built in 1755 near the junction of the La Chute River and the lake, the sprawling stone fort was constructed around the same time as Fort de Chartres, the only stone French fort on the Mississippi. It was built in typical Vauban style, with four bastions at the corners. These two relatively sophisticated structures were ordered by Pierre Rigaud de Vaudreuil, the French Governor General of Louisiana, and were far superior to the flimsy, wooden palisaded forts, some also built in Vauban style, that the French employed elsewhere in the Louisiana Territory.

But when the British attacked on July 8, 1758, the battle did not take place at the fort. The French commander, Montcalm, decided to position his defenses in a row of trenches and zigzag log walls on a hill known as the "Heights of Carillon". Though Montcalm was known as a cautious commander, in this case his strategy, thanks largely to British incompetence, proved to be the right one. He placed the pointed ends of tree trunks in front of the trenches and covered the area with snares of brush and felled trees.

The British, while far superior in numbers, were severely handicapped by the loss of their leader, Lord Howe, killed shortly after his troops landed at the end of Lake George. His replacement, General James Abercromby, a poor strategist, decided to rush the French positions without cannon support and without trying to outflank the trenches. Row after row of the massed redcoats were mowed down, four charges in all, the last led by Scottish Highlanders. The British defeat became a rout; the army fled, leaving arms and provisions on the ground. Almost two thousand had been killed in an afternoon.

The victory of Fort Carillon proved to be only a temporary boost to the French. The following year, the British General Jeffrey Amherst arrived with a large army and retook the fort.

During the American Revolution, Fort Ticonderoga changed hands three more times: in 1775, when Ethan Allen, Benedict Arnold and a small American force took it in a daring daylight raid; in 1777, when General Burgoyne's army forced an evacuation by the Americans; and in 1780, when the British too abandoned the fort following their defeat at Saratoga.

ROCHAMBEAU: ANOTHER FOUNDING FATHER

While almost every American schoolchild knows the name "Lafayette", Lafayette's countryman Rochambeau has not received the same acclaim. Yet Rochambeau, using his military and diplomatic skills, was the French officer most responsible for the victory of the colonists in the American Revolution and should rightfully be considered to be one of the founding fathers of the new republic.

∧

Le Comte de Rochambeau.

(Charles-Philippe Larivière.

Châteaux de Versailles et de Trianon)

©Photo RMN – D. Arnaudet/G.Blot

Born in 1725 in Vendôme, southwest of Paris, Jean-Baptiste Donatien de Vimeur, Comte de Rochambeau was the third son of a family with a military tradition that extended back to the Crusades. Like Washington, he assumed his military responsibilities early. He was promoted to captain at the age of eighteen, following his service in the War of the Austrian Succession. Other important military posts followed: brigadier general, major general, and in 1760, as a result of his skillful command of the Auvergne infantry regiment, *Maréchal de Camp*.

Known for his coolness, charm and diplomatic skills, Rochambeau was handed the task of leading the six thousand men of the French expeditionary force that set out from Brest to reinforce the American rebels. On July 11, 1780, he and his men anchored off Newport, and for the next year his troops were quartered in and around the city. They behaved with courtesy and tact, and Rochambeau overcame provincial suspicion by hosting several balls, having his officers meet with local citizens and placing himself under Washington's command. The discipline of his troops was due in no small measure to the respect they had for their commanding officer, who provided for their needs and recognized the isolation they felt in the unfamiliar surroundings of the colonies.

Rochambeau faced a daunting challenge: he was five thousand miles from home, blocked in Newport by the British fleet, and at odds with Lafayette and Washington, who wanted to attack the British in New York. Though Washington became impatient, Rochambeau continued to resist, counseling instead to marshal all of the French and American forces in the south, where the French admiral, Comte de Grasse, stationed in the West Indies, was ready to come to their support.

Washington finally acceded to Rochambeau's counsel, and in June 1781 American and French forces joined at Philipsburg, New York for an overland march south. Near the end of September, the two armies, joined by a detachment under Lafayette, were ready to begin the siege of Cornwallis and the British at Yorktown. The French, unlike the Americans, were skilled in the use of siege warfare; Washington's siege of Boston had not required fighting trench by trench, supported by cannon fire. With the Cornwallis surrender on October 19, the decisive battle for independence was won.

Rochambeau returned to France where he was awarded the Cordon Bleu of the Order of the Saint-Esprit by Louis XVI and made commander of the Northern District. Like Lafayette, he had an ambiguous relationship with the French Revolution. Though he was appointed *Maréchal de France* by the revolutionary war minister, Narbonne, he became disturbed by the increasing politicization of the army and returned to Vendôme, only to find his home and grounds ravaged by the revolution. After Robespierre came to power, Rochambeau was imprisoned and only saved from the guillotine at the last minute. Freed in October 1794, he retired to his château. After Napoleon came to power, he recognized Rochambeau's service to the nation, and in 1803 awarded him the Legion of Honor. The gifted commander died in 1807.

The French base during the American Revolution – Newport

Founded in 1639, Newport, at the entrance to Narragansett Bay, has the largest number of early colonial houses of any city in the northern United States. Its first settlers were English, led by a remarkable woman, Anne Hutchinson, who fled Boston in search of liberty of conscience and religion. They were later joined by Jews and Quakers, who first came in the 1650s, and in time Irish, Italian and Portuguese immigrants all contributed to the ethnic diversity of the town.

Newport was once one of the five largest ports in America. Ironically, this haven of religious tolerance was for a time a key link in the notorious triangle trade, when African slaves were traded for West Indian sugar and molasses, which was later made into Newport rum.

Newport's link to the French was forged in the American Revolution, when the French army, under Rochambeau, camped in the city for more than a year and later linked up with Washington's troops to bring victory at Yorktown.

In the 1800s, wealthy Americans discovered Newport and constructed their elegant summer homes along Bellevue Avenue and Ocean Drive. Thanks to persistent preservation campaigns, most of these mansions, some designed by American architects, such as Richard Morris Hunt and Henry Hobson Richardson, who were trained in the French *École des Beaux-Arts*, are part of the city's architectural heritage.

There are still reminders of the French presence in Newport. One is Vernon House, Rochambeau's headquarters during his year-long stay in the city, where he planned strategy with Washington and carried out his diplomatic duties with local officials. Another is Rochambeau's statue, which stands overlooking Newport's harbor.

< ∧

The statue of Rochambeau in Newport harbor memorializes the commander's arrival in the city in 1780 with the first French allies of the American colonists. The statue depicts him directing his forces and wearing the uniform of a major general of the Continental Army. Rochambeau's headquarters, Vernon House, is one of Newport's most elegant townhouses, dating from the early eighteenth century.

<

Plaque commemorating Rochambeau on the front of Vernon House in Newport.

^

The Paul Revere house,
built of earth and wood,
is medieval in style
with a high pitched roof
and huge timber posts.
Upstairs there are
two chambers containing
period furnishings
belonging to the
Revere family.

>

The present renovation
of Faneuil Hall, dating
from 1805, is linked
to one of America's great
architects, Charles
Bulfinch. Bulfinch's work
included doubling the
width and height of the
building without altering
its basic style.

First battles of the American Revolution – Boston

Founded in 1630 by a group of Protestants who fled England to escape religious and political persecution under James I and Charles I, Boston remains the most English of America's larger cities. The Massachusetts capital, founded in 1630, was named after the town of Boston in Lincolnshire, north of London. The English town was a hotbed of religious nonconformism during the seventeenth century. Some of its inhabitants relocated to what became the American Boston. In all, more than twenty thousand people left England between 1620 and 1640 to establish their homes in the Bay State.

The American Revolution that later brought France in on the side of the colonists had its genesis in Boston. It was here on March 5, 1770, that five citizens were killed by British troops in the "Boston Massacre" that inflamed American colonial opinion against the mother country. And it was here on December 16, 1773, that a group of colonists, dressed as Mohawk Indians, dumped some 342 crates of tea from British ships into Boston Harbor to protest against the

proposed monopoly of the British East India Company over the tea trade. These events led directly to the first battle of the Revolution on April 19, 1775, at nearby Lexington, where the "shot heard around the world" started the fighting in earnest. A year later, in May 1776, France sent fourteen ships with war supplies to aid the colonists.

Though Philadelphia, the first capital of the new United States, drew more French *émigrés* than Boston, there are French links to the Massachusetts capital as well. The son of a French Huguenot, Apollos Rivoire, Paul Revere became one of the heroes of the American Revolution. His fame as a revolutionary is based on his famous "midnight ride" of April 18, 1775, immortalized in a poem by Henry Wadsworth Longfellow, in which Revere set out to warn other American patriots that British troops were marching to Lexington to arrest them. Borrowing a horse, he roused the countryside before arriving at his destination. Later arrested by the British, he returned to see part of the battle on Lexington Green.

The Paul Revere House, dating from around 1680, still stands in Boston; it is the oldest colonial building in the city.

Another son of French Huguenots, Peter Faneuil, also made his mark on the city. Born in the Huguenot settlement of New Rochelle, New York, Faneuil inherited considerable wealth from his uncle and augmented it by amassing a fortune in shipping and the slave trade. Aware of Boston's need for a public market house, he agreed to erect a suitable building at his own expense. Faneuil Hall, completed in 1742, became a market house on the ground floor, and a town hall on the second floor. Destroyed by fire in 1761, it was rebuilt in 1763.

During the early days of the Revolution, the hall became the focal point of colonial protest against the British. Under the leadership of James Otis, Samuel Adams and Dr. Joseph Warren, meetings held in the hall assailed the Sugar Tax of 1764, the Stamp Act of 1765 and other British impositions on the colonists. Reports of the debates carried throughout the colonies and earned Faneuil Hall the title of America's "cradle of liberty".

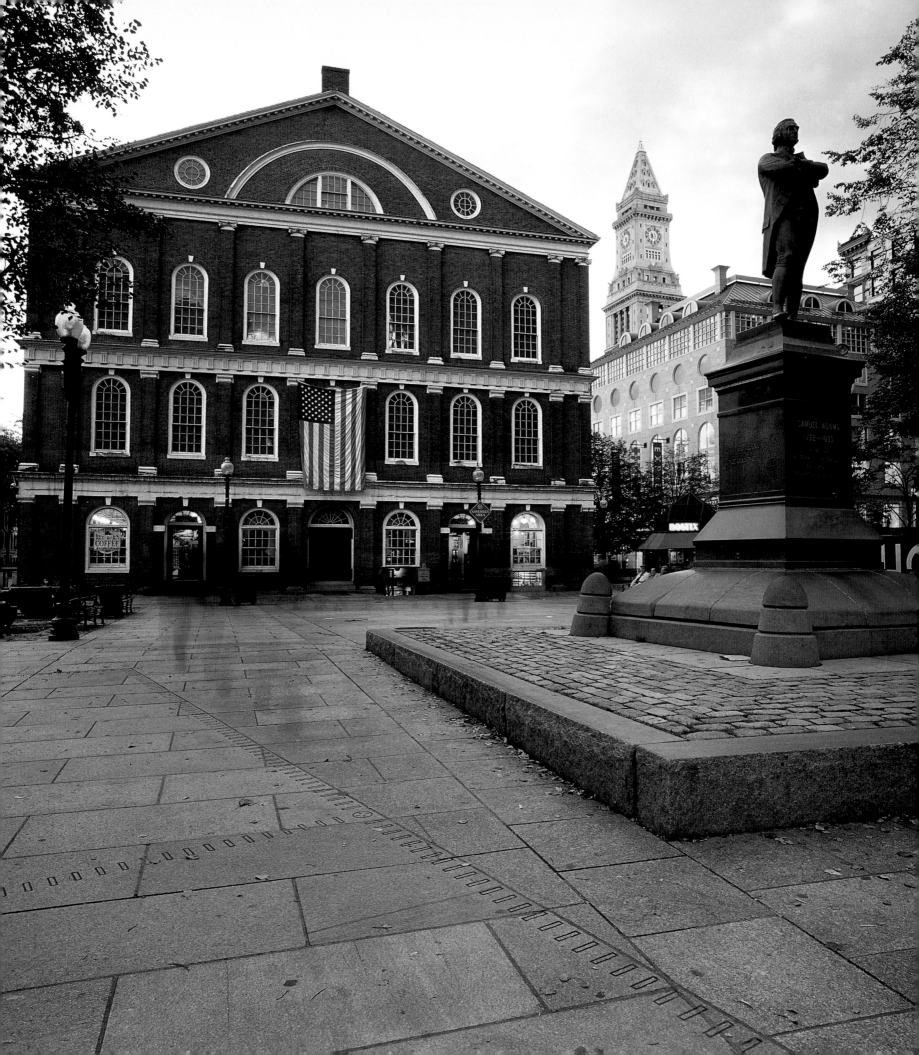

LAFAYETTE: AN ENTHUSIAST FOR AMERICA

The name "Lafayette" has a special resonance in America: more than forty American towns and cities are named after him, as are innumerable streets and schools and the park facing the White House. Almost every American schoolchild knows his name.

Born in 1757 at the castle of Chavagnac in Auvergne, Marie-Joseph, Marquis de Lafayette inherited a fortune at the age of twelve when his mother and grandfather died the same year. At sixteen, he also married into wealth, his wife being a member of the Noailles family, one of the richest in France. Lafayette's interest in America was kindled in 1775, and two years later, accompanied by some French officers, and against the wishes of the Crown, he sailed to the colonies and volunteered to serve in the army as an unpaid volunteer. Named a major general at the age of twenty, he became a protégé and lifelong friend of General Washington, with whom he spent the terrible winter at Valley Forge. He fought gallantly in several revolutionary battles – at Gloucester Point, Barren Hill and at Brandywine, where he was wounded in the leg.

Back in France, Lafayette repaired his relationship with the French court, which had suffered because of his disobedience in traveling to the colonies. He worked ceaselessly to raise money for the American cause, so much so that the Comte de Maurepas, a minister in the French government, said of him: "It is fortunate for the King that Lafayette does not take it into his head to strip Versailles of its furniture, to send to his dear Americans; as his Majesty would be unable to refuse it."

>

Lafayette was only twenty years old when he became a major general in George Washington's army.

(Joseph-Désiré Court, Châteaux de Versailles et de Trianon)

©Photo RMN

Lafayette returned to America aboard the frigate *Hermione* in 1780 and was appointed by Washington to command a special corps of two thousand light infantry. In Virginia, reinforced by troops from the French fleet, he harassed the British army as efforts were made to resupply it, clearing the way for Washington and Rochambeau to defeat the British in the decisive battle for American independence.

The revolution won, Lafayette returned once again to France, where he sat in the Estates-General of 1789 as a representative of the nobility of Auvergne. An early supporter of the French Revolution, he nonetheless was charged with protecting the king and queen from personal danger. He rescued Queen Marie-Antoinette from the mob that stormed the Palace of Versailles on October 5, 1789, but later issued orders to stop King Louis XVI when he sought to escape from France.

Lafayette fell out with the radicals and fled to Belgium, where he was taken prisoner by the Austrians and incarcerated in a dungeon for four terrible years before being finally freed in 1797. A lifelong supporter of constitutional liberty, he declined several positions offered by Napoleon. In 1830, as commander-in-chief of the National Guard, he was instrumental in placing Louis-Philippe on the throne.

Even in his later years, his thoughts turned to America. In 1824-25, accompanied by his son, George Washington Lafayette, he returned to America for a triumphal tour. Congress made him an honorary citizen, and his descendants still have the right to carry an American passport.

Decisive French aid during the American Revolution – Yorktown

The Battle of Yorktown, the decisive battle for American independence, ended with the British surrender to French and American forces on October 19, 1781. Less than two months later, the British House of Commons voted against further war in America, and eighteen months later, peace talks were held in France between Benjamin Franklin and Richard Oswald of Britain, culminating on September 3, 1783 with the signing of the Treaty of Paris, in which "His Brittanic Majesty [acknowledged] the said United States … to be free and sovereign and independent states …".

The Yorktown victory came after a series of defeats. In the south the British had captured Savannah and Augusta, and in May 1780, in the worst American defeat of the Revolutionary War, Charleston, South Carolina fell, with its 5,400 man garrison, four ships and a military arsenal.

In the summer of 1780, the arrival of 5,500 French troops at Newport, Rhode Island under the command of Comte de Rochambeau marked the beginning of a new stage in the fight. The French motives were complex: there was strong support in France for the American struggle, especially among young nobles nurtured with the ideals of the Enlightenment; but of foremost political importance was the desire of the French government to block British expansion in North America and to avenge the loss of settlements in Canada and in the Mississippi Valley.

Rochambeau discreetly placed his army under Washington's command, then convinced his American colleague that defeating a large British army in the south would be more decisive than attacking heavily defended New York. Washington agreed, and the two armies, French and American, marched five hundred miles south to encounter Cornwallis's British forces.

The tired British army, some 8,300 men, was seeking resupply from the British fleet following a long campaign in the Carolinas. But the French admiral, Comte de Grasse, sailed from the West Indies to the Chesapeake Bay and defeated a British fleet. Lafayette, reinforced by troops from the French fleet, blocked the Williamsburg peninsula. The pursuing French/American force of 17,600 men reached the area shortly after, linked up with Lafayette, and began bombarding Cornwallis's positions. The siege lasted three weeks.

The French corps of engineers built trenches, moved up their artillery and took the British redoubts one by one. Cornwallis, his supplies depleted and under constant fire, was compelled to give up. On October 19, after a long exchange of letters between Washington and Cornwallis, the British army marched out of Yorktown in formation and into a field where they laid down their arms.

The contribution of the French to the victory was considerable: the majority of Washington's army was French; many of the rifles they used were French; and French gold paid the soldiers' wages. Moreover, the French government loaned the Americans millions of livres to keep them in the war.

∨

Cornwallis surrendering the British troops in "Surrender Field" at Yorktown.
("Victory at Yorktown" by L.-C.-A Couder, Châteaux de Versailles et de Trianon)
©Photo RMN

A NOBLE CAUSE — THE FRENCH ARISTOCRACY AND THE AMERICAN REVOLUTION

As American revolutionary fever spread to France, the nobility, steeped in a long and rigorous military tradition, answered the call to arms. The contribution of the French nobility weighed heavily on the course of events in America, just as the insurgency captured the popular imagination of the times in France and was reflected in the fashions and tastes touching virtually every aspect of life, from the serious to the frivolous.

King Louis XV had just died as the American struggle unfolded. His young successor, King Louis XVI, gave secret financial

assistance to the insurgent cause for the purchase of weapons and equipment, a financial burden so great as to imperil France's frail economy. His Minister of Foreign Affairs, the Comte de Vergennes, took the pragmatic view that helping America hindered England, while many nobles found in this struggle glory and the romanticism of fighting in a foreign land for an idealistic cause.

Aware that the American Continental Army needed engineers, experienced artillerymen and staff officers, the U.S. Congress asked Silas Deane and Benjamin Franklin to secure professional French officers with these skills. Even before being recruited, a number of French military officers drawn from the nobility sought to join the American Army as forerunners to France's official military and naval participation in 1778. The Marquis de Lafayette was the most famous of many French nobles who volunteered to serve with the American forces before the French officially entered the war. Their ranks also included the Comte de Rochambeau, who made perhaps the most significant military contribution as commander of the French expeditionary force of nearly six thousand men. He was accompanied by scions from some of France's most illustrious families: the Comte de Ségur, diplomat, historian and author; the Duc de Lauzun, who raised, then commanded Lauzun's Legion, four colorful companies of lancers and hussars numbering more than one thousand men; the Marquis de Chastellux, known for his journal *Travels in North America in the Years 1780, 1781, and 1782*; the Vicomte de Noailles, Lafayette's brother-in-law; the Marquis and the Vicomte de Vaudreuil, descendants of the last Governor of *Nouvelle France*; Hayes de La Radière, an engineer involved in the early design and construction of fortifications at West Point and many others. The Chevalier Achard de Bonvouloir, as the French emissary to America, initiated contacts to bring about official French support. The Comte de Beaumarchais, the celebrated author, conducted secret negotiations to obtain ships, arms and supplies for clandestine aid to the colonies.

Around 80 per cent of the muskets and almost 90 per cent of the artillery

and gunpowder used by the colonists at their first major victory at Saratoga in 1777 had been supplied by France. America could not produce the military equipment and supplies it needed because there was little manufacturing capacity in the colonies. This victory would not have been possible without the still secret aid from France.

One of Admiral de Grasse's ships for his naval squadron, the *Ville de Paris,* was financed by collections solicited on the streets of Paris. When he set sail from Brest in the Spring of 1781, de Grasse had a powerful fleet at his command. The collection frenzy even reached the Court of Versailles, where noble women raised enough to purchase a battleship for John Paul Jones, the popular American admiral who had previously fought

but also in the intellectual and philosophical struggles that marked the age. The Duc Louis-Alexandre de La Rochefoucauld translated thirteen American state constitutions into French and was a passionate advocate for republican ideals. Even the skeptical Voltaire was moved to speak enthusiastically of the American cause.

At the war's end, in honor of the strong bond forged between officers, French and American, who had fought at Washington's side, the Society of the Cincinnati was created to perpetuate the aims of the American Revolution and the friendships of those who served. It was named after the Roman Emperor Lucius Quintus Cincinnatus.

with the French against the English. Admiral d'Estaing sailed from Toulon with a fleet of twelve battleships and eighteen frigates and landed in Newport.

The future Maréchal Alexandre Berthier was among the French officers who sought passage on ships bound for America. He served at Yorktown, where he drew the battle maps for the encounter. Berthier, later to become famous as Napoleon's Chief of Staff, was the son of a military engineer and cartographer, as well as chief of the Royal French Army Map Service. Berthier himself was proficient in map-making according to the highest standards of the day, and his maps reflect the best French cartography of the period. In 1800, Bonaparte sent Berthier to Spain to negotiate the acquisition of the Louisiana Territories ceded by Louis XV in 1762 to the King of Spain at the end of the French and Indian War. With the secret Treaty of San Ildefonso, France retook possession of Louisiana.

By October 1781, American currency was virtually worthless, and the Continental Congress' coffers were so empty they could not pay for Washington and the troops sent

to Yorktown. The French again provided funds and military strength to win the battle. The Allied forces with Rochambeau, de Grasse, LaFayette and Washington's troops numbered 5,700 Continentals, 3,100 militia and seven thousand French troops, whose land and sea forces with their military skill and experience proved decisive.

George Washington's Huguenot roots, Thomas Jefferson's francophilia and Benjamin Franklin's enduring favor in France ensured that the American struggle held a personal appeal for the French. And of course, the fashions of the day drew inspiration from the insurgency across the ocean. Queen Marie-Antoinette proudly donned a hat "à la John Paul Jones"; others sported coats "à l'Insurgente" and "Lightning Conductor" dresses in honor of the ever-popular Franklin, whose image also graced a panoply of items ranging from hats, gloves, rings and bracelets to snuff boxes and medallions. For fashionable ladies, coiffures "à la Boston", "à la Philadelphie" and "à l'Indépendance" were all the rage.

French nobles joined forces with the Americans, not only on the battlefield,

PENNSYLVANIA

BENJAMIN FRANKLIN AND THE FRENCH

A man with a breathtaking range of interests, Benjamin Franklin had several successful careers before ending his days as a diplomat and a statesman. His early profession was as a printer in Boston, the city of his birth, then in Philadelphia, where he purchased the *Philadelphia Gazette*, considered one of the colonies' best newspapers. He turned to writing, and his *Poor Richard's Almanac*, published under the pseudonym of Richard Saunders, became popular as a journal of satire, aphorisms and lively writing. He then ventured into civic improvements, starting up the nation's first subscription library in 1743, and helping to establish the first fire department, the first hospital, a police force and the Academy of Philadelphia, which later became the University of Pennsylvania.

Franklin's next incarnation – and the one for which, apart from his years as a statesman, he is most widely known – was as an inventor. In 1744, he conceived the Franklin stove, which reduces excessive chimney smoke and which is still in use today. And in 1748, he gained international fame through his experiments with electricity and the invention of the lightning rod.

Franklin's links with the French covered a period spanning almost twenty years. He first traveled to France on business in 1767 and returned to that country nine years later, a member of the Continental Congress, a signer of the Declaration of Independence and as the first American Commissioner to France. He remained there for the next nine years, having been appointed in 1779 as the Minister to France.

Among other tasks, Franklin's role in Paris was to secure funds from the government of Louis XVI for the young American republic. In negotiations with the French foreign minister, the Comte de Vergennes, he first succeeded in receiving an oral promise of two million livres, followed by grants of over twenty million livres over the next several years.

Franklin formed a friendship with Voltaire, and the two men were recognized by the French Academy of Sciences as leading intellectual paragons of their respective nations. Honored by Louis XVI, Franklin saw his portrait placed on everything from chamber pots to snuff boxes.

>

Benjamin Franklin.
(Jean-Baptiste Greuze (1777))
©Photo American
Philosophical Society

Along with other French and American dignitaries, Franklin was on hand to sign the Treaty of Paris, ending the American Revolution, in 1783. A plaque has been placed on the building where the Treaty was signed, just off the Place de la Concorde.

In his last years, Franklin served as a delegate to the Constitutional Convention and was a signer of the Constitution. When he died in 1790, at the age of eighty-four, his funeral was attended by more than twenty thousand people. He has been called by some "the first American".

Home of French artists, architects and political refugees – Philadelphia

Site of the nation's capital from 1790-1800, Philadelphia has roots that are fundamentally English. But its long history has been enriched by the presence of French architects, artists, statesmen, philanthropists, military men and refugees from the turmoil of the French Revolution and the Napoleonic wars.

In 1681, King Charles II of England made a land grant to Quaker William Penn to establish the colony of Pennsylvania. Penn envisioned it as a "Holy Experiment" with guarantees of religious and political freedom. Because of its strong appeal to people of many faiths, countries and skills, his city of Philadelphia (from the Greek for "brotherly love") became the largest and most prosperous city in the American colonies by the time of the Revolution.

Philadelphia's French links were forged during the American Revolution. On their way to join General Washington at Dobbs Ferry, six thousand French troops under the command of the Comte de Rochambeau marched through the town in full regalia, leading one observer, Abbé Robin, to write: "All Philadelphia was astonished to see people who had endured the fatigue of a long journey so ruddy and handsome, and even wondered that that there could be Frenchmen of so genteel an appearance!"

Philadelphia's historic buildings were where French diplomats huddled with leaders of the soon-to-be republic to secretly discuss French assistance to the American cause. The first contacts with the French government were made as early as December 1775, when Benjamin Franklin

Carpenters' Hall has been owned and operated by the Carpenters' Company of Philadelphia, the oldest trade guild in America, since 1770. The Hall has been home to a host of firsts, including the First Continental Congress.

The main building
of Girard College,
which sits on Girard
Avenue in North
Philadelphia, is a superb
example of the Greek
Revival Style. It contains
Stephen Girard's massive
personal collection,
including paintings
of ships, books of
philosophy, silverware
and dishes.

∧

Independence Hall sits
in Independence National
Historical Park, a space
of some forty-five acres in
Philadelphia's center city.
The two most significant
documents in American
history – the Declaration
of Independence and
the Constitution – were
signed here, the latter
following a debate from
May to September 1787
presided over by George
Washington and
involving delegates from
twelve of the original
thirteen colonies.

and John Jay met in secret with Louis XVI's emissary,
Achard de Bonvouloir in Carpenters' Hall, where the first
Continental Congress had met in 1774.

The city's other architectural symbol of the American
Revolution is Independence Hall, where the two most significant documents in American history – the Declaration of
Independence and the United States Constitution – were
signed. The Constitution's central doctrine, the separation
of powers, has both French and British roots. The French
set of those roots extends through the work of the French
political philosopher, Charles-Louis de Secondat, Baron de
la Brède et de Montesquieu, whose *Spirit of Laws* (1748),
– with its concept of the separation of powers among the
executive, legislative and judicial branches of government –
was read by many of the constitutional framers, including
Jefferson, Hamilton, Madison and Jay.

Over the years, French citizens from a range of disci-
plines made their imprint on Philadelphia, including the
statesmen Talon de Baumetz, le Vicomte de Noailles
(Lafayette's brother-in-law); the Duc d'Orléans (the future
King Louis-Philippe), briefly a refugee here; Joseph
Bonaparte (le Comte de Survilliers), banished from France
with the rest of the Bonaparte family after Waterloo; and
the French diplomat and foreign minister, Charles Maurice
de Talleyrand-Périgord. In architecture and the arts,
Philadelphia has been enhanced by the work of the French
architects Napoléon LeBrun, Jacques Gréber and Paul Cret,
and the sculptors, Gaston LaChaise, Joseph Alexis Bailly,
Antoine Louis Barye and Emmanuel Frémiet.

One of the French sculptors, Jean-Antoine Houdon, was
much admired by Thomas Jefferson. Houdon is responsible
for the life-size statue of Washington that sits in Washington

Square. Jefferson recommended Houdon for the commission, and the Frenchman traveled to Mount Vernon so that Washington could sit for him in person. Houdon was also commissioned to sculpt statues of other prominent Americans – John Paul Jones, Jefferson, Franklin and Robert Fulton.

French philanthropists and educators have also made important contributions to the city. Stephen (Etienne) Girard, born in Bordeaux in 1750, was a shrewd business-man who amassed a fortune in ships and later in land and mines. One of the young nation's richest men, his fortune helped to finance the War of 1812. Girard also had a highly developed social conscience. He bequeathed a fortune to set up Girard College for poor orphan boys. The school, which sits on Girard Avenue in North Philadelphia, was designed according to specific instructions in Girard's will.

Another illustrious Frenchman, the Prince de Talleyrand, stayed in Philadelphia for a short time, from 1794 to 1796. One of the most brilliant and controversial men of his age, Talleyrand held high office in five succes-sive French regimes, walking a tightrope between the excesses of the French Revolution and the restoration of the Bourbons, both of which he supported. Under suspicion of having offered his services to the Crown, he fled France during the Revolution, settling first in England, where he was suspected of being a French secret agent and later expelled. Joining other French refugees in Philadelphia, he took a modest house in Elfreth's Alley and proceeded to alternately charm and outrage Philadelphia society with his rapier wit and disdain for American mores. Pardoned and received back in France, he became foreign minister during the *Directoire*, the Consulate, the Napoleonic Empire and the Restoration.

∧

The cobblestoned street along which the Prince de Talleyrand resided is said to be the oldest residential street in America, dating from 1702. Named after Jeremiah Elfreth, a blacksmith and large property owner, it contains some thirty-three houses of mixed Georgian and Federal Styles.

<

A statue of Stephen Girard sits in front of the main building of Girard College. It shows Girard flanked by images of the poor ophan boys that his school was founded to educate.

After the Revolutionary War, the newly formed United States set about creating federal institutions and strengthening the nation. The ratification of the Constitution closed an era of political instability, and a Bill of Rights supplemented the broad framework of the Constitution when it was ratified in 1791.

In France, the American Revolution had an impact on the fate of the *ancien régime*. The French Revolution, which flared up only a few years after the American upheaval, succeeded in reforming many areas of French life. But it soon convulsed into political executions and violence that engulfed the country and the continent. For twenty-five years, the aftermath of the Revolution, which brought on the Napoleonic Era, dominated Europe and much of the western world.

By 1789, France had lost virtually all of her North American possessions. She did keep the Caribbean Islands and regained her West African colonies, but kept only small enclaves in India. Under the Consulate and Napoleonic Empire, St. Domingue revolted and gained independence. Louisiana, re-acquired by France in 1800, was sold to the United States in 1803 when Napoleon, strapped for funds, abandoned his dream of an American Empire to concentrate on European conflicts.

The United States was, in turn, impacted by the wars that emanated from the French Revolution. Thomas Jefferson and his followers, the Republicans, admired France and believed in the democratic promise of the Revolution. The Federalists, by contrast, led by John Adams and Alexander Hamilton, saw the excesses of the Revolution as a threat to republicanism everywhere. These disagreements helped to create an unanticipated political party system which tested the capacities of the Constitution.

The British, in fighting the French and later Napoleon, also launched attacks on American shipping. John Jay formulated a treaty with Great Britain, which delayed a war with the English for seventeen years while the new nation grew stronger. During John Adams's presidency, the relations between the United States and France deteriorated into a "quasi-war". The Convention of Mortefontaine in 1800 ended this tense period and restored good relations between the two countries.

The federal capital was moved from Philadelphia to Washington, D.C. in 1800; Lewis and Clark's expedition of 1804 helped open the West; and Jefferson's successor, James Madison, led the nation through another war with Great Britain, the War of 1812, which ended in 1815 with an American victory. The successful outcome of the war established once and for all the credibility of the new nation, which now began to look West in earnest, rather than to Europe, for its commercial sustenance.

EASTERN CIVIC AND URBAN ARCHITECTURE

"CHERCHEZ LES FRANÇAIS"

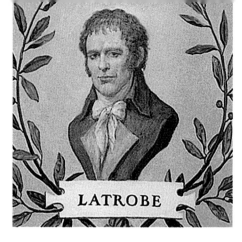

LATROBE

There is an easy way for someone who lives on the East Coast of the United States to observe the effects of French taste in architecture upon our country. It is to start with the national Capitol, and then move outward through the national capital. The architect whose talent most benefited the Capitol was a man of Huguenot descent who sometimes chose to write his name "Benjamin Henry Latrobe de Boneval". True, after our quasi-war against France at the end of the 1790s as "Benjamin Henry Latrobe", and true as well that he learned his architecture not in his ancestral France, but in Silesia and then in England. But he acknowledged that, like his friend and employer, Thomas Jefferson, he often "fished" architectural ideas "from old French books".

Latrobe actually designed and managed most of the work on the Capitol, including its spectacular interiors, but Étienne Sulpice Hallet was the first professional architect to do so. Hallet had been encouraged by Jefferson to submit the design for the building after he showed Jefferson a sketch. It was not possible at that juncture to select an unknown foreigner who spoke barely any English, so Dr. William Thornton got the job – Latrobe was not yet in the United States. Thornton was a medical doctor, botanist and amateur architect, who – so far as we know – had never managed a construction job, so Jefferson put Hallet in charge. Hallet did not suffer amateurs easily, and was far better qualified than

Thornton. He persisted in making suggestions, and was fired. Not long thereafter, Latrobe was put in charge, and stayed in the post long enough to produce an acceptable building – twice, actually, because the British burnt the first version during their second concurrent war against France and the United States, that Americans call "The War of 1812".

The domed central section of the Capitol was, however, Hallet's idea, a grand one, though not nearly so grand as the immensity that had been suggested for the space by Major Pierre-Charles L'Enfant. Irascible and thought by some to be eccentric, L'Enfant died unthanked, forgotten and poverty-stricken in 1825, but his French genius shaped the physical context of American national political life more than anyone else. He was a military engineer, neither a city planner nor an architect. He had, however, served George Washington well during the previous concurrent war beside the French and against England, which had brought independence. (He had also slipped an aristocratic apostrophe into his name, which had previously been simply Lenfant in much the same way that Baron von Steuben, the Prussian drill-master of the Revolution, provided himself with a Baronage unknown in his native land.) Washington engaged L'Enfant to remodel an existing building into the first Capitol building, Federal Hall in New York City, and the President's House in that city. His work was successful. The President then recommended him to design the federal city to be built on a 10-mile square on the Potomac River just above Washington's estate at Mount Vernon. L'Enfant obliged with a plan manifestly derived from that of Versailles, with a huge building – perhaps ten times the size of the structure actually built – in the site equivalent to that of the royal château of Louis XIV – and an executive mansion in roughly the place of the Petit Trianon on a cross-axis to a grand mall – all to be the center pieces of the radial avenues that to this day exasperate taxi drivers at rush hour.

It is a cliché of architectural writing to invoke Daniel Burnham, the next great urban designer of the federal city, as saying to his clients: "make no little plans," but Burnham was a finicker when compared to L'Enfant. Things were much smaller in 1789 than in 1919, yet even in 1789 L'Enfant made no apologies for his imperial vision for the United States: "No nation perhaps had ever before the opportunity offered them of deliberately deciding on the spot where their capital city should be fixed. And altho' the means now within the power of the country are not such as to pursue the design to any great extent it will be obvious that the plan should be drawn on such a scale as to leave room for that aggrandizement and embellishment which the increase of the wealth of the nation will permit it to pursue at any period however remote."

The mention of wealth and embellishment points us toward New York City. Its City Hall is the most patently French building in that city, more French than any couturiers' or cosmeticians' uptown by a 1990s celebrity architect. It is as light, airy and ingenious as anything achieved since, but considerably more poised, manifesting the conjoint genius of the Mangin Brothers and their contractor-partner, John McComb. After a fire and rebuilding, there are only bits left of their first St. Patrick's Cathedral on Mott Street, but it may well be that their thumb-prints are on the only remaining residential structure fronting on Battery Park and at the other end of Manhattan Island on Alexander Hamilton's "Grange". Hamilton was the Mangin's sponsor, prevailing in the City Hall design competition over Aaron Burr, who backed Latrobe. It is a pity that L'Enfant's house for Washington, in lower Manhattan, went to the wreckers before Brendan Gill, Kent Barwick and Jacqueline Bouvier Kennedy Onassis renewed New York's sense of its past after Pennsylvania Station was demolished.

Two Virginia capitals have done better, perhaps out of relative poverty, perhaps out of relative diffidence in the face of the past. Richmond retains its Capitol building, designed by Jefferson in emulation of the Gallo-Roman Maison Carrée in Nîmes. The square of public buildings surrounding Jefferson and Charles-Louis Clérisseau's temple-Capitol was laid out by Maximilien Godefroy, who left in Baltimore the finest expression in North America of French neoclassicism, its Unitarian Church, the oldest building in United States

NEW YORK · 1785

continuously occupied by a Unitarian congregation. Godefroy also gave that city St. Mary's Chapel for the Suplician priests, the nation's oldest Roman Catholic seminary. He won a competition for that building against Latrobe, who had already contested against the Mangin Brothers, and would shortly feel the bitter loss of a commission to Joseph Jacques Ramée. But Latrobe's relationship to the first Roman Catholic Bishop to be appointed to serve in the United States, John Carroll, gave him an edge in Catholic competitions, the most important of which, and the most important of Latrobe's career, was the Baltimore Cathedral. Unlike his service in making good buildings out of the Capitol and the White House, which had been started by others, this was an opportunity to do a great building on his own.

From Baltimore, let us skip over the Capitol, the White House and the Capitol at Richmond to descend upon Williamsburg, where Virginians created their first grand Capitol building in the time of good, if cold and mercenary, King William, or, if we prefer, Willem, for he was also chief of state of Holland. Williamsburg, or Willemsburg, like Washington, is laid out upon the plan of Versailles, though through a Dutch filter. Its Governor's Mansion sits in for the Petit Trianon, and its Capitol for the Château. William of Orange's architects for the capital of Virginia – he was also King of England at the time – deferred to the

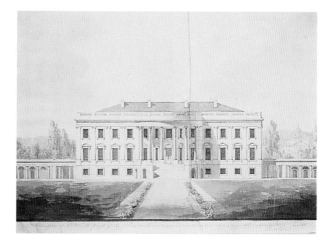

great city of the French a half century before the French were able to send their own architects to help the United States through its eaglet stage.

Jefferson preceded them, and the Monticello we now see at Charlottesville is very French, though not so in its first version. He had built to the level of the window-lintels a very pleasant bi-loggial English Palladian villa when he went off to Paris to become Minister to France. On a fund-raising expedition to Holland, he rode through ripe tulip fields on a summer afternoon, and groggily drew a picture of a really splendid version of that design, Welgelegen, the mansion of an American-born banker named Hope. It was all of marble and very large. Beside it, his little Monticello was a shed – an ambitious shed. (French château owners may be inspired when writing their own guidebooks in English to draw upon the example of the English-language tourist guide to Welgelegen, which informs us that "Hope hasn't actually lived here, he used it as a museum for his collection of art. In 1808 it was sold to Lodewijk Napoleon, brother of the famous French emperor.")

Jefferson abandoned the idea of a bi-loggial building, ordering construction at Monticello to stop. Then, in Paris,

∧
After the White House was burned by the British in 1814, it was reconstructed incorporating Latrobe's semi-circular South Portico.
©Photo White House Historical Association

<
Latrobe sought to improve Hoban's design of the White House by adding pavilions at each end, interior alterations and porticos on both fronts.
(Latrobe, *The President's House* (White House), south front elevation, watercolor, (1807))
©Photo Library of Congress

The Yellow Oval Room of the White House, which features Louis XVI Style furniture, was one of the last renovations undertaken by First Lady Jacqueline Kennedy.
©Photo White House Historical Association

he saw how the taste of the élite had turned toward the scrupulous, restrained and understated. Especially was he impressed with the relatively modest in-town villa of the Princes of Salm, to which they repaired during the social season from an eleventh-century castle at Anholt. It was still in his mind when he returned home as Washington was dealing with L'Enfant. The Hotel de Salm was the most powerful influence upon the final design for Monticello, which disguises its considerable size by burying much of itself in the ground and pretending to be only a single story high. It is a triumph of French elegance, whereas the first Monticello invited comparison to the marble mansion of a jumped-up banker from Boston. The present Monticello, in which so much French music was played, French wine consumed and anecdotes of the *ancient régime* imparted, does not require acre after acre of tulips to give it an appropriate setting. It whispers its opulence in a French accent.

Jefferson briefly succeeded in giving the new American Republic a taste for expensive modesty. The ruins of his most ambitious domestic design, Barboursville, are now a backdrop for the wine-tasting room of a vineyard near Charlottesville, but even Governor Barbour's rotunda house was not much more pretentious than Monticello, and it sat in a valley, invisible from the public road. Jefferson's other French villas, in Kentucky and Virginia, are still more shy. Then, however, came Andrew Jackson. The Jacksonian style was that of the University of Virginia, the grand Franco-Roman of the mid-eighteenth century rather than Parisian of the almost embarrassed reticence of Jefferson's friends among the aristocracy of the last years of the *ancien régime*.

There is nothing French about the American Greek Revival that succeeded Jacksonian Romanism. It is American. Its virtues are to be found in its innumerable meticulous, beautifully proportioned and detailed folk expressions, from the remote northeast extremity of Maine to the Oregon coast. There is, indeed, nothing like it in any other country. The Canadians did not follow suit, and the Greek Revival in

Scotland and Germany was grand rather than popular. America's was both, as the country celebrated its triumphant nationalism – with its dark side all too prominently displayed – after Jackson's victory at New Orleans. The displacement of the Greek Revival occurred in the 1850s with another wave of French influence, the mark of which was the Napoleonic mansard. Fortunately, we can also thank the mid-century French for educating Richard Morris Hunt, Henry Hobson Richardson and Louis Sullivan. Their works are all about us, showing us what a good thing a good education can be when it reaches people of genius, as it had earlier with Latrobe, Ramée, the Mangins, Jefferson and Godefroy.

Roger G. Kennedy

Latrobe won the commission for the Baltimore Cathedral, the first monumental Catholic church built in America. His design included a classical porch and two belfry towers.
©Photo Mary Ann Sullivan

The shaping of a city is an historic act – as indeed it was with Washington, District of Columbia. Born of a profound utopian notion rooted in eighteenth-century ideals, the nation and its federal city were envisioned as hallmarks of equality, justice and liberty. The innovative shaping of a wilderness and farmlands into a coherent city plan, assimilating spatial features of common American urban fabric with those models from the great European cities, was the implicit challenge that President George Washington put forth in 1791 to Pierre-Charles L'Enfant – the inspired designer on whose seminal design Washington's foundations were laid. The national capital would be an icon of an exemplary city, an ordered place in which the physical environment would influence individual deeds. Classicism, as the architectural lexicon, would provide a setting for formal ritual.

In America, L'Enfant, a young Frenchman with only a formal art education, rose to the rank of major by the end of the Revolutionary War – despite his lack of military, engineering or architectural schooling. He was known as an artist to George Washington for his portraits of officers and later for his designs for the Society of the Cincinnati. In 1783, following the war, as Washington's emissary to King Louis XVI he visited France at an opportune moment to find an outpouring of urban projects. Subsequently, he established himself as an architect, working in New York and Philadelphia. In New York, he redesigned the old city hall on Wall Street, which

became Federal Hall, and created the Federal Banquet Pavilion to serve marchers supporting the new constitution.

Thus known to President Washington, L'Enfant was selected as the designer of the new federal city – a rare opportunity to reinforce a national iconography of democratic ideals and republican space. The artistic and urban precedents culled from his French past and post-colonial American experiences inspired a unique design in a new place for a new order. A new urban narrative would ascribe meaning, amass collective memory and place-making – accommodating growth, evolving through time. Design of the public realm in France had become high art, and L'Enfant's Plan reflects this poetic acumen. He anticipated the potential flowering of the city, infusing his Plan with elements of his French heritage. In spite of a myriad of pressures, for two hundred years this powerful design has not unraveled.

Washington is an elaborately developed and controlled composition. The Plan – itself the physical symbol of the grandeur of the country and its people, its social goals and noble democratic ideals – was conceived as a setting for human civilization and achievement. As a late eighteenth-century "new town" Plan, it is an artful and articulate model for urban culture and civic function, icon of city as garden personifying rational order and aesthetic harmony. The Plan serves as a metaphor for a just humanity and the glory and valor foreseen for the nation – an experiment upon which the eyes of the world were focused.

During the eighteenth century, a keen interest in history was a prevailing influence upon architecture, urbanism and the arts. The design and redesign of cities, especially in France, evoked genuine images of classical imagery derived from antiquity, partly as a result of the rediscovery of Pompeii, Herculaneum and ancient Rome. The L'Enfant Plan's triumvirate placement, separating the major branches of government – president, congress and judiciary – underscores the separation of powers and the ideology espousing purity and reconstruction of society in a universe reminiscent of the Golden Age of Rome (an inherently Masonic image), representing a utopian ritualized landscape journey of moral and spiritual enlightenment.

A sensibility of eighteenth-century historicism influenced L'Enfant's formative years. Born in 1754, he grew up and was educated in the art curriculum at *Manufacture des Gobelins* national tapestry factory, where his artist father, Pierre, painter *ordinaire du roi*, specialized in military battle scenes and landscapes. The father became his son's professor at the *Academie Royale de Peintre et Sculpture* in 1771. In this milieu, the Baroque garden and hunting forest as a quintessential archetype informed the city planner. André Le Nôtre's landscape metaphor joining town and garden was applied routinely following his renowned work at Versailles for Louis XIV. Radial *patte d'oie* (crows-feet road pattern) imposed upon orthogonal streets, emanating from a symbolic space, offered an urban typology for expedient circulation and enchanting bursts of the unexpected, as advocated by l'Abbé Marc-Antoine Laugier.

Throughout France, as national unity was being achieved, older cities were enlarged and connected to one another by a network of roads. Civil engineers and architects modeled their grand urban projects after prolific playgrounds of the élite, such as Versailles and Marly-le-Roi (formerly within Versailles' forest), Saint Germain-en-Laye, Saint Cloud and the Tuileries in central Paris, thus altering the French urban landscape. The hunting forest typology at Château de Chanteloup near Amboise and Tours, where his father and colleague Charles Cozette were painting local maps and views between 1767-1770, offered a cogent urban design example for L'Enfant's future Washington Plan. Responding to terrain and natural features, Chanteloup's grid-patterned pathways integrated with radial tree-lined *allées* (avenues) that created a multiplicity of views and open spaces.

When L'Enfant returned to Paris from America in 1783, he found many changes. Innovative mediation between the old town and new, large or small, emphasized an identity with evolving ideas about republican space. Celebratory public spaces, named on behalf of nobility, gave towns an air of grandeur. These royal squares and hemicycles paired national-political goals with economic necessity. Jacques-Ange Gabriel's treatment of the Place de la Concorde vies with equally exquisite set pieces across France – Rheims, Dijon, Nancy, Nantes and others. The newly built Pantheon and its urban setting, designed by Jacques-Germain Soufflot, resulted in the clearing of numerous structures for the huge plaza and wide avenue terminating at the Luxembourg Palace. In these plans, as in Washington, D.C., often streets fanned out in an ordered radial composition with their morphology adhering to the undulating terrain.

L'Enfant's Washington Plan recognized the significance of episodic interplay of linear movement and spatial volume, vista and narrative in a continuous urban theme. Executed on the scale of an entire city, his brilliant design exhibited obvious connections with these compositions. In France, L'Enfant grew up in the midst of a public debate over the urgency for reform in the urban environment with concerns for the well-being of the populace and considerations of health and corollary legal

V

The Thackara and Vallance engraving of L'Enfant's Plan of the city of Washington (1792) shows the interplay of broad perspectives leading to public squares and monuments.

©Photo Library of Congress

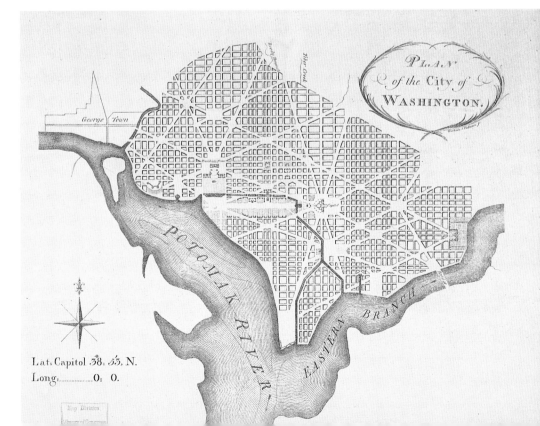

and architectural issues. For sanitary reasons, new garden-esque cemeteries were designed on the outskirts of town. Building heights were limited, while streets were broadened with large squares added to allow sunlight and pure air, according to established height-width ratios. In his Plan for Washington, L'Enfant attains a spatial quality to accommodate both dramatic visual effect and rational adaptations of similar regulations, endorsed by both Washington and Jefferson.

Thomas Jefferson played a major role in the design and development of the District of Columbia and offered specifics for its layout, the particular use of certain parcels and the means to acquire land for the "10 Mile Square" or one hundred square mile boundary of the territory. From the initial planning process for the new capital, for which he submitted his own city design proposal, Jefferson's involvement was substantial. He consulted directly with President Washington regarding the precise site and regu-lations, worked on city land acquisition, guided survey work, drew concept sketches, suggested a diamond-shaped, north-south orientation and coordinated the design process. Between 1790-1791, as the President's represen-tative, he corresponded with L'Enfant and provided him with plans of recently transformed cities, such as Lyon, Bordeaux, Montpellier, Marseille and other European urban centers. Jefferson made numerous notations and cor-rections on L'Enfant's Plan and followed its progress.

The L'Enfant Plan, with derivatives in French and European design, is unique to its site. Its loose grid overlaid with diagonals follows the topography in a gardenesque manner, displaying great sensitivity for the terrain. The repetitive system of open spaces, envisioned as neighbor-hood centers, was determined by the visual effect of grade changes spanning the gently rolling hills, a morphology developed in baroque gardens and urban landscapes. "The

positions for the different Grand Edifices, and … Grand Squares [were] on advantageous ground," said L'Enfant on his Plan, with extensive perspectives and space for improvement and growth. "Lines or Avenues of direct communication have been devised to connect the separate and most distant objects with major ones, preserving reciprocity of sight" and overall consistency while "passing … over the most favorable ground for prospect and convenience," he wrote. North and south lines (streets) intersected with east and west ones to form a hierarchy of grand and smaller city streets and squares "so combined as to meet at certain given points with those divergent Avenues … all proportional in magnitude … ". Two east-west baselines can be discerned, one a commercial thoroughfare at K Street leading to Georgetown, the other a virtual axis across The Mall.

Due to ensuing problems, President Washington later replaced his talented designer by surveyor Andrew Ellicott, who had worked with L'Enfant, though Ellicott failed to understand aspects of the Plan's underlying urban design nuances and significance. Nonetheless, L'Enfant's Plan fascinated Americans and Europeans alike who followed the development of the new American democracy and its capital. Maps of Washington began to appear in America and abroad. The nineteenth-century picturesque landscapes glorifying nature stimulated alterations to The Mall, but the dramatic 1902 Senate Park (McMillan) Commission Plan restored L'Enfant's principles of classical formality in the civic core and the grid street pattern of the "in-town" suburbs. While Washington is unique in many ways, the tradition from which is was created and its profound influence remain enduring models for civic design and vitality in urban life, representing a powerful symbol of national unity and civic pride.

Iris Miller

∧

This perspective looking from Memorial Cemetery to the Lincoln Memorial in Washington illustrates Versailles' influence on the L'Enfant Plan, which included a grand design of broad avenues leading to public squares and gardens, built on a vast scale to allow for the capital's growth.
©Photo Linda C. Durkee

JEFFERSON, MONTICELLO AND "L'ESPRIT FRANÇAIS"

> The five years spent
> by Thomas Jefferson
> in France were among
> the most fulfilling and
> stimulating of his life and
> left a lasting influence
> on his development
> as an architect.
>
> (An eighteenth-century portrait
> by Bouch, Châteaux de
> Malmaison et Bois-Préau)
> ©Photo RMN – D. Arnaudet

Thomas Jefferson was a man uniquely suited to absorb the lessons of European political, social and architectural aspirations and transplant them to a new nation. The young nation's public and political structures would be modeled on the ideals of the Enlightenment that Jefferson witnessed in Paris as America's Minister to France from 1784 to 1789. So too, Monticello would serve as his personal theater to apply architectural ideas from that rich period.

Jefferson's intellectual and aesthetic tastes inextricably drew him to eighteenth-century France. Third President of the United States, first Secretary of State, politician, diplomat, author, architect, horticulturist and landed gentleman, Jefferson benefited from a classical and rigorous education, which made him one of the best educated men in America. He began to study French at the age of six and later introduced it into the curriculum at his alma mater, William and Mary College in Virginia. By the time he entered college, Jefferson was well versed in Greek, French, Latin, Italian

and Spanish. His personal library grew to more than 2,600 volumes, the largest in the colonies. It included a full range of the classics and literature from the Enlightenment: Molière, Racine, Fénelon, Montesquieu, Rousseau, Diderot, Bossuet, Buffon and Voltaire.

When Jefferson arrived in Paris in August 1784, the city was experiencing a dynamic modernization despite the advancing deterioration of the *ancien régime*. The economy had revived, and a building spree caught hold of the capital. Jefferson delighted in exchanging ideas with an array of talented individuals – writers, scientists, artists, philosophers. He lived in a stimulating cosmopolitan environment, sampling widely the art, music and theater available in Paris, frequenting salons and bookstores and observing French architecture. He considered the five years he spent in France to be among the happiest of his life.

Jefferson's circle shared faith in a constitutional revolution. Louis-Alexandre, Duc de La Rochefoucauld, from one of the most illustrious families in France, lent unfaltering support to the American cause. The Marquis de Lafayette, who first met Jefferson at the end of the American Revolution, was a dedicated advocate for both nations. The Marquis de Condorcet – mathematician, academician, *philosophe*, pamphleteer – had been one of the earliest defenders of the insurgency, and both he and Jefferson saw the American and French Revolutions as linked. Lavoisier, a member of the Academy of Sciences, was a close friend of Benjamin Franklin, Jefferson's predecessor in Paris. Upon Franklin's recommendation, Lavoisier was elected to the American Philosophical Society in Philadelphia, along with La Rochefoucauld, Condorcet and Buffon, reinforcing American-French relations among scientists and intellectuals. With a highly personal interest, these men avidly followed the new country's development as an embodiment of the ideals of the Enlightenment.

Progressive ideas, debated in Paris salons, about representative government, the government's role in economic production, public education, religious freedom, the separation of church and state, slavery and architectural reform, were being put into practice in the formulation of the American Republic. Jefferson firmly believed in man's intellectual and social progress, and his prologue to the Virginia statute establishing religious freedom drew from Voltaire, Diderot and other *philosophes*. A great admirer of Montesquieu, Jefferson used abstractions from the Frenchman's writings in his own work.

The Paris Jefferson was thrust into was alive with intellectual and artistic ferment. France was experiencing changes in ideas and taste. The influence of the Enlightenment produced a strong reaction against the Rococo Style, which emphasized the play of curves and the proliferation of ornamentation. The trend toward classical ideas with clear and simple forms was hastened by the earlier excavations of Pompeii and Herculaneum and

the discovery of Greek temples. This neoclassicism, as reflected in the hotels and houses of the aristocratic world, proved a revelation to Jefferson.

Private investors and entrepreneurs spurred the Paris real estate boom of the 1780s as the *nouveaux riches* had spectacular new palaces created throughout the city. The avant-garde went in for the Neoclassical Style of architects such as Brongniart and Ledoux. At the same time, their libraries were filled with literature inciting revolutionary changes in society, changes already evident as nobles socialized with financers and entrepreneurs. The erosion of class barriers was undermining the old social and political structure as fast as the ancient buildings were being razed all over Paris in the name of progress and profit.

Jefferson's association with French architects showed him "the flexibility and logic of French rational planning". His Parisian residence, the two-story Hôtel de Langeac, with a

The colonnaded interior courtyard and portico of the Hôtel de Salm in Paris were greatly admired by Jefferson for their neoclassical elegance. He later had a colonnaded portico built at Monticello, his estate in Virginia.

∨

The Hôtel de Salm's façade was the prototype for the west front of Monticello. The prominent exterior dome that Jefferson added to his home, inspired by the eighteenth-century Parisian townhouse, was the first of its kind in a private residence in America.

∧

Jacques-Ange Gabriel's
neoclassical façade
on the north side
of the Place Louis XV
(now the Place de
la Concorde), between
the Tuileries gardens
and the Champs-Elysées,
was an impressive
example to Jefferson
of public architecture.

dignified neoclassical façade, perhaps most influenced Jefferson's architectural development in Paris. Here, he fully enjoyed the amenities of a new architecture. Langeac taught him a number of architectural lessons, later incorporated into his home at Monticello, including the use of weather-tight skylights to illuminate interior windowless rooms.

The Hôtel de Salm, now the Palace of the Legion of Honor, fascinated Jefferson. He confessed to being "violently smitten" with the building and went to the Tuileries almost daily to admire it from across the Seine. Begun in 1782 by Pierre Rousseau for the Prince de Salm, the building brought together the elegance of the French townhouse and the grandeur of the ancient world. Comfort, privacy and classical references coexisted harmoniously. The gate on the side away from the river, inspired by a Roman triumphal arch, framed an inner courtyard of a colonnaded peristyle.

Jefferson was also intrigued by Mézières' Halle au Blé, (now the site of the Bourse de Commerce), completed in 1783 to house the grain market. The light-filled building had an inverted glass dome held in place by wooden-ribbed framing. This "enlightened space" embodied the idealism of the age, combining practical engineering and beauty. It left such an impression that nearly twenty years later, as President, Jefferson urged Latrobe to model the ceiling for the House of Representatives after the Halle.

Jacques-Ange Gabriel's façades decorating the new public space between the Tuileries gardens and the Champs-Elysées – Place Louis XV (now Place de la Concorde) – were popular, as France still had little architecture for public use. Jefferson understood the underlying political implications of the development of Paris with the Palais Royal, the Place Louis XV and the new public theaters. In

> This eighteenth-century painting of the Maison Carrée in Nîmes in the south of France, by Robert Hubert, captured the allure that antiquity held for the imagination of the time. Jefferson considered it one of the finest architectural achievements of the ancient world.

(Musée du Louvre)
©Photo RMN – Gérard Blot

∨ The Capitol in Richmond, Virginia, designed by Jefferson and Clérisseau, was inspired by the Maison Carrée. It was the first structure in either America or Europe built specifically to house government offices and embodied the aesthetic ideals Jefferson sought for the new republic.
©Photo Mary Ann Sullivan

the final decades of the *ancien régime*, the élite and the popular coexisted in the public theaters open to both worlds, such as the Théatre des Italiens and the Théâtre Français (now the Théâtre de l'Odéon), which presented Beaumarchais' *Le Mariage de Figaro*.

The Palais Royal, the Duc d'Orléans' innovative shopping mall, featured commercial areas along with animated street theater. Jefferson had once considered creating such an area next to the new Virginia Capitol, which he designed with Clérisseau, inspired by the Maison Carrée in Nîmes. Jefferson relied on the architecture of classical antiquity, which alone had the beauty he felt symbolized contemporary republican principles. Jefferson's search led him to the ancient Roman ruins of the south of France, and in particular to the Maison Carrée, which he described as the "most beautiful and precious morsel of architecture left us by antiquity". The Virginia Capitol was the first structure on either continent designed specifically to house offices of a modern government.

Paris was the culmination of Jefferson's education in architecture and provided the inspiration that transformed him from the gentleman architect of his early years into a chief proponent of the neoclassical movement in America.

The worldly diplomat who sailed home in September 1789, just after the outbreak of the French Revolution, had also become a dedicated and talented architect.

In 1790, as Secretary of State planning the federal city, Jefferson sought out aesthetic and ideological models of modern public architecture, commenting: "for the President's house [later the White House] I should prefer the celebrated fronts of Modern buildings … [such as] the Galerie du Louvre, the Gardes meubles [by Gabriel on the north side of Place Louis XV], and two fronts of the Hotel de Salm."

On his return to Virginia, Jefferson designed, built and then remodeled his home, Monticello, over a period of forty years, seeking the delicate balance between the pragmatic and the aesthetic. A red-brick structure with a white dome and Doric portico, Monticello served as a laboratory for his ideas and reflected his interest in the Neoclassical Style.

The Hôtel de Salm, with a prominent exterior dome over the center front room, was the prototype for the west front of Monticello. Jefferson's house was the first in America to feature such a dome. This addition caused the loss of a second story, but this was compensated for by doubling the width of the house. The new section included a mezzanine and alcove bedrooms, features of French architecture which he admired. The house has a great variety of rooms, spacious service areas, and a separation between the public and

private areas, due to the clever arrangement of the private rooms in two tiers around the double-height public rooms. All of these are distinctly French traits, yet adapted to Jefferson's own taste and way of life.

While in France, Jefferson had visited the Château de Laye in the Beaujolais region, and was later to use the floor as inspiration for Monticello. He used a number of French sources, laying out a *ferme ornée*, or ornamental farm, in the French-American tradition. He pored over Buffon's *Histoire Naturelle*, and acquired a vast knowledge of gardens, which he put to good use at Monticello. In 1796, as the remodeling of the house was taking shape, Monticello was visited by the French exile the Duc de La Rochefoucauld-Liancourt, who viewed the new design as fully comparable with similar European houses. Jefferson's tastes were French in food, wine and furnishings as well. During his years in Paris he avidly collected furnishings, *objets d'art* and books, shipping eighty-six crates back to Monticello, a repository of all that he cherished in an exceptionally full life.

In 1819, Jefferson founded and designed the University of Virginia, highlighting the importance of education to the development of the new republic. The new American Republic was weak; only its ideas were strong, but classical architecture lent it the language of power, authority and continuity. Each of the pavilions at the university was designed with elements drawn from classical models as published by Palladio, Fréart de Chambray and Charles Errard. The layout was influenced by a number of sources, including Marly-le-Roi, that rivaled Versailles. At Marly, individual pavilions were grouped in two lines leading up to the casino of the *Roi Soleil*. Jefferson's design for the campus included a central domed rotunda, inspired by the Pantheon, which served as the library with classrooms, and two rows of pavilions con-taining student rooms and faculty lodgings on either side of the "lawn". A striking, half-domed doorway and curved double doors dominate Pavilion IX, the faculty house, inspired by Ledoux's pavilion in Paris for the dancer and opera singer, Mademoiselle Guimard. Jefferson devoted his last years to the project, and the Rotunda was completed the same year he died, in 1826.

As much as the Declaration of Independence and Jefferson's other political and literary achievements, his architecture is symbolic of his hopes for the new nation and for humanity. Through the masterful implementation of republican ideals of universal freedom and self-determination, coupled with the design and construction of the edifices to embody those ideals, Thomas Jefferson left an enduring legacy as the architect of a nation.

<

Jefferson founded and designed the University of Virginia, his last architectural achievement. For The Lawn, pictured here, he drew inspiration from several sources, including the two rows of pavilions leading up to a central pavilion at Marly-le-Roi, which Jefferson often visited, near Versailles.
©Photo Mary Ann Sullivan

>>

The west façade of Jefferson's home, Monticello, was directly inspired by the Hôtel de Salm in Paris. Its colonnaded portico and central dome testify to the Parisian structure's strong influence on Jefferson's architectural tastes.
©Photo Mary Ann Sullivan

As this book attests, the preservation of historic structures hinges on the generosity and devotion of those who care about the significance of the universally shared French heritage, relevant to us all. These buildings are the architectural testimony to our history, a bridge from the past to the present. They have come down to us thanks to the dedication of those who came before us, and will continue to stand thanks to our efforts to maintain and preserve them for future generations. French Heritage Society, an American charitable organization, was founded in 1982 by Michèle le Menestrel-Ullrich to help fund preservation for these architectural and historic treasures.

Initially called Friends of Vieilles Maisons Françaises, the organization consists of sixteen chapters of volunteers across the United States – in Arizona, Atlanta, Boston, Charleston, Cleveland, Dallas, New Orleans, New York, North Carolina, Northern California, Palm Beach, Philadelphia, Ste. Genevieve (Missouri), Southern California and Washington D.C. – as well as in Paris. Its purpose is to provide support for buildings exemplifying the French heritage in America and France. Restoration grants totaling millions of dollars have been awarded.

Educational and cultural exchange programs between the two countries keep alive preservation arts and traditions through travel grants and work on specific restoration projects. Talented professionals are exposed to practices and experiences in both France and the United States. Practicing American and French architects investigate preservation methods and techniques in each other's country. Seminars in French architecture and decorative arts bring together specialists at the highest level. An Artisans Exchange Program permits skilled craftsmen from both countries to master preservation techniques ranging from stone wall construction to stained glass, gilding and carpentry. A Student Exchange Program offers reciprocal internships for French and American undergraduates for architectural and historic preservation projects. Educational grants are awarded to curators, architects, artisans and students.

French Heritage Society seeks to ensure the preservation of this living heritage, while reinforcing the cultural bonds between the two countries. Grant awards, with the help of foundations, corporations and individuals, cover a wide range of projects.

Numerous projects reflecting France's historic influence in America have been funded by French Heritage Society in addition to projects in France. They represent a broad selection, as detailed below, that testifies to the diverse historic French presence and enduring architectural legacy in America.

The East Coast

Wye Mill in Wye Mills, Maryland

In 1671, a gristmill was built on the Wye River, and still operates on the site, making it the oldest commercial enterprise in the area. Owned by the Society for the Preservation of Maryland, the mill, completely restored, uses the traditional stone grinding technique, drawing water from a nearby lake to power the mill's ten-foot waterwheel. Wye Mill is twinned with a fortified manor house and historic mill at Sorans-les-Breurey in France, which uses the same techniques.

Gore Place in Waltham, Massachusetts

In 1806, French architect Jacques-Guillaume Legrand designed a Palladian-style brick mansion for Governor Christopher Gore and his wife. The couple, prominent members of Boston society, purchased four hundred acres in Waltham for their summer home. In time, it hosted a range of celebrated personalities: the Marquis de Lafayette, Daniel Webster and James Monroe. For the Great Hall, Mrs. Gore selected French wallpaper. In 1946, a small fragment of the paper was found behind the mantelpiece, and more recent research in Paris uncovered a larger piece of the same pattern, revealing

©Photo Gore Place Society, Waltham, Massachusetts

the full floral and geometric design. With a FHS grant, the wallpaper was restored, using the same technical processes employed for the original paper.

The Mount in Lenox, Massachusetts

In 1902, the American writer Edith Wharton constructed her estate, The Mount, inspired by her many visits to France. She centered the home on the vast entrance hall, decorated and designed in French classical style and incorporating a French-style wrought-iron staircase. Wharton moved to Paris following her departure from The Mount in 1911, and spent the last twenty-six years of her life in France. An FHS grant helped restore the staircase.

©The Mount, Lenox, Massachusetts

Trinity Church in Boston, Massachusetts

Trinity Church was commissioned in 1869 and designed by H.H. Richardson. After Richard Morris Hunt, Richardson was the second American to study architecture at the *École des Beaux-Arts* in Paris. He commissioned French and French-trained designers to work on the church. Eugène Oudinot, who studied under Delacroix

©Photo Trinity Church, Boston

and was the official stained glass artist for the city of Paris, created the stained glass windows in the south transept, now being restored in part by an FHS grant.

City Hall in New York, New York
City Hall in New York, designed by Joseph Mangin and John McComb, among the city's most active builders, was completed in 1811. It continues to house the Mayor's office and City Council Chambers. Mangin, a French *émigré*, is responsible for the elegant French Renaissance details and graceful ornamentation of the exterior. FHS's grant assisted in the restoration of the President's Room.

©Photo The Art Commission of the City of New York

DuBois Fort in New Paltz, New York
The DuBois Fort was built in the late seventeenth century by Daniel DuBois, great-grandson of the Huguenot New Paltz patentee, Louis DuBois. In 1677, DuBois and other Huguenots purchased land from the Esopus Indians for which they were granted a patent with the condition that they build a redoubt as a place of safe retreat. The FHS grant was used for masonry consolidation.

Jean Hasbrouck House in New Paltz, New York
This historic Huguenot house, built in 1721, features one of the largest chimneys to be found in colonial homes. With the help of an FHS grant, the north stone wall is being restored to its eighteenth-century appearance.

Morris-Jumel Mansion in New York, New York
The mansion, built in the Palladian Style, features a two-story octagon at the rear, believed to be the first of its kind anywhere in the colonies. In 1790, George Washington is said to have entertained his guests in the dining room, and Eliza Jumel wed Aaron Burr in the parlor in 1833. An FHS grant served to restore the main staircase.

Fort Ticonderoga in Ticonderoga, New York
Designed in 1756 by Michel Chartier de Lotbinière, Fort Ticonderoga, on the banks of Lake Champlain, was originally known as Fort Carillon. It is the only intact example of a stone fort in North America. The last French fort built in the United States, inspired by the classic designs of Vauban, it housed, among other structures, a bakery and brick ovens. The bakery chamber is the largest remaining intact element of French construction on the site. FHS is supporting repairs of the bread ovens.

Old Fort Niagara in Youngstown, New York
The French Castle at Old Fort Niagara was built in 1726. The Governor of Montreal entrusted Gaspard-Joseph Chaussegros de Lery with the creation of a French defensive outpost constructed almost entirely of stone, making it essentially fireproof. It featured machiolated dormer windows and is reminiscent of military barracks blocks erected in France during the reigns of Louis XIV and Louis XV. The oldest standing building in the Great Lakes region, an FHS grant supports window repairs where precipitation has entered, causing extensive structural damage.

Coustou Statuary, Apollo and Aphrodite; Mathurin Moreau Statuary, The Faun, at The Elms, Newport, Rhode Island
The Elms, a *Beaux-Arts* Style summer residence, was built for Edward J. Berwind in 1901. Design elements were inspired by the Château d'Argenson, built in 1750 by Jacques Hardouin-Mansart de Levy outside of Paris. Two life-size figure groups, featuring Apollo and Aphrodite, carved in demi-relief on the façade in French limestone by Guillaume II Coustou, required restoration. Moreau's white marble statue, *The Faun*, exhibited at the Universal Exposition in Paris in 1900, was purchased for the formal sunken gardens at The Elms. To restore the statue, an expert from the Louvre traveled

©Photo Jane Bernbach

©Preservation Society of Newport County

to Newport to take impression casts in silicone of the missing fingers, wing tips, water reeds and diadem, which were later recarved in marble matching the original. FHS grants helped fund these two projects.

Salon Doré at the Corcoran Gallery of Art, Washington, D.C.
The Corcoran Gallery's French room, the eighteenth-century Salon Doré, is entirely gilded and paneled and contains a variety of furniture and art. The Salon was bequeathed to the Corcoran by Senator William A. Clark along with his collection of European art. The FHS grant helped restore the eighteenth-century French doors with decorative painted panels surrounded by a gilt molding.

©Collection of The Corcoran Gallery of Art

Octagon House, Washington, DC
The Octagon House's link with France dates to the war of 1812, when it served as home to the French minister, Louis Serurier, who saved the house from destruction while the British burned Washington. After the White House was destroyed, President James Madison and his wife lived at the Octagon for six months, and it was there that Madison signed the Treaty of Ghent, formally ending the war. The FHS grant aided restoration of the portico.

Decatur House, Washington, D.C.
Completed in 1818, Decatur House is one of three surviving residential buildings designed by America's first professional architect, Benjamin Henry Latrobe de Boneval, who was of Huguenot descent. Located across from the White House, Latrobe's design and layout borrowed extensively from nineteenth-century French concepts. Stephen Decatur had an extensive collection of French decorative arts. Other furnishings were acquired with the help of President and Mrs. James Monroe, who at the time were decorating the White House.

The Midwest

The Louis Bolduc House, Green Tree Tavern, Guibord-Vallé House, the Vital St. Gemme Bauvais House, Amoureux House and Jean-Baptiste Vallé House II (Dorlac House) – Ste. Genevieve, Missouri

These six significant buildings are some of the earliest examples of French colonial architecture in the United States :
Green Tree Tavern, built in 1790, is thought

©Photo private collection

to be the oldest house in Missouri. Its basement suffered damage during floods in 1993, and once restored will house the Charles E. Peterson Institute Library on French colonial architectural studies. FHS support enabled installation of sash windows.
Vital St. Gemme Bauvais House, built in the late eighteenth century, is one of three *poteaux-en-terre* structures in Ste. Genevieve. Restoration of the French Creole house focused on a French colonial well, a rare vestige of its kind, and a fruitful site for archaeological investigation.
Louis Bolduc House was built in 1785 and carefully restored by the Colonial Dames of America. FHS grants aided in the stablization of the chimney.

©Photo private collection

Guibord-Vallé House, built around 1806, is now a museum operated by the Foundation for the Restoration of Ste. Genevieve. FHS has supported restoration of the cistern and the gallery.

Amoureux House is a rare example of *poteaux-en-terre* construction in eighteenth-century French colonial architecture. An initial FHS grant helped enable the purchase of the house, and title was thereafter given to the Department of Natural Resources of the State of Missouri. FHS also provided grants to restore the window shutters and to assist the State in the development of a study center and exhibition space.

©Photo private collection

Jean-Baptiste Vallé House II (Dorlac House), a *poteaux-sur-sole* vertical-log construction, built during the first decade of the nineteenth century, is listed as one of the important structures in Ste. Genevieve's National Landmark Historic District. Restorations include replacing the existing standing-seam metal roof with a new sawn-cedar shingle roof, tuckpointing and the repair of a brick chimney.

Cemetery, Ste. Genevieve, Missouri
FHS is contributing to the restoration of the final resting place of the town's numerous French settlers, including Jean-Baptiste and Jeanne Vallé, Vital St. Gemme Bauvais, Jacques Guibourd, Louis Bolduc and Felix and Odile Pratte Vallé.

The South

Houmas House in Burnside near New Orleans, Lousiana
Built in 1840, Houmas House fell into ruin after the Great Depression, but in 1940 the house and remaining grounds were bought and restored. Hexagonal brick *garçonnières* stand at each side of the mansion, and housed visitors who had traveled long distances by riverboat or horseback. The *garçonnières* received an FHS restoration grant.

Laura Plantation in Vacherie, Lousiana
Laura Plantation, built in 1805 by a Frenchman who fought in the American Revolution and with the Spanish against the British in Florida, tells the story of the gradual Americanization of Creole Louisiana. Built by slave carpenters, it is in traditional Creole and West Indian Style. FHS awarded a grant for the recreation of the *jardin français*.

Pitot House in New Orleans, Lousiana
The only Louisiana colonial style home in New Orleans, Pitot House was built by James Pitot, a Frenchman who became mayor of New Orleans, and who lived in the house from 1810-1819. In the 1960s, to save the house it was disassembled and moved two hundred feet. Consequently, some brick columns supporting the ground floor had to be rebuilt. Today the building is a museum of living history of life on Bayou St. John. An FHS grant is repairing damage caused by termites, rain and museum traffic.

Prudhomme-Rouquier House in Natchitoches, Lousiana
The Prudhomme-Rouquier House is located in the Cane River National Heritage Area, home to a unique blend of African, Creole, French, Native American and Spanish cultures. The boundary of the Heritage Area lies around Natchitoches, now a National Historic Landmark District. The Prudhomme-Roquier House, constructed of *bousillage* walls, received an FHS grant to treat water damage and remove termites that threatened the *bousillage*.

Longwood House in Natchez, Mississippi

Longwood is America's greatest octagonal house. Its exterior was virtually completed by 1861, when the Civil War brought construction to a halt. The unfinished interior of the house testifies to the devastating impact of the war on the cotton economy of the South. Of the planned thirty-two rooms, only nine on the ground floor were completed. Indirect lighting is provided by large mirrors in the dome reflecting sunbeams to smaller mirrors to light the interior below. An FHS grant aided the repair and installation of four light boxes to ventilate and light the basement.

French Huguenot Cemetery in Charleston, South Carolina

The first Huguenot Church in Charleston was built in 1681 by refugees who had fled persecution in France. The Gothic Revival church that stands on the same site today was constructed in 1844. For more than three centuries, the adjoining cemetery has been the final resting place for the Huguenot settlers. Exposure to the elements, fallen trees and expanding tree roots have deteriorated

©Photo Jane Bernbach

the headstones and eroded the inscriptions. In cooperation with the School of Building Arts in Charleston, an FHS grant funds restoration of the headstones through a workshop, in which professionals in cemetery conservation use the work site to pass their skills on to artisans of the future.

©The Middleton Place Foundation

Gardens of Middleton Place in Charleston, South Carolina

Believed to be the nation's oldest existing designed landscape, Middleton Place was conceived in 1741 to rival the finest European gardens. Henry Middleton, who owned fifty thousand acres in South Carolina, chose this rice plantation upriver from Charleston to lay out his gardens. He built a large brick house and spent ten years constructing the gardens with the help of one hundred slaves. Middleton was inspired by the precise patterns and formal symmetry of the seventeenth-century French landscape architect, André Le Notre. An FHS grant aided the restoration of the rose garden.

Joseph Manigault House in Charleston, South Carolina

The house was built in 1803 by Gabriel Manigault, a wealthy planter, for his brother, Joseph. The Manigault family had played an important role in the history of Charleston since their arrival as Huguenot refugees in 1685. The house is furnished with an important collection of Charleston, American, English, and French pieces from the period, reflecting the cosmopolitan lifestyle of a wealthy rice planter. An FHS grant permitted the restoration of a Palladian window damaged by Hurricane Hugo.

Nathaniel Russell House in Charleston, South Carolina

The Federal Style brick house was built in 1808 by Charleston merchant Nathaniel Russell. The structure suffered from the long-term effects of salty air as well as Hurricane Hugo, which did extensive damage to the slate roof. FHS provided a grant for the restoration of the portico over the entrance door.

©Photo Jane Bernbach

©Photo Jane Bernbach

The Southwest and West

Gila Chapel in Florence, Arizona
The Gila Chapel, built by French missionary priests in 1870, along with the adjoining Convent of St. Joseph of Carondelet, are major historic landmarks of the Southwest and important examples of French influence on the American frontier. The complex, the last surviving mission of the territorial period in Arizona, has suffered from heavy rains. An FHS grant helped restore structural damage.

Ursuline Convent in San Antonio, Texas
Bishop Odin, a native of France and the first bishop of the Republic of Texas, asked the

©Photo Richard Q. Kroninger, Southwest School of Art & Craft

New Orleans-based Ursuline Order to establish a convent and school for girls in San Antonio. French architects François Giraud and Jules Poinsard began construction in 1848, employing the *pise-de-terre* method compressing rock, straw and clay by hand. The building is the only major site in Texas from the period of its early statehood that reflects direct French architectural influence. It is now a museum and home of the Southwest School of Art and Craft. FHS supported a major program to restore the chapel, including work on the pressed tin roof of the sacristy.

©Courtesy of the Kimac Co. Ltd., Guilford, CT

Notre Dame des Victoires Church in San Francisco, California
When the gold rush brought Catholics of all nationalities to San Francisco, the French abandoned an earlier smaller church in 1856 in favor of a more spacious site. An FHS grant aided restoration of the current church.

©Photo by Robert Canfield, courtesy of City and County of San Francisco

War Memorial Opera House in San Francisco, California
The War Memorial Opera House, one of the most beautiful and technologically advanced performing arts centers in the nation, was designed in 1932 in the French Renaissance Style by Arthur Brown Jr., architect of Coit Tower and City Hall. Both a local and international landmark, the Opera House was used for the signing of the United Nations charter by President Truman on June 26, 1945.

©Photo by T. McCarthy

An FHS grant was awarded to make seismic upgrades and repair damage following the 1989 earthquake.

Marie-Sol de La Tour d'Auvergne

1524
Verrazano explores the east coast of North America from Charleston to Maine

1534
Jacques Cartier's first voyage to North America

1562
The first Huguenot *émigrés* attempt to settle in Florida; are massacred by the Spanish in 1565

1603
Samuel Champlain's first voyage to North America

1605-1606
Champlain explores coast of New England

1609
Champlain explores the Green Mountains and Adironacks and discovers Lake Champlain; engages Iroquois Indians near the present Fort Ticonderoga

1626
Peter Minuit, a Huguenot of Walloon background, is said to purchase Manhattan Island from the Indians

1660s
More Huguenot and Walloon settlers arrive in New Netherland (renamed New York after the British conquest in 1664)

1666
René-Robert Cavelier, Sieur de La Salle arrives in New France

1673
Jolliet and Marquette reach the Mississippi River via the Wisconsin River; they descend to its junction with the Arkansas River

1674
Marquette establishes the Kaskaskia Parish of the Immaculate Conception in the Illinois Country

1678
French-speaking Huguenots and Walloons found the village of New Paltz, New York

1680
La Salle and Henri de Tonty build Fort Crèvecoeur in what is now Peoria, Illinois; it is destroyed three months later

1682
La Salle descends the Mississippi to its mouth; claims all of the Louisiana Territory for France

1683
La Salle has Fort St. Louis built on the Illinois River at Starved Rock

1684
Henri de Tonty establishes the settlement of Arkansas Post, the first French settlement on the lower Mississippi

1683-1684
La Salle sets out to find the mouth of the Mississippi from the south; overshoots by four hundred miles, sets up Fort St. Louis and a colony in Texas near present-day Victoria

1685
Two to three thousand Huguenot refugees arrive in British North America, following the revocation of the Edict of Nantes by Louis XIV

1686-1697
Pierre Le Moyne d'Iberville commands five expeditions to the Hudson Bay area

1687
La Salle, on his way north to seek help for the Texas colony, is assassinated by his own men near present-day Navasota, Texas

1688
Huguenots begin to settle the village of New Rochelle, New York

1698
D'Iberville founds the colony of Biloxi in present-day Mississippi; his brother Jean-Baptiste le Moyne, Sieur de Bienville, has Fort Maurepas built at Ocean Springs

1699
French Canadian missionaries establish the settlement of Cahokia in the Illinois Country

1702
D'Iberville establishes a settlement at Mobile; builds Fort St. Louis de la Mobile to the north of it

1714
Natchitoches, in what is now north Louisiana, is founded by Louis Juchereau de St. Denis

1717
John Law, a Scot, is granted a twenty-five-year monopoly on the commerce and trade in Louisiana by the French Crown; establishes Company of the Indies

1717
Fort Toulouse, at the easternmost edge of Louisiana, is established by the French

1718
New Orleans is founded by Bienville; becomes capital of Louisiana in 1723

1719
John Law's "Mississippi bubble" bursts, bankrupting thousands of French investors

1729
Natchez Indians massacre some 250 French settlers and soldiers at Fort Rosalie in what is now Natchez, Mississippi

c. 1749-50
Founding of Ste. Genevieve in what is now Missouri by French Canadian settlers

mid-1750s
Fort de Chartres, the only stone French fort on the Mississippi, is erected in what is now Illinois; Fort Carillon (later to become Fort Ticonderoga) is built in New Amsterdam around the same time

1754
George Washington is defeated by the French at Fort Necessity in what is now southwest Pennsylvania

1755
Acadians are expelled from Nova Scotia and New Brunswick by the British in *le Grand Dérangement*

1756-1763
French and Indian War (called the Seven Years War in France)

1759
French Army, under Montcalm, is defeated by the British Army under Wolfe at Québec. This is the decisive battle of the French and Indian War

1762
Louisiana is ceded by France to Spain in the Treaty of Fontainebleau

1763
Treaty of Paris signed; France cedes all of its territory east of the Mississippi to the British

1764
St. Louis founded by Pierre de Laclède Liguest and Auguste Chouteau

1765
First Acadian settlers arrive in Spanish Louisiana

1766
First Spanish officials arrive in New Orleans to administer Louisiana

1776
American Declaration of Independence signed; Benjamin Franklin appointed the first American Commissioner to France; he returns there three years later as a full minister

1780
Jean Baptiste de Vimeur, Comte de Rochambeau disembarks at Newport with six thousand French soldiers to aid the colonists in the American Revolution

1781
Rochambeau and Lafayette team with Washington to defeat the British at Yorktown, in what is the decisive battle for American independence

1783
Treaty of Paris signed; the British agree to grant independence to the American colonies

1790
Destrehan, the oldest documented plantation home in the Mississippi Valley, is built by Robin de Logny

1800
Spain, in the Treaty of San Ildefonso, retrocedes Louisiana to France

1803
Thomas Jefferson's government purchases the Louisiana Territory from Napoleon for $15 million; called "the greatest real estate deal in history"

GLOSSARY

BALUSTER. An upright support for the handrail on a flight of stairs, a balcony, or a *GALERIE*.

BALUSTRADE. A row of BALUSTERS supporting a rail.

BANQUETTE. A sidewalk (from the French term for a footway of a road).

BAY. Any of a series of major divisions or units in a structure, as window, door, or archway openings, or the spaces between columns or piers. A reference to the number of bays usually concerns the number of openings across an elevation.

BAY WINDOW. A window or set of windows projecting from an outer wall and creating a polygonal, rounded, or rectangular alcove for the room inside.

BEAUX-ARTS. A style based on designs developed at the *École des Beaux-Arts* in Paris. Buildings in the style manifest a grandiose Classicism and are often faced in stone and embellished with monumental, frequently paired columns, heavy BALUSTRADES, enriched details (such as cartouches) and moldings, and pronounced CORNICES and PEDIMENTS.

BOUSILLAGE. A mixture of mud, Spanish moss, and animal hair laid in loaf shapes on a series of horizontal laths as NOGGING between the posts of a timber-FRAME structure.

BRIQUETTE-ENTRE-POTEAUX. A form of construction with low-fired bricks as NOGGING between the posts of a timber-FRAME structure.

CAPITAL. The uppermost part of a column, PILASTER, or the like, usually molded or otherwise decorated.

CASEMENT. A window that swings open on hinges, as opposed to one with sashes that can be raised and lowered.

CAST IRON. Iron that, when molten, is poured into sand molds. Elaborate *GALERIE* railings, window hoods, and *FAÇADES* are possible in cast iron.

CHINKING. The material, usually a clay mixture, that fills the gaps between the logs of a log house.

CLAPBOARD. A board with one edge thicker than the other, so as to permit horizontal overlapping.

COLOMBAGE. A heavy timber FRAME.

COLONNETTE. A wooden column or turned post of the TUSCAN ORDER having the shape of an elongated vase and used as a *GALERIE* support on the principal level of some CREOLE houses.

CORNICE. The horizontal projecting member at the top of a wall.

CREOLE. 1. A person born in the New World of parents from France or Spain, or with ancestors from these countries and from Africa. 2. Resulting from the blend of European with African, and sometimes also Native American cultures. 3. Of the architecture in Louisiana derived from this heritage. 4. Of a sort specifically Louisianian.

CUPOLA. A small structure on top of a roof for observation or ventilation or simply to complete a design.

DORIC ORDER. The oldest and simplest of the three Classical Greek orders, with a rounded CAPITAL, a frieze of triglyphs and metopes, and a shaft with flutes.

DORMER. A window set vertically in a small GABLE that projects from the slope of a roof.

EAVES. The edge of a roof, usually overhanging a wall.

FAÇADE. The face of a building, usually the front elevation.

FANLIGHT. A semicircular or semielliptical window, with radiating muntins or tracery, placed over a door, a window, or FRENCH DOORS.

FAUX BOIS. Painted with a grain to resemble a decorative wood.

FEDERAL STYLE. A style developed in the new republic of the United States and reaching Louisiana during the first three decades of the 1800s that was based on an Adamesque interpretation of imperial Rome, with light, airy Classical features.

FRAME. 1. The wooden or steel structural members of a building fitted together to form a skeleton. 2. A basic structural unit that when fitted with other parts forms a whole.

FRENCH DOOR. A door the upper section of which is multipaned and the lower section paneled, often in pairs within a single doorframe, both doors opening from a central vertical axis.

GABLE ROOF. A roof having two pitched slopes that meet at their uppermost edge.

GALERIE. A covered porch, veranda, or piazza, usually functioning as an outdoor living space.

GARÇONNIÈRE. A building near a main house for the young men of the household.

GOTHIC REVIVAL. A style based on medieval castles and churches that in its castellated form shaped monumental buildings in the 1840s and 1850s.

GREEK REVIVAL. A style widely embraced in Louisiana from the 1830s through the 1860s based on temples exhibiting the Doric, Ionic, and Corinthian orders, with columns, friezes, pediments, and low roofs.

HIP(PED) ROOF. A roof with four uniformly pitched sides.

LEVEE. A man-made embankment along waterways to prevent flooding.

LOUVER. One of the horizontal slats in a FRAME, as of a shutter, spaced for ventilation and shade and tilted to admit air but to shed rain.

MANSARD ROOF. A roof with two slopes on each of four sides, with steeper lower slopes. It is named for the seventeenth-century French architect François Mansart.

MOLDING. A decorative contoured surface or strip, usually of wood, plaster, or stucco, and frequently combined with others, often to function as a CORNICE.

MORTISE AND TENON. A technique of joinery in which the pieces are put together by projecting parts, that is, tenons, which fit into holes, that is, mortises. In timber-FRAME construction, a wooden peg is driven through two members to secure a joint.

NOGGING. The fill in the open spaces of a wood FRAME.

NORMAN TRUSS. A form of timber roof construction employing MORTISE AND TENON and associated with Normandy.

PEDIMENT. 1. A wide low-pitched GABLE above the FAÇADE of a Classical building. 2. Such a triangular form over a door, window, niche, or the like.

PIEUX. A fencing of cypress planks with pointed tops, and bottoms set in a trench.

PIGEONNIER. A pigeon house or dovecote. In Louisiana, this is a substantial square or polygonal building with the pigeons roosting in the upper level.

PORTE COCHÈRE. 1. A gateway by which vehicles enter a courtyard. 2. A covered porch attached to a building at ground level where passengers alight.

PORTICO. A porch or walkway with a roof supported by columns, often at the entrance to a building.

POTEAUX-EN-TERRE. A method of early CREOLE building construction in which sharpened logs are set in the ground and held in place by the framing of a roof.

POTEAUX-SUR-SOLE. A method of early CREOLE building construction in which the SILL is laid directly on the ground.

SCORING. Marking with lines or notches to resemble stone blocks, usually on exterior stucco.

SILL. 1. A heavy horizontal timber or masonry wall supporting the walls of a structure. 2. The horizontal timber at the bottom of the FRAME of a wooden structure, resting on brick, stone, or cypress piers, or directly on the ground in some early CREOLE houses.

TRANSOM. A horizontal, usually rectangular, window over a door or full window.

WROUGHT IRON. Iron soft enough to be pounded into shapes, usually for railings, gates, and fences.

FRENCH AMERICA CONTRIBUTORS

Ron Katz

Author of *French America*, Ron Katz is an American who has lived in Paris since 1978 and who has been a professional journalist and editor for more than twenty years. He has written extensively on travel and business issues for several newspapers and magazines, including the *London Sunday Times*, *The International Herald Tribune*, *The Business Traveller*, *Europe* and *Airline Business*. He is currently an editor for ICC Publishing S.A. in Paris.

Arielle de La Tour d'Auvergne

Photographer of *French America*, Arielle de La Tour d'Auvergne is a French citizen. She has had commissions from several international organizations, including *Comité des Parcs et Jardins de France* and the *Fondation Théodora pour les enfants*. She has done photographic spreads for Magazines such as *Monsieur, Montres Magazine, Bilan*, as well as portraits and CD covers. She is currently working on a *reportage* on Argentina. Based in Paris, she has spent some time in the U.S. and has a knowledge of both cultures.

Daniel B. Baker

Dan Baker is currently the Representative of the United Nations Population Fund (UNFPA) in the new country of East Timor. In 1982, he undertook research and studies at the Université de Moncton in New Brunswick on Acadian history and French Canadian culture. During that time, he published a scholarly article on the Acadian National Congress of 1921 in the *Cahiers de la Société Historique Acadienne*. Following this experience, he returned to the United States and began working for the United Nations in 1988.

James Baker

James Baker, a native of Ohio, has served as the historic site administrator of the Felix Vallé House State Historic Site in Ste. Genevieve, Missouri since 1983. His interest in French colonial Ste. Genevieve has developed during his tenure at the site. Baker is currently restoring his own vertical log home in Ste. Genevieve, the 1807 Dorlac House.

Carl J. Ekberg

Carl J. Ekberg is Professor Emeritus of History, Illinois State University in Normal, Illinois. An acknowledged expert on the French colonial period in the U.S., he has published a number of articles on the subject in scholarly journals, and is the author of several books, among them: *François Vallé and His World: Upper Louisiana Before Lewis and Clark; French Roots in the Illinois Country: The Mississippi Frontier in Colonial Times;* and *Colonial Ste. Genevieve: An Adventure on the Mississippi.*

Jesse Francis

Jesse Francis, who has researched French buildings for more than twenty years, is a restoration and historical curator at Faust Park in St. Louis County, Missouri. He has consulted and worked on the restoration and conservation of many of the historic edifices in Ste. Genevieve, Missouri.

Hilliard J. Goldman

Hilliard J. Goldman is a retired professor of history living in Kirkwood, Missouri. Long interested in history and old buildings, he purchased The Green Tree in Ste. Genevieve, Missouri soon after the Mississippi River flood of 1993. Since then, he and his wife Bonnie have been restoring it to its 1791 state.

Arnaud d'Hauterives

Arnaud d'Hauterives is a member of the Institut de France and is the *Secrétaire Perpétuel de l'Académie des Beaux-Arts*, in Paris. A painter, he was the recipient of the Premier Grand Prix de Rome in 1957. He spent four years at the Villa Medici in Rome and three years at the Casa Velasquez in Madrid. He is an official painter for the French Navy, Vice President of the *Société Internationale des Beaux-Arts* and a member of the *Comité du Salon Comparaisons* and the *Salon d'Automne*.

Roger G. Kennedy

From 1993 to 1997, Roger G. Kennedy was Director at the U.S. National Park Service. Prior to that, he served for thirteen years as Director of the National Museum of American History, Smithsonian Institution, and for the ten years before that as Vice President of the Ford Foundation. His books include: *Minnesota Houses; Figures on a Moving Frontier; American Churches; Greek Revival America; Architecture, Men, Women and Money; Orders from France; Rediscovering America; Mission; Hidden Cities; Burr, Hamilton, and Jefferson;* and *Mr. Jefferson's Lost Cause.*

Iris Miller

Iris Miller maintains a practice in landscape architecture and urban design in Washington, D.C., where she is Director of Landscape Studies in the School of Architecture and Planning at The Catholic University of America. She is the author of the book *Washington in Maps 1610-2000.*

Adams, William Howard. *The Paris Years of Thomas Jefferson*. New Haven, CT: Yale University Press, 1997.

Ambrose, Stephen E. *Undaunted Courage*. New York: Simon and Schuster, 1996.

Arrigo, Joseph. *Louisiana's Plantation Homes*. Stillwater, MN: Voyageur Press, 1991.

Balesi, Charles J. *The Time of the French in the Heart of North America*. Chicago: Alliance Française Chicago, 2000.

Bannon, Lois Elmer, Martha Yancy Carr and Gwen Anders Edwards. *Magnolia Mound*. Gretna, LA: Pelican Publishing Company, 1998.

Butler, Jon. *The Huguenots in America*. Cambridge, MA: Harvard University Press, 1983,1992.

Casanova, Jacques-Donat. *Une Amérique française*. Québec: La Documentation Française et de L'Editeur Officiel du Québec, 1975.

Chartrand, René. *Ticonderoga 1758*. Oxford, United Kingdom: Osprey Publishing Ltd., 2000.

Cooper, Duff. *Talleyrand*. London, U.K.: Phoenix, 1997.

Crouse, Nellis M. *LeMoyne d'Iberville*. Baton Rouge, LA: Louisiana State Univerity Press, 2001.

Daspit, Fred. *Louisiana Architecture 1714-1830*. Lafayette, LA: The Center for Louisiana Studies, 1996.

Davis, Edwin Adams. *Louisiana: The Pelican State*. Baton Rouge, LA: Louisiana State University Press, 1976.

DeHart, Jess. *Louisiana's Historic Towns*. New Orleans, LA: Hamlet House, 1983.

Derleth, August. *Father Marquette and the Great Rivers*. San Francisco: Ignatius Press, 1955.

de La Rochefoucauld, Gildine. Research of family documents concerning Duc Louis-Alexandre de La Rochefoucauld and Duc François-Alexandre de La Rochefoucauld.

de Tocqueville, Alexis. *Democracy in America*. Edited by Richard D. Heffner. New York: New American Library, 1956.

Donnelly S.J., Joseph P. *Jacques Marquette*. Chicago: Loyola University Press, 1985.

Downs, Tom et al. *Louisiana and the Deep South*. Melbourne, Australia: Lonely Planet Publications, 2001.

Eccles, W.J. *France in America*. Vancouver, Canada: Fitzhenry & Whiteside Limited, 1972.

Eccles, W.J. *The French in North America, 1500-1783*. East Lansing, MI: Michigan State University Press, 1998.

Ekberg, Carl J. *Colonial Ste. Genevieve*. Gerald, MO: The Patrice Press, 1985.

Ekberg, Carl J. *French Roots in the Illinois Country*. Urbana, IL: University of Illinois Press, 1998, 2000.

Emgarth, Annette H. *French Philadelphia: Exploring the French Cultural & Historical Presence in the Delaware Valley*, 2nd edition. Philadelphia: Alliance Française de Philadelphie, 1991

Evans, Mark L. *The Commandant's Last Ride*. Cape Girardeau, MO: Ten-Digit Press, 2001.

Foley, William E., C. David Rice. *The First Chouteaus*. Urbana, IL: University of Illinois Press, 1983,2000.

Franzwa, Gregory M. *The Story of Old Ste. Genevieve*. Tucson, AZ: The Patrice Press, 1998.

Fricker, Jonathan, Donna Fricker, and Patricia L. Duncan. *Louisiana Architecture*. Lafayette, LA: The Center for Louisiana Studies, 1998.

Fry, Macon, Julie Posner. *Cajun Country Guide*. Gretna, LA: Pelican Publishing Company, 1999.

Gannon, Peter Steven, ed. *Huguenot Refugees in the Settling of Colonial America*. New York: The Huguenot Society of America, 1993.

Hafen, LeRoy R., ed. *French Fur Traders and Voyageurs in the American West*. Spokane, WA: The Arthur Clark Company, 1995.

Holbrook, Sabra. *The French Founders of North America and their Heritage*. New York: Atheneum, 1976.

Huber, Leonard V., Samuel Wilson, Jr. *The Basilica on Jackson Square*. New Orleans, LA: Laborde Printing Co., Inc., 1965.

Huber, Leonard V., Samuel Wilson, Jr. *Baroness Pontalba's Buildings*. New Orleans, LA: The Friends of the Cabildo, 1964.

Jouve, Daniel, Alice Jouve, and Alvin Grossman. *Paris: Birthplace of the U.S.A.* Paris, France: Gründ, 1994.

Kennedy, Roger G. *Orders from France*. Philadelphia: University of Pennsylvania Press, 1991.

Kever, Jeannie. "The First French Colony in Texas." *Texas* 17 Sep 2000: 8-12.

Kever, Jeannie. "Hot on their tracks." *The Houston Chronicle* 3 Dec 2000: 1E+.

Laughlin, Clarence John. *Ghosts along the Mississippi*. New York: Bonanza Books, 1961.

Ledet, Michael. *Capturing Oak Alley*. Oak Alley Foundation. Vacherie, LA: 2002.

Marmillion, Norman & Sand. *Memories of the Old Plantation Home*. Vacherie, LA: The Zoë Company, Inc., 2001.

Mazel, Jean, Robert Laffont. *Louisiane Terre d'Aventure*. Paris, France: Éditions Robert Laffont S.A., 1979.

Miller, Iris. *Washington in Maps 1610-2000*. Rizzoli International Publications, 2002.

McJoynt, Albert Durfée. "Rochambeau." *Journal of Early Modern Warfare* III:4. Gorget & Sash (1990).

Nolan, Charles E. *A History of the Archdiocese of New Orleans*. Strasbourg, France: Éditions du Signe, 2000.

Parkman, Francis. *The Discovery of the Great West*. Paulton, England: Purnell & Sons Ltd., 1869,1962.

Peterson, Charles E. *Colonial St. Louis*. Tucson, AZ: The Patrice Press, 2001.

Pfeiffer, Maria Watson. *School by the River*. San Antonio, TX: Maverick Publishing Company, 2001.

Poesch, Jessie, Barbara SoRelle Bacot. *Louisiana Buildings 1720-1940*. Baton Rouge, LA: Louisiana State University Press, 1997.

Primm, James Neal. *Lion of the Valley*. Boulder, CO: Pruett Publishing Company, 1981.

Stacey, Truman. *Louisiana's French Heritage*. Lafayette, LA: Acadian House Publishing, 1990.

Taylor, Alan. *American Colonies: The Settling of North America*. New York: Viking Penguin Books, 2001.

Taylor, Joe Gray. *Louisiana*. New York: W.W. Norton & Company, 1984.

Toledano, Roulhac. *The National Trust Guide to New Orleans*. New York: John Wiley & Sons, Inc., 1996.

Walthall, John A., ed. *French Colonial Archaeology*. Urbana, IL: University of Illinois Press, 1991.

Weil, Tom. *The Mississippi River*. New York: Hippocrene Books, 1992.

Wilson, Samuel. *A Guide to the Architecture of New Orleans 1699-1959*. New Orleans, LA: Louisiana Landmarks Society, 1960.

Printed by Star Standard, Singapore
in October 2004
Reprinted in February 2005